PRAISE FOR HI HONEY, I'M HOMO!

"Every chapter serves up a slice of queer history with a rich scoop of fascinating, juicy asides and shocking behind-the-scenes insights—like having dishy late-night cheesecake with a witty, wise friend."

—Anthony Oliveira, PhD, author, film programmer, and pop culture critic

"For a medium so aligned with queer sensibilities, with its brazen artifice, showy wit, and over-the-top performances, the network sitcom was slow to embrace actual queer people. In *Hi Honey, I'm Homo*, Matt Baume takes us on a highly entertaining tour of queer representation in television comedy, from the be-bad-with-metaphor and you'll-miss-it winks of *Bewitched* to the out-and-proud-ish center stage of *Will & Grace*. Baume brings his trademark mix of childlike enthusiasm and intellectual rigor to a medium he clearly loves. He calls out cowardice and appeasement where he sees it, but is also careful to place each show inside its moment in queer history. This not only broadens the scope of the book, it helps us understand why sitcoms failed queer people where they did, and allows us to appreciate each step of progress on its own terms. Mainly, he never allows the many times sitcoms failed queers to diminish his appreciation for the form. I came away from *Hi Honey, I'm Homo* with not only a broader understanding of the medium I've spent over thirty years writing, but a big smile, too."

—Richard Day, TV writer and producer on *Arrested Development*, *Spin City*, *The Drew Carey Show*, *Ellen*, and more

"What an absolute honor to read Matt Baume's *Hi Honey, I'm Homo*. Matt's exhaustively researched episodes of pivotal television shows makes us realize how important these scripts were to change public attitudes. Matt breaks down this queer visibility by integrating history, character motivation, actual dialogue, and political agendas. His clarity and cohesive reflection brings context to what was happening in the world at the time and how, at first, these seemingly innocuous shows brought about change to queer history. Queer visibility didn't just happen overnight. It is and continues to be a series of wins and setbacks, which Matt chronicles with each painstaking step it took to move equality forward. This in turn shaped public perception and acceptance about queer life/lifestyles. All twelve television shows that Matt reviews unpack the parallels drawn to real life using not-so-cryptic analogies. When you read his examples, you will say, "It was so obvious!" But perhaps not at the time. The tremendous amount of curated minutia reads like Matt's love letter to the television pioneers of queer culture. His granular exploration of decisive episodes distills it all down to civil equality, which made the audience care about people they had been fearful of or biased against. Matt's use of such palatable clarity makes *Hi Honey, I'm Homo* an absolute joy to read."

—Deven Green, award-winning comedic chanteuse, DevenGreen.com

HI HONEY, I'M HOMO!

Also by Matt Baume

Defining Marriage

HI HONEY, I'M HOMO!

SITCOMS, SPECIALS, AND THE QUEERING OF AMERICAN CULTURE

MATT BAUME

Smart Pop Books
An Imprint of BenBella Books, Inc.
Dallas, TX

Smart Pop is an imprint of BenBella Books, Inc.
10440 N. Central Expressway
Suite 800
Dallas, TX 75231
SmartPopBooks.com | BenBellaBooks.com
Send feedback to feedback@benbellabooks.com.

Smart Pop and *BenBella* are federally registered trademarks.

Printed in the United States of America
10 9 8 7 6 5 4 3 2 1

Library of Congress Control Number: 2022049039
ISBN 9781637743010 (trade paperback)
ISBN 9781637743027 (electronic)

Editing by Vy Tran and Leah Wilson
Copyediting by Leah Baxter
Proofreading by Denise Pangia and Marissa Wold Uhrina
Indexing by WordCo Indexing Services, Inc.
Text design and composition by Jordan Koluch
Author photo by Nate Gowdy
Cover design by Brigid Pearson
Cover image © Shutterstock / bug34
Printed by Lake Book Manufacturing

Special discounts for bulk sales are available.
Please contact bulkorders@benbellabooks.com.

To Skeletor, with love from Snagglepuss

CONTENTS

Introduction   1

Bewitched   9

All in the Family   27

Alice   49

Barney Miller   67

Soap   93

Cheers   119

The Golden Girls   135

Dinosaurs   165

Friends   179

Ellen   189

Will & Grace   207

Modern Family   229

Conclusion   247

Acknowledgments   253

Notes   255

Index   269

INTRODUCTION

Marsha Posner was working late one night when the phone rang. She picked it up, and a man's voice bellowed, "I want the address of where I can write a letter about this show!"

Posner knew this meant trouble. It was 1977, and she'd recently been hired as a secretary on a new sitcom called *Soap* that was set to premiere on ABC that fall. Although the public had yet to see a single frame of the program, it already had the country up in arms, thanks to a *Newsweek* reporter who'd read a leaked script and declared that *Soap* was "impure," full of sacrilegious sex, gay love affairs, nymphomaniacs, cross-dressers, and kink.

"*Soap* needs its mouth washed out," fumed the head of one ABC affiliate.[1]

A national outcry had ensued. Conservatives were furious that a television show would attempt such boundary-pushing themes; gay community leaders feared negative depictions of queer characters would set their movement back by years. Groups that were normally on opposite ends of the ideological spectrum now organized complementary nationwide protests and letter-writing campaigns against the show.

Over the spring and summer of 1977, a steady parade of twenty to thirty protestors had taken up a picket outside Posner's street-facing office window. She made sure to keep the curtains closed. "We were afraid somebody was going to throw a brick through our window," she recalled.[2]

As a production secretary—and, before long, a script supervisor and then associate producer—Posner knew that *Soap* would indeed push television boundaries, but also that it would do so thoughtfully. In particular, the sitcom's leading queer character, Jodie (played by then-unknown comedian Billy Crystal) would provide a nuanced portrayal of coming out, examining one's gender and attractions, and eventually co-parenting as a gay man. It would also be extremely funny, thanks to writer Susan Harris, who had blazed a similarly controversial trail five years earlier with an episode of *Maude* that tackled abortion with equal parts heart, humor, and smarts. But none of that mattered to an angry public whipped into a frenzy by salacious news coverage.

Until now, the picket lines had remained outside the building. But the moment Marsha picked up the phone that night, it was as if the protests had invaded the production office. And in that moment, she decided she'd had enough.[3]

*

To understand the position Posner—now Marsha Posner Williams—was in, it's important to note that the late 1970s was a particularly volatile time for television, particularly when it came to depictions of queer characters. It wasn't quite ten years from the Stonewall uprising, an anti-police uprising in New York that catalyzed the modern LGBTQ+ liberation movement, and public attitudes toward queer individuals were still generally hostile. Television programs of the time frequently resorted to disparaging tropes: pansy perverts, insane transvestites, criminal dykes.

For example, a few years prior to *Soap*, the medical drama *Marcus Welby, M.D.* depicted a doctor helpfully offering a patient advice for overcoming homosexuality; *The Ernie Kovacs Show* presented comedy sketches in which audiences howled at a sissy poet; current affairs program *The David Susskind Show* presented an episode titled "Are Homosexuals Sick?" (Yes, Susskind concluded, they are; but he conceded that there's no reason to be rude about it.)[4]

Whether Americans tuned in to watch sitcoms, dramas, or the nightly news, TV reflected the prevailing belief that queer people were, at best, mincing freaks and, at worst, a public menace.

Exasperated by these portrayals and emboldened by a growing queer liberation movement, community organizers in the early 1970s began pressuring the three major networks to stop airing cruel stereotypes. Their tactics ranged from letter-writing campaigns to tense meetings with broadcast executives to sit-ins at network headquarters. And to everyone's surprise, these methods sometimes worked, with occasional depictions popping up on broadcast television that were not entirely mortifying—and even, on a very good night, positive.

This newfound prominence presented a valuable opportunity. In decades past, homophile organizations had maintained a low profile, staying largely hidden in order to avoid oppressive laws and social stigma that could ruin a person's life. With the rise of Pride events and more confrontational activism, the 1970s marked a time of unprecedented queer visibility, but this was limited primarily to major cities. Achieving visibility in Middle America was a challenge for queer people, but their cause was aided by television, the "vast wasteland" that beamed conversations, stories, jokes, and news to the 95 percent of American homes that owned a TV set by the decade's start.[5]

But queer visibility faced formidable opposition from powerful conservative forces that were equally determined to stake a claim on the airwaves. Throughout television's history, from its earliest transmissions in the 1920s to the present, television has been the site of a never-ending tug-of-war for control of the dial.

The man whose call Marsha Posner Williams received that night wasn't acting in a vacuum; his outrage had been stoked by pearl-clutching groups like the National Federation for Decency (NFD) and the Coalition for Better Television (CBTV), created by conservative media activists Donald Wildmon and Jerry Falwell with the intention of bending the medium to their will through church-based protests and nationwide boycotts of any programs they deemed offensive.

By the 1970s, these conservative campaigns had become a point of considerable concern for networks.

"We at CBS see in Mr. Wildmon's coalition perhaps the greatest assault on intellectual freedom that we have witnessed in many years," said Gene Mater, CBS's vice president in the 1970s and '80s. Speaking from his experience as news director of Radio Free Europe in East Germany after World War II, he continued, "The efforts of the coalition are only half a step removed from book burning."[6]

"They called me a bunch of names," gloated Wildmon in a speech. "They called me Hitler, they called me McCarthy . . . That ain't bad for a country preacher from Mississippi."[7]

*

Comedy programs like *Soap* were a focal point in this ideological back-and-forth. Sitcoms had become a staple of weeknight schedules starting in 1947 with the DuMont Network's *Mary Kay and Johnny*; since then, they have been among television's most popular programs, from *I Love Lucy* to *The Andy Griffith Show* to *All in the Family* to *Friends*. They have also been among the most widely syndicated programs, thriving in an afterlife of reruns for successive generations.

And crucially, tucking controversial topics in among farcical families and wacky workplaces can have a disarming effect. Jokes make challenging ideas more palatable, whether audiences are watching Archie Bunker grapple with the discovery that the woman he saved with mouth-to-mouth was actually a man in drag; or Blanche Devereaux obtusely failing to recognize what her brother means when he introduces his "very special friend"; or Jerry Seinfeld insisting, "Not that there's anything wrong with that!"

Particularly after the boundary-pushing success of *All in the Family* in the early '70s, sitcoms used comedy as a medium to deliver provocative ideas about bigotry, tolerance, and sexuality—topics that audiences might avoid if they were not sweetened by laughter. And thanks to the pervasiveness of sitcom syndication, they were seldom further than a dial-turn away, even in the most remote parts of the country.

"Laughter is an intravenous," sitcom pioneer Norman Lear said in a 2005 interview with the Television Academy Foundation. "Causing people to think while they're laughing is the intravenous of messaging through laughter."[8]

Lear's observation described my own personal experience as a teenager, nearly twenty years after Marsha Posner Williams took that angry phone call. I was an anxious, closeted kid living in a small Connecticut suburb in the mid-1990s, and gay role models weren't exactly in plentiful supply . . . that is, until I landed on *Soap* reruns on Comedy Central. The sitcom drew me in with laughs, but I kept watching it for Jodie, the gay character—one who was witty, sophisticated, aspirational, and cute.

At the time, I was keenly aware that there were large, powerful organizations out there opposed to my existence, but seeing Jodie on *Soap* was a signal that I might also find others like me; that queer people could thrive; and that I might manage to find not only a community where I belonged, but an entire culture.

That was the power of a syndicated sitcom, and it's why I became fascinated by primetime comedy as a means to shape public perception.

I started tracking down the moments in shows that told me I wasn't alone, from a lesbian kiss on *Roseanne* to homosexuals hiding out at *Cheers*. It was around this time that the internet was gaining widespread adoption, which provided me with an opportunity to learn about the real-life history of queer liberation, and I was struck by some surprising parallels.

For example, I noticed how the 1960s' *Bewitched* could only drop subtle hints about Uncle Arthur's queerness, just as gay men of the time might avoid openly sharing their identities. (Little did I know then just how many of the show's cast harbored such secrets.) As I read about the surge of visibility in the 1970s, I saw a clear example in *The Mary Tyler Moore Show* featuring Phyllis's openly gay brother. In my adulthood, I became an activist for marriage equality, and I gained a new appreciation for the episode of *The*

Golden Girls in which Sophia explains to Blanche why her brother wants to marry a man, and for the episode of *Roc* that dared to marry Russell Emerson (played by Richard Roundtree, better known for *Shaft*) to a man.

Across each decade, the story of social progress plays out through the characters of primetime sitcoms—if you know where to look. Fascinated by this history, I created a YouTube channel where I could hunt for the comedy moments that mark real-life civil rights milestones. That channel forms the basis of the book you're reading now, expanded with more research, interviews, and insights from behind the scenes of some of television's most iconic programs.

*

Holding the receiver that night in her office, Williams knew that she couldn't singlehandedly defuse the national outrage over *Soap*, which was still so far from its premiere date that they hadn't even finalized the pilot. But she could at least deal with this one person on the phone who was demanding the network's mailing address.

"Okay," Williams told him, "no problem, happy to give you the address. But may I just ask, what are you writing about?"

"Well, I'm writing about this show," the man said, and recited a familiar list of complaints cribbed from the exaggerated news coverage about *Soap*.

"Oh, have you seen it?" she innocently replied.

"No," he said.

"Really? How come?"

"It's not on the air yet."

"Okay," she told him. "So, what you want to write a letter about is not what you think, but what somebody else thinks."

This was not how the man expected the call to go. A fifteen-minute conversation followed, and by the end of it, Williams had persuaded him to change his plans.

"You know what, you're right," he told her. "I'll wait and watch the show and make my own opinion."

They ended the call on relatively cordial terms, considering how the conversation had begun. In the tug-of-war over television, their hands were on opposite ends of the rope, holding tight and waiting for the start of the next round to pull. A few months later, *Soap* would premiere to a generally positive response, Jodie would become one of the most positive depictions of a queer person on American television to date, and controversy would move on to other shows. Waiting in the wings was a scandal that rocked *Cheers*; a brush with gay marriage on *The Golden Girls*; the rise and fall (and rise again) of *Ellen*; and the gay Trojan horse of *Modern Family*. *Soap* constituted a stepping stone in television's gradual evolution from the mortifying stereotypes of the 1950s to the diverse queer leads that programs would embrace in decades to come. It was a fight that would be waged show by show, boycott by boycott, angry phone call by angry phone call.

"I like to think I won that one," Williams later said, recalling her late-night response to one viewer who sought to halt the queering of the American sitcom. She smiled sweetly. "I'm sorry, but fuck off."

BEWITCHED

ENDORA: What is normal to you, young man, is to us... asinine.

Something strange was afoot with the young husband and wife who had just moved into the home at 1164 Morning Glory Circle.

A neighbor, peering through her curtains across the street, gasped at the sight of the wife's colorful, campy mother—to say nothing of the flamboyant visiting uncle. Then there was the British gentleman with a penchant for vibrant male companions, and a supposedly strait-laced husband with a two-faced secret.

Yes, this much was certain: there was something very queer indeed about Darrin and Samantha Stephens.

Airing from 1964 to 1972, *Bewitched* was a show laden with gay subtext—despite its main characters being a heterosexual couple. When placed alongside the shows that followed it, *Bewitched* seems relatively straight: across its eight seasons, there was never an explicit mention of homosexuality, while *All in the Family* (which debuted the year *Bewitched* ended) featured explicitly gay characters starting in the very first season. Not long after *Bewitched* finished its run, *Soap* featured a gay dad as a core cast member, *M*A*S*H* had a coming-out episode,[1] and *Mary Hartman, Mary Hartman* contemplated gay marriage.[2] But though *Bewitched* didn't tackle any of those topics (at least not directly), there's a certain undercurrent that makes the show feel far gayer than its contemporaries.

In an odd twist, the element of *Bewitched* that originally seemed like its most heterosexual would be revealed, decades later, to be its queerest.

*

You can trace the inspiration for *Bewitched* back to the Salem witch trials, but more direct roots can be found in two Columbia Pictures films: *I Married a Witch* (1942) and *Bell, Book and Candle* (1958), both breezy fantasy romances about the chaotic, magical power of pretty young witches in love.[3] The films were adapted for Columbia's television arm, Screen Gems, by a seasoned television producer named Danny Arnold, but oversight of the show quickly fell to lead actress Elizabeth Montgomery and director William Asher—who, just like the characters on the show, were two young newlyweds head over heels in love.

The premise of the show is cute: a witch named Samantha marries a mortal named Darrin, and the happy couple decides to keep her witchcraft a secret so they can blend in as a nice, normal, suburban family. Sitcoms being what they are, something always seems to go haywire, and the more the Stephenses try to blend in, the more their lives become utterly abnormal. Upending the old TV-family conventions of the docile obedient housewife and her commanding husband, Samantha is portrayed as a powerful woman, in love with the eternally flustered Darrin but never subservient to him.

Bewitched wasn't the only sitcom concerned with domestic secrets and unusual families in the mid-1960s.

For television's first few decades, sitcoms tended to focus on one flavor of nuclear family, with shows like *The Honeymooners*, *I Love Lucy*, and *Father Knows Best*: a career-oriented husband and his housebound wife, usually with kids, and almost always white.

Then, in the 1960s, something changed. Where the airwaves were once dominated by monolithic depictions of the American family, the TV schedule began to give way to shows in which American families were, occasionally, out-and-out freaks.

Take, for example, the transition away from *Leave It to Beaver*, a show about a Midwestern family dealing with such sober topics as going to church, making new friends, and choosing a college. It debuted in 1957 and lasted until 1963; the next year, the same creative team introduced *The Munsters*, a sitcom that was also about a suburban family—but this time, the family are monsters in a haunted house, cheerfully tackling werewolves, cursed jewels, and dancing bears.*

In the 1960s, sitcom families wandered away from the template of ordinary married couples and kids, opting instead for bizarre chosen clans and satires of the suburbs. Many of these new shows had secrecy baked into the premise: on *Bewitched*, witches must stay hidden lest they be burned at the stake; on *Mister Ed* (created by gay director Arthur Lubin),[4] a man keeps his companion, a male talking horse, hidden from his wife; on *My Favorite Martian*, a local reporter hides his alien friend; on *My Living Doll*, a doctor hides a robot from the military; *Get Smart* features undercover spies; *Occasional Wife* is about a man who hires his best female friend to pose as his wife to advance his career. There was even a show called *My Mother the Car* about a man whose secret is that his mother has been reincarnated as an automobile.†

That sitcom families were getting exponentially weirder in the 1960s wasn't a result of executives dabbling in psychedelics (though that can't be ruled out as a contributing factor). This shift was happening amid the Civil Rights Movement, a period of widespread organizing, protest, and legal victories for minority groups, who had been ignored or denigrated by mass media in the past. Sitcoms, traditionally an escape from real-life turmoil, were slow to reflect this shift in American life. But, producers found, fantasy scenarios could provide a convenient metaphor for social change.

---

* *The Munsters* was produced by *Leave it to Beaver*'s creators, Joe Connelly and Bob Mosher.
† Rein-*car*-nated, get it?

Bewitched was one of the most potent examples—a show about a younger member of an invisible minority group who takes up residence in the heart of traditional suburbia, struggling to fit in without losing the qualities that make her distinct. Samantha's marriage to Darrin could be read as a metaphor for mixed-faith marriages, for people with disabilities, for sexual minorities, or for any number of groups that experience tension between being outcasts and joining the mainstream.

Samantha's conflict is evident in the second episode of the show, when she goes house-hunting in the suburbs and is confronted by her mother, Endora, a more traditional witch who is disgusted by the idea of assimilation:

SAMANTHA: All young married people dream of owning their
    own home.
ENDORA: It's fine for them, Samantha, but not for us. We are
    quicksilver, a fleeting shadow, a distant sound. Our home has
    no boundaries beyond which we cannot pass. We live in music,
    in a flash of color. We live on the wind and in the sparkle of a
    star! [Looking disgusted.] And you want to trade all that for an
    acre of crabgrass.[5]

This dialogue wasn't written specifically for gay viewers, but its resonance is clear. We're not like them, Endora says; we're something far more marvelous. It's a message delivered with moving panache by actress Agnes Moorehead, and with deep appeal to a wide range of outcasts, whether they're set apart by religion, race, gender, or family structure. In the world of *Bewitched*, Endora revels in her life outside of mortal limitations, and cannot fathom why Samantha would want to hitch her wagon to tedious, traditional what's-his-name:

DARRIN: I don't mean to be disrespectful, but we want to live
    normal lives.
ENDORA: What is normal to you, young man, is to us . . . *asinine*.[6]

Endora's breezy, confident dismissal of the mainstream is a luxury that many viewers could only dream about. At the time that *Bewitched* debuted, for many queer people, blending in was a matter of survival, as had been the case in the United States for centuries. American history is filled with examples of queer peoples' persecution, including records from the early 1600s (the same century as the Salem witch trials) that document the discovery of "5 beastly Sodomiticall boyes [who] confessed their wickednes not to bee named."[7] Criminal records note that in 1637, two men named John Allexander and Thomas Roberts were accused of "lude behavior and uncleane carriage one w[ith] another, by often spendinge their seede one vpon another."[8]

Though such offenses could carry the death penalty, these transgressions were often overlooked in the early days of colonization. To apply consistent punishment would overwhelm early European settlers. "Puritans became inured to sexual offenses," wrote historian Edmund Morgan, "because there were so many."[9]

American persecution of homosexuals has waxed and waned over the centuries, and *Bewitched* aired in a period that was particularly unwelcoming toward public discussion of same-sex romance. In the 1960s, homosexuality was a crime, and although it was no longer punishable by death, it wasn't uncommon for queer people to face extrajudicial beatings or to turn up dead. Police conducted relentless raids on businesses suspected of catering to queers. Newspapers printed the names, addresses, and workplaces of those arrested. The people whose names were publicized could expect to lose their jobs; to be ostracized by family; and to be subjected to cruel "cures" that included electroshock therapy, induced vomiting, and lobotomies.

Such witch hunts were common even in relatively liberal Hollywood. Two years before *Bewitched* premiered, a Los Angeles newspaper called the *Citizen News*—now defunct—launched a campaign to expose and persecute queer people.

"It is time for the greater Hollywood area to do something about a very ugly problem," declared the *Citizen News* in January of 1962. "The problem is the large concentration of homosexuals in the area."[10]

The editorial, signed simply "S.G.," continues, "It is time that the interests of normal men, women and children be protected . . . It is important to see that the deviates are treated . . . [and] more men must be assigned if this community is to stop being a mecca for queers." The piece concludes that the paper would assign several staff members to cover "the homosexual blot."

This marked the start of a years-long crusade against Hollywood's homosexuals. The *Citizen News* splashed its front page with headlines like "Officer Spells Out Sex Deviate Data," alongside articles fuming that nearly two dozen bars in Hollywood "cater almost exclusively to these people," and expressed outrage over a masquerade party held by homosexuals, "some of whom were dressed as chorus girls."[11]

"Police records say most homosexuals are driven by a vital urge to convert the non-deviate to their way of life," the paper reported. "Your teenager is not safe."[12]

The steady drumbeat of moral outrage, which leaned heavily on the claim that children needed protection from homosexuals, soon pushed officials to action. "Sex deviates are being rounded up by Hollywood police today in efforts to break up a ring of homosexuals which has been luring out-of-town juveniles into motels and homes," read a May 1962 article that listed the names and addresses of men arrested in stings.[13]

The police claim of "a ring of homosexuals . . . luring out-of-town juveniles" is not particularly credible. In interviews with biographer Robert C. Steele, longtime gay activist Jim Foshee described how, as a teenage runaway in Los Angeles in the 1950s, LAPD cops detained him and pressured him to lie about having been molested by a local drag performer whom they wanted to frame.[14]

Like the false claim that "homosexuals are driven by a vital urge to convert," police reports of the time were often flights of fancy concocted to justify bigotry.

Local judges praised the *Citizen News* for supplying information about the location of gay gatherings, which were then passed along to vice officers. California attorney general Stanley Mosk commended the paper's "series of articles on sex deviates" as "a fine journalistic service" and promised that an even stronger law enforcement response was coming. Sure enough, by 1963, the paper reported that police had ramped up sex deviate ("SD") patrols around Hollywood and were arresting around twenty-five men a week, an increase of 10 to 12 percent over the past year—but still not enough for the Hollywood Chamber of Commerce, which complained of ten to twenty thousand local homosexuals "who bother the public."[15]

The most iconic impact of this crackdown may be the work of Sid Davis, a film producer who teamed up with the Inglewood School Board to address the problem of "SDs" with a series of educational short films—among them 1961's now-infamous *Boys Beware*. The ten-minute film, screened in schools for decades, explains that homosexuality is "a sickness of the mind."[16]

"One never knows when the homosexual is about," warns a narrator, accompanied by images of a sinister man leering at boys outside a public bathroom. "He may appear normal, and it may be too late when you discover he is mentally ill."

Coverage of sex deviate arrests must've been good for *Citizen News* circulation, because the paper kept the Hollywood homosexual hunt going for years. Articles published the addresses of suspected gay hangouts, as well as locations where perverts practiced "wife swapping" and "nude swimming." Editorials called for "SDs [to] be forced to live in restricted areas" and for gay men to be punished with "commitment to [a] psychiatric hospital for the mentally ill until it is determined [they] can live safely within society."[17]

This was the climate in which much of the nation's television was being produced. Like the rest of America, Los Angeles was a place in which one wrong move, one slip of the tongue, one malicious piece of gossip could ruin a person's life.

But with the rise of the Civil Rights Movement, there also came glimmers of hope for the future. In 1961, San Francisco drag performer José

Sarria became the first openly gay candidate to run for public office in the United States.* In 1962, a small group of queer people in Philadelphia had formed an early activist coalition known as the East Coast Homophile Organizations; it was out of this organizing that the first Prides would occur. In 1965, another activist group called the Mattachine Society organized the first picket for gay rights outside the White House.[18]

Little by little, queer people were starting to emerge from the closet, to risk declaring their existence, and to make demands—if not for acceptance, at least tolerance. It was a revolutionary time, and that spirit is reflected in an early episode of *Bewitched* titled "The Witches Are Out."[19]

Samantha has invited over some witch friends—a coven, if you will—for an afternoon tea that quickly turns into a venting session about how intolerant mortals are:

SAMANTHA: I guess they just don't realize we're like anybody else . . . almost.

MARY: I don't know why we don't simply tell everyone we're witches. And then they'll see what wonderful, nice people we really are.

As the title of the episode suggests, they're talking about coming out—but remembering what happened in Salem in 1692, they agree it's not safe for them to reveal themselves.

It's not hard to connect this storyline to queer life. In fact, later in the episode the witches propose a public relations strategy to highlight their normalcy, with a theme similar to one message favored by queer protests of the time: that gay people are no different from straights.

The parallels deepen when Samantha's husband, Darrin, comes home

---

* He lost, but his campaign infrastructure stuck around in the form of San Francisco's Tavern Guild, fighting back against police crackdowns and eventually helping Harvey Milk win a seat on the city's board of supervisors.

from work. An ad executive, he's been tasked with managing a campaign for Halloween candy that features stereotypical haggard witch images:

SAMANTHA: That picture, it's offensive.
DARRIN: That's the way most people think witches look.
SAMANTHA: Is that any reason to discriminate against a minority group?

It's a far cry from anything that sitcoms were talking about ten years earlier. This couple is straight and white and middle-class, but they're at least talking about minorities, stereotypes, inequality, and media representation. Samantha is directly accusing her husband of perpetuating stereotypes, and pushing him to acknowledge that painting with such broad, ugly strokes does harm:

SAMANTHA: When we see those children running around on Halloween with blacked-out teeth and warts, well, don't you understand? It hurts.

The episode climaxes with the witches staging a protest—not in public, but in the mind of the candy company executive who wanted to use ugly witches in his ads. Samantha and her friends march on the executive's bedroom as he sleeps, invade his dreams, and wave furious signs at him reading "WE DEMAND A NEW IMAGE" and "WITCHES ARE PEOPLE TOO." Shown that witches aren't what the media has led everyone to believe, he promises not to rely on stereotypes anymore.

The image of an outraged minority holding picket signs was surprisingly timely. On September 19, 1964—less than a week before this episode aired—five people organized what is believed to be the first public protest for queer equality in the country. Led by activist Randy Wicker, the protestors stood outside the US Army Building in Lower Manhattan to protest the Army's policy of rejecting gay recruits, issuing less-than-honorable discharges to homosexuals, and sending discharge records to current and potential employers.[20]

Their signs bore slogans like "LOVE AND LET LOVE" and "HOMOSEXUALS DIED FOR U.S. TOO." And although the protest garnered no media attention at the time, many of the participants would go on to have a major impact on queer life: Craig Rodwell, then twenty-three years old, would go on to found the Oscar Wilde Memorial Bookshop; twenty-year-old Renée Cafiero would be one of the first openly gay delegates to attend the Democratic National Convention in 1972.

The year that followed saw a surge in public demonstrations by queer community leaders, with actions outside the White House, the United Nations, and other places. One of the most important pickets took place in Philadelphia on July 4th; known as "The Annual Reminder," these protests featured well-dressed, well-behaved homosexuals holding cleanly lettered signs reading "HOMOSEXUALS SHOULD BE JUDGED AS INDIVIDUALS" and "DISCRIMINATION AGAINST HOMOSEXUALS IS IMMORAL," and established early organizing networks for what would become, just a few years later, the first Prides.

By aligning itself with the revolutionary spirit of the times on just its seventh episode, *Bewitched* set a clear expectation: for all its goofy humor, this was a show unafraid to reflect the anger of misunderstood outcasts. That the central metaphor of *Bewitched* could apply so easily to sexual minorities—or, for that matter, to numerous other groups demanding equality in the 1960s—is one reason why the show feels so much queerer than others of the time, even when compared to those that would follow with one-and-done gay guest characters. Without talking about sexuality at all, *Bewitched* depicted a situation that many viewers could find startlingly familiar.

The showrunners were aware that their silly sitcom could be read as a more serious metaphor for the closet. In 1994, a reporter from *The Advocate* asked Elizabeth Montgomery if *Bewitched* was specifically meant to be an allegory for queer liberation. She replied:

Don't think that didn't enter our minds at the time. We talked about it on the set, certainly not in production meetings, that this was about people not being allowed to be what they really are. If you think about it, *Bewitched* is about repression in general and all the frustration and trouble it can cause. It was a neat message to get across to people at that time in a subtle way.[21]

While the early episodes of *Bewitched* established a balanced tension between stuffy conservative tradition and modern liberation, later seasons of the show showed liberation gaining a firm upper hand.

In season three, for example, Samantha and Darrin have a daughter named Tabitha. The parents fret about whether Tabitha's orientation is human or mortal, and when Tabitha begins to exhibit signs of having magic powers, Samantha has a tough conversation with her toddler:

SAMANTHA: I know what fun it is to be a part of the magical life, to have so much at your fingertips. But we're living in a world that's just not ready for people like us, and I'm afraid they may never be. So you're going to have to learn when you can use your witchcraft, and when you can't.[22]

These words were broadcast in September of 1966, two and a half years before the Stonewall uprising. It's a speech about caution, discretion, and social stigma that in the mid-sixties many queer elders were giving to their younger counterparts (maybe not as young as Tabitha, but still).

But if that speech makes *Bewitched* seem a little somber, it's important to also acknowledge its more uplifting and empowering moments. In season six, Samantha's magic begins to mysteriously break down: in one episode, she loses control of her powers and magically traps herself and her family in their house. In another, her magic unexpectedly causes what seem like random objects to appear around their home. In both cases,

Samantha's problem turns out to be that she's feeling trapped by self-imposed rules about not using magic, and the solution is for her to give herself permission to use magic more often so that she can have an outlet for self-expression.

"You must stop feeling guilty about doing witchcraft," insists Samantha's witch doctor, a fancy man given to playing a miniature Liberace-style piano.[23]

It was 1971 at that point, and family sitcoms still didn't talk about homosexuality directly. But if the show can be seen as an allegory for the closet, as Elizabeth Montgomery acknowledged was on the creators' minds, it's not hard to imagine how those words must have been received by queer viewers: "You must stop feeling guilty."

*

Not much is publicly known about the personal lives of everyone who worked on Bewitched, but we do know that there was a contingent of queer people in the cast.

Maurice Evans, who played Samantha's father (as well as The Puzzler on Batman and Dr. Zaius in Planet of the Apes) was said to be gay, though he never discussed it publicly. (His memoir laments the "intrusion into one's private life" experienced by actors "and the necessity . . . to titillate speculation about your personal conduct."[24]) Evans was a resident of New York's Greenwich Village, and his home later passed to gay playwright Edward Albee (of Who's Afraid of Virginia Woolf?),[25] and then gay songwriter Jerry Herman (of Mame and Hello, Dolly!).[26]

Far more memorable was actor Paul Lynde, who played Samantha's Uncle Arthur as a dandy prankster—and also served as the witty and suggestive center on Hollywood Squares:

PETER MARSHALL: Paul, why do Hell's Angels wear leather?
PAUL LYNDE: Because chiffon wrinkles too easily.

In truth, there were really two Paul Lyndes—the fun public persona, and the unhappy man who drank in private. On screen, he was usually typecast as the bumbling straight father with a limp-wristed affect, but behind the scenes, he was deeply frustrated about having to stay closeted for the sake of his career. In one particularly telling *Tonight Show* appearance, Johnny Carson asked Lynde why he did so few interviews, and Lynde replied, "I really don't know . . . other than I'm just absolutely scared to death of coming out and being myself."[27]

If *Bewitched* was made today, Uncle Arthur might be portrayed as the quintessential gay uncle, popping in to entertain the kids, telling some whimsical jokes, and then gallivanting off on some flamboyant adventure with his husband. Alas, he could only be coded as gay on the show with sassy one-liners.

We have Lynde to thank for an unsolved mystery regarding another cast member, Agnes Moorehead. In one interview, Lynde declared that Moorehead was "classy as hell, but one of the all-time Hollywood dykes."[28] It's hard to know how much truth there is to the claim; the actress was guarded about her private life, and Lynde was known for vengeful, alcohol-fueled outbursts that were not entirely reliable.

But of all the show's cast members, the one with the most unexpected journey was Dick Sargent,* who took up the role of Darrin after the original actor, Dick York, left the show. Sargent, who was in the closet at the time, must've had a particularly difficult time with episodes that could be read as gay allegories. For years, he worked on a show about the unfairness of negatively portraying oppressed minorities, about the danger of being discovered, about how important it is to throw off shame about who you are—all the while, trapped behind a secret himself.

Sargent's careful guarding of his private life is evident in the few interviews he granted. When *TV Guide* visited him at home in 1970, he was

---

* Sargent's real name, believe it or not, was Dick Cox.

eager to deflect questions away from himself and toward the decor (antique French pewter colanders, enormous plants, Mexican embroidered pillows, and the lives of the saints painted on sheets of tin). He offered a few words of regret about the dissolution of his marriage a few years earlier—a marriage that did not actually exist, and was fabricated for interviews—and then steered the conversation to the landscaping and his new backyard pool.[29]

Sargent was by no means alone in concocting distractions from the truth of his personal life. *Perry Mason* actor Raymond Burr, for example, would describe entirely fictitious dead wives and a son in interviews, covering for his thirty-year relationship with fellow actor Robert Benevides.[30] Such deception was unpleasant, but it was necessary armor against the social disapproval of the time, which would have destroyed the career of any actor known to be gay—and in fact nearly did in the case of two other stars, Rock Hudson and Jim Nabors.

Close friends, Hudson and Nabors often vacationed together, attended theater, spent holidays together, and guested on each other's shows. Then, disaster struck in 1971. It's hard to say exactly how it started; according to Hudson, a group of gay men outside of LA sent party invitations to a small group of friends that contained a joke about a supposed marriage between Hudson and Nabors.* Somehow, those invitations found their way into the hands of a gossip columnist, without the context of it being a joke, and soon the rumor was being repeated in magazines, by radio DJs, and even parodied in *Mad Magazine*.

At first, Hudson and Nabors both ignored the gossip, hoping it would blow over, but it managed to endure though the summer of 1971. There was just enough of a kernel of truth to the rumor to keep it alive, as they were indeed both gay (though Nabors wasn't Hudson's type—"He's not even blond," scoffed Hudson's housekeeper). But the longer it went unaddressed, the more it circulated, and eventually they realized they'd have to respond.

---

* The joke was that Hudson would take the last name of Nabors's character on *The Andy Griffith Show*, thus: "Rock Pyle."

Hudson gave an interview to a friendly gossip columnist in which he denied everything, including their friendship: "They're not even good friends," read the headline.[31]

Meanwhile, Nabors began granting interviews with entertainment magazines that pointedly emphasized what a ladies' man he was. In one such profile, his friend Olan Mills* effuses about Nabors's dream of starting a family with the right girl. "I'm always fixing him up with dates," Mills told a reporter from *TV Radio Mirror*, adding in an aside that was perhaps poorly phrased: "When we were in Jamaica three years ago, Jim said I just about wore him out."

As a result of the rumors, Hudson and Nabors cut off all contact with each other. The risk was too great; not only were their careers at stake, but queer people were still frequently arrested, and homosexuality was considered a mental illness requiring torturous treatment. For their own safety, they sacrificed their friendship.

But damage had been done to both men's reputations. Hudson's career as a film star was already entering a decline, and work became harder to come by following the months of rumormongering. And Nabors's variety show, which had been one of the top-rated programs on television, was quietly canceled.

This is all to say that by the late 1960s and early 1970s, the seeds of social change had been planted but had yet to fully sprout. Yes, there were protests; yes, there were Pride parades; yes, there were enclaves in major cities where same-sex couples might dare to hold hands in public without fear of violence. These actions would, in the coming years, help shift public opinion, but it was a process that would take decades.

For the time being, being openly, vocally queer was still a risk that few could safely take, and so *Bewitched*'s queer cast members were forced to keep their personal lives hidden, from Paul Lynde to Maurice Evans to Dick Sargent to those actors whose secrets remain no more than speculation.

---

* Yes, the portrait studio guy.

*

After an eight-season run, *Bewitched* took its final bow on March 25, 1972. By that time, primetime television was undergoing another transformation—this time, moving away from wacky premises and toward a franker depiction of shifting American culture. There was a new feminist sitcom about a young single woman pursuing a career, called *The Mary Tyler Moore Show*; another that tackled controversial topics—including homosexuality—head-on called *All in the Family*; and a groundbreaking made-for-TV movie about a gay couple called *That Certain Summer*.

In the gritty, realistic seventies, silly shows like *Bewitched* felt awkwardly passé.

But it left a lasting impression, particularly on Dick Sargent. After the show's conclusion, he stepped back from public view, taking on voice acting roles and occasionally appearing as a guest star on various programs. Reduced media scrutiny seemed to suit him fine, but then a tabloid threatened to out him in the early nineties.

In a panic, Sargent consulted with a friend who'd been through a similar gauntlet: Sheila Kuehl, who played Zelda Gilroy on *The Many Loves of Dobie Gillis* in the 1960s. Kuehl had tried to keep her relationship with another woman secret, but their love letters were discovered, and Kuehl soon found acting work drying up—the result, she later suspected, of an unspoken blacklist. She left showbiz and pursued politics, becoming the first openly queer person elected to the California legislature in 1980.

When Sargent came to her, distraught about the impending outing, she advised him to beat the tabloid at their own game by coming out first.

"Dick was just beside himself," Kuehl recalled in an interview with the Archive of American Television. "I said, 'You know, you have to really come out.'"

At her urging, on October 11, 1991, Sargent attended a fundraiser at the Los Angeles Gay and Lesbian Community Services Center, throwing off the burden of the closet at last in a speech. "Finally telling the truth about who I am gives me more pleasure than any acting job I've ever had," he said, adding, "Most actors wait until they're dead before they come out. I'm glad I did it now."

Those who knew him could see what a relief it was.

"I think he was happier than I've seen him in a long time," Kuehl recalled, "because there's just nothing freer than being yourself."[32]

Sargent's happiness was evident in interviews from the time. "My life is better than it's ever been," he said, "because of coming out."

Public reaction was overwhelmingly positive as well. Sargent was invited to be the grand marshal of the 1992 Pride parade in Los Angeles, and he arrived with his friend Elizabeth Montgomery at his side.

"Elizabeth, what are you here for today?" asked a reporter.

"My buddy," she replied, gesturing with a big smile to Sargent. "In or out of the closet, I love him. He's a super guy and a good friend. I'm happy for him and proud of him."[33]

The journey from the closet to Pride grand marshal left Sargent reflecting on what might have been—and how the show that made him famous could revisit the issue. In one interview, he described his wish for a *Bewitched* reunion special; it could be set twenty years later, he said, and he envisioned a story in which Darrin meets another mortal man married to a witch, and then another, and another.

"He forms a support group for the mortal spouses of witches and warlocks," Sargent mused, describing a not-too-thinly veiled metaphor for a common coming out experience. "Finally, when Darrin marches in the first Mortal Pride Day parade, his still-beautiful wife still at his side, he turns to her and tells her he should have done this years ago."[34]

This imagined reunion special ends with Darrin catching a glimpse of Endora, Samantha's mother, who never respected him on the show and could never remember his name. At this protest, she's holding a sign aloft, Sargent says: "I'm proud of my mortal son-in-law ... Derwood."

ALL
IN THE
FAMILY

BEVERLY: I'm afraid you don't understand, Mrs. Bunker. I'm a transvestite.

EDITH: Well, you sure fooled me. I mean, you ain't got no accent at all.

On January 12, 1971, Edith and Archie Bunker came home early from church to find their twentysomething daughter, Gloria, in a passionate embrace with her husband, Michael. Archie regarded the amorous couple, then shook his head with disapproval and muttered, "Eleven-ten on a Sunday morning."[1]

The studio audience laughed at his assumption about what they were up to, but network executives didn't see the humor.

"They wanted that line out," recalled *All in the Family* creator Norman Lear.[2]

Loosely inspired by a British sitcom and by Lear's own parents, *All in the Family* was a departure from what audiences had come to expect from American comedies—it was a half-hour primetime show about a working-class family that seized topics from newspaper headlines and tackled the country's cultural upheaval head-on.

Getting it on the air had already been an uphill battle. Two different versions of the pilot had been rejected by ABC before it found a home on

CBS, and even then the network had difficulty selling ads to run alongside this controversial experiment.

But CBS reps felt that the "eleven-ten on a Sunday morning" line was a step too far. Censors strongly objected, Lear recalled, "because it put a picture in the audience's mind" of Mike and Gloria getting up to something scandalous. They told Lear the line would have to go; or, at the very least, they'd have to shuffle air dates and broadcast a milder episode first, saving the intended pilot for sometime mid-season—if the program even lasted that long.

Lear was steadfast. "Somehow," he said, "I realized if I gave into that, there's no way I could stand up against anything."

But he wasn't exactly in a strong bargaining position. An unfamous TV writer with no producing credits, he was fighting for a show that had already gone through two failed pilots, based on an off-putting overseas property few had even heard of.

Nevertheless, his response to CBS: No changes. Keep the line. Broadcast the pilot as is, or else. "I said, 'Take the line out and I won't be in tomorrow,'" Lear recalled. "I gather I came across as meaning it."

The night that *All in the Family* was set to debut, Lear had no idea what CBS was going to put on the air. He was at his Los Angeles home when the phone rang at 6:30 PM—his family on the East Coast were watching the 9:30 broadcast and the line, they reported, remained intact. CBS had backed down, clearing a path for *All in the Family* to push the boundaries of what television could air.

The early 1970s was a time of new possibilities both on television and real life, particularly when it came to queer liberation—a topic that Lear's shows would go on to repeatedly explore. The first Prides were starting to blossom around the country; in New York, a recently fired Wall Street analyst named Harvey Milk was thinking about growing out his hair and moving to San Francisco; and by the end of the decade, the public perception of homosexuals would be completely upended, transformed from that of frightening perverts to members of the family. And this revolution would be televised.

*

All in the Family wasn't the first American television program to feature queer characters, though it was among the earliest to do so with any measure of respect. A 1965 episode of *Alfred Hitchcock Presents* is representative of depictions of the era, featuring a sensational story about a killer transvestite. In comparison, *All in the Family*'s fifth episode, "Judging Books by Covers," puts forth the radical idea that queer people might not be a monolithic bunch of perverts.[3]

The episode, aired in February of 1971, begins with Archie meeting a friend of Gloria and Mike's, a fussy young man named Roger whose mannerisms are affectedly precise and whose ascot is assertively purple. Archie clocks Roger from a mile away, calling him a "strange little birdie" and "queer" when he's not present. Mike objects:

> MIKE: You know something, Archie, just because a guy is sensitive and he's an intellectual and he wears glasses, you make him out a queer.
> ARCHIE: I never said a guy who wears glasses is a queer. A guy who wears glasses is a four-eyes. A guy who is a fag is a queer.

But Archie's powers of deduction may not be as strong as he believes. Later, Mike gets into a conversation with the local bartender, Kelsey, who drops some particularly juicy innuendo about one of Archie's friends—a muscular, deep-voiced football player named Steve.

> KELSEY: Well, now, don't get me wrong. I don't mind Steve. His camera store is just down the street here. He only comes in for a drink once in a while on his way home. Besides, he don't, uh, camp it up, you know? And he don't bring in none of his friends.
> MIKE: Kelsey, are you trying to tell me that Steve is . . .

KELSEY: I just wouldn't want my place to become no, uh . . . hangout.*

In the next scene, Archie and Mike get into another argument about Roger. Mike, eager to prove that Archie is too quick to judge, lets it slip that macho Steve "could prance and flit all over this room."

Archie is at first furious at the insinuation, then laughs it off. The next time he sees Steve, the two get into a friendly arm-wrestling tournament, and as their hands are clasped together, eyes locked across the table, Archie mentions what he thinks is Mike's ridiculous mistake.

ARCHIE: I don't know where he gets these brainstorms, but he thinks that you're a . . . jeez, I can't even say it to you, Steve.
STEVE: He's right, Arch.
ARCHIE: Hah?

Archie's face passes through several distinct emotions in the span of a few moments—first confusion, then horror, then amused dismissal of what he believes is a practical joke, transforming into dismay that it might be true, all before landing on a final resolve that it can't possibly be. Steve just shrugs and allows Archie to believe what he wants. (The word *gay* is never said out loud.) The episode concludes with Archie momentarily considering that his prejudices might be unfounded—before waving the idea away with a "nahhhh," though it's clear to the audience that his judgment is buffoonishly wrong.

That this struggling show was willing to tackle homosexuality so early in its run—the fifth episode!—is nothing short of amazing, but it was by design.

_____

* In a strange twist, by making the gay character a camera store owner, writers Norman Lear and Burt Styler forecasted what would be Harvey Milk's occupation several years before Milk himself contemplated opening his shop in the Castro.

"Read whatever you're reading, *LA Times*, *New York Times*, and pay a lot of attention to your kids," Lear recalled telling the writing staff. "We're going to work with what exists by way of problems in your neighborhood, your family, your memory, et cetera."[4]

Queer visibility would certainly have been reflected in headlines of the time, particularly if writers glanced at newspapers from New York. The Stonewall uprising marked a dividing line between two very different approaches to queer liberation: whereas previous protests had tended to be orderly and polite, now they were growing steadily louder and more raucous. The old "Annual Reminder," a solemn and well-dressed procession of sign-carrying homosexuals in Philadelphia, had given rise to the "zap."

Zaps were bold, disruptive confrontations, often organized by the newly formed Gay Activists Alliance (GAA) in New York. Instead of standing on the sidewalk in conservative suits and dresses and handing out fliers, this new style of protester invaded institutions, made noise, and started fights. One zap involved a crowd of rowdy queers descending on the New York City Marriage Bureau, taking control of the office and denying licenses to heterosexuals.[5] A particularly intrepid activist named Mark Segal, identifying his group as "The Gay Raiders," was known for infiltrating television studios, handcuffing himself to cameras, and shouting slogans at startled newscasters.

These actions didn't always achieve their stated goals, but those goals were often something of a red herring: protestors might demand gay marriage, for example, but the unstated mission was publicity.

"Gays who have as yet no sense of gay pride see a zap on television or read about it in the press," GAA leader Arthur Evans told writer Toby Marotta.[6] "And the no-longer-closeted gays realize that assimilation into the heterosexual mainstream is no answer: gays must unite among themselves, organize their common resources for collective action, and resist."*

---

* Another benefit of these actions: catharsis. As another activist told Marotta, "One good zap is worth ten years of analysis."

As headline-grabbers, zaps were highly effective. The *New York Times*, which had ignored the Stonewall uprising when it happened, paid instant attention to a GAA protest after cops raided a gay bar called The Snake Pit. "Homosexuals Hold Protest in 'Village' After Raid Nets 167," read the headline.[7]

While groups like the GAA led raucous guerilla actions, other organizers took bold legal steps, like activist Richard John Baker, who sued a Minnesotan county clerk when he and his male partner were denied a marriage license. Around the same time, a group of medical professionals pushed the American Psychological Association to stop treating homosexuality as a mental illness. And when television shows like *Police Woman* and *Marcus Welby, M.D.* aired episodes depicting queers as cruel criminals and freaks, gay viewers didn't just write angry letters; they stormed the networks' offices and refused to leave until executives promised the episodes would never air again.

Queers were tired of waiting. The seventies marked a rapid tactical shift: *no more asking nicely; now we're issuing demands.*

*

As *All in the Family* gained recognition for its groundbreaking approach to current events, Lear expanded his primetime footprint with more programs. There was *Hot L Baltimore*, a short-lived series featuring one of the first recurring same-sex couples on television; *Mary Hartman, Mary Hartman*, an odd soap opera spoof that showed a gay couple contemplating marriage; *The Jeffersons*, which featured a compassionate depiction of a transgender woman; and then there was *Maude*, which in one episode made a compelling argument in favor of gay bars.

But of all Lear's shows, it was *All in the Family* that most frequently commented on homosexuality. One of the show's most memorable storylines, playing out over three years, involves a drag queen whose depiction is shockingly nuanced and touching even by the standards of modern television.

The character's name is Beverly LaSalle, and she first appears in the season six episode "Archie the Hero," initially aired in September of 1975. It opens with Archie, who has been moonlighting as a cab driver, bragging about having saved the life of a "big, tall, beautiful-looking, classy dame"—she was one of his passengers and fainted, he tells the family, so he rushed to perform mouth-to-mouth and revived her.

After getting the woman to a hospital, he'd left his name and address (expecting her to look him up to pay her cab fare), and headed home to bask in his family's praise. After a bit, he steps away, and that's when the woman shows up at the house. She explains to Edith that she'd passed out from exhaustion because she'd been working a lot of shows lately:

EDITH: Oh, are you in show business?
BEVERLY: Yes. I'm a female impersonator. [Explosive audience laughter.]
EDITH: [Considering.] That's smart, too. I mean, who can imitate a female better than a lady?

Though Edith doesn't quite understand what's happening, she soon will. Archie returns and is happy to see that Beverly is well—and even happier when she offers him a fifty-dollar bill in payment. Beverly tries several times to explain herself as gently and euphemistically as she can—"I'm no lady," she says, to which thick-headed Archie shrugs, "How you earned this fifty is no business of mine." Finally, impatient, she cuts to the chase:

ARCHIE: . . . I'll just say "Thank you, Miss." Unless youse girls like to be called Ms?
BEVERLY: Why don't you call me . . . mister.

With this, she yanks off her wig. Archie's crestfallen face, accompanied by even more explosive audience laughter, is the last thing we see before cutting to commercial.

The character of Beverly LaSalle was based entirely on the performer, a San Francisco drag artist who went by Lori Shannon on stage and Don Seymour McLean off stage. McLean, who called himself "a stand-up comic in a dress,"[8] was a fixture of San Francisco's famed club Finocchio's, a drag institution in the city's North Beach where Lear happened to catch the show. When it came time to create the character of Beverly, the writers got out of Lori's way, allowing her to play the drag persona she'd perfected on stage.

"We didn't influence Beverly LaSalle to be anything but what [Lori] was," Lear laughed, recalling their collaboration. "I thought she was wonderful, wonderful."[9]

After the commercial break, Edith struggles to recount the story of Beverly's visit while slipping frantically between pronouns: "I would never have guessed she was a man until she took his hair off," she says to Mike, "Well, anyway, his hair came off, and there she was, a man."

Archie, on the other hand, is less kind. "This freak took my breath under an assumed sex," he fumes. If he'd known what Beverly was when she needed rescuing, he "would have got a fag fireman."

It's uncomfortable dialogue to hear, but Archie's attitude is in line with that of many Americans of the time.

Drag was rarely seen on TV or in film, and when it was, it was generally awkward—or shorthand for mental illness. Though there had been many female impersonators working in live venues throughout the twentieth century, television censors were generally quite effective at keeping such performances off the air.

When drag did appear in movies and television, it was usually in the context of a trick rather than artistry. On film, Charlie Chaplin set the template in 1914's *The Masquerader*, the title of which makes its attitude clear; a few decades later, two men dress as women to deceive the mob in the comedy *Some Like It Hot*; in 1974, *Freebie and the Bean* features an appalling gender-bending killer, just one year before audiences were to meet Beverly LaSalle.

On television, one of the first shows to regularly depict female impersonation was a 1968 series called *The Ugliest Girl in Town*, in which a man disguises himself as a female model in order to be close to his girlfriend. In the late seventies, Jack disguised himself as a woman from time to time on *Three's Company* for the purpose of various schemes; and in the eighties, trickery was the entire premise of *Bosom Buddies*, with two men posing as women to obtain cheap housing at a women-only hotel.

It's a trope one might call "deceitful drag"—the idea being that a man who dresses as a woman is trying to pull off a scheme, either because they're running a con or because they're desperate. It makes drag seem like a particularly unsavory practice.

That's not to say that deceit was the only reason audiences would see drag on television; it was also common for performers to don dresses for comedy. Milton Berle involved frequent cross-dressing in his sketches, as did Jonathan Winters, Harvey Korman, Danny Kaye, and Flip Wilson. In contrast to drag-as-deceit, these comedians were intentionally obvious about being men in dresses. The joke is the inconsistency of their gender presentation, or the perceived humiliation—and misogyny—of a man "lowering himself" to being seen in feminine attire.

Beverly embodies a different kind of drag, one that was far rarer at the time on TV: she is an empowered drag character. She's not deceitful at all; she's straightforward about who she is, introducing herself as a female impersonator. And although she is entirely believable as a woman, she doesn't mind removing her wig and correcting those who misperceive her. Beverly isn't playing a trick, or desperate, or an obvious frumpy man. She's in drag because she's good at it, and because it's her highly skilled craft. Although such performances weren't uncommon in the live venues of major cities at the time, they were relatively new to television.

Over the next few years, audiences would see more characters like Beverly in mainstream entertainment, such as Charles Pierce playing a Mae West–impersonating nightclub performer in *Starsky & Hutch*, Jim Bailey as Judy Garland in the opening ceremonies of the 1984 Olympics, and

Divine breaking out of midnight movies with *Hairspray*. By the 1980s, the term "drag queen" was catching on, as was mainstream fandom, and the regal terminology perfectly fit these powerful, extravagant, larger-than-life performers.

But back in the mid-seventies, Archie isn't keen to be connected to Beverly. He tries to keep their association under wraps, which gets complicated when the publicity-seeking owner of the cab company tracks Archie down at a local bar, a reporter in tow who expects to write an article about how Archie saved a woman's life. As luck would have it, Beverly arrives just as Archie's trying to escape the attention.

The reporter soon suspects something's amiss about Beverly:

REPORTER: I just saw your lady friend in the men's room.

ARCHIE: She must've made a mistake.

REPORTER: No way, I was a medic in the army, there's no mistake.

That's followed by a chilling scene in which the men in the bar all turn to stare at Beverly. She sees their look and understands just how volatile the situation has become: a bunch of straight men in a bar have just sniffed out a queer person in their midst. The scene could easily turn ugly.

Beverly thinks fast and concocts a little lie, telling the reporter that she received mouth-to-mouth from a passing truck driver, not Archie. The reporter runs off to track down the nonexistent driver, much to Archie's relief. "For a dame," he tells her, "you're one hell of a guy."

The experience leaves them both changed—Beverly from an object of Archie's scorn to his savior, and Archie from a thoughtless bigot to someone ever-so-slightly more respectful. And although Archie is eager to boast about saving Beverly's life, it's her intervention that rescues them both. The episode may be called "Archie the Hero," but in the end, Beverly comes off as the true champion.

Another groundbreaking aspect of the character: she was one of the first openly queer television characters to return for more than one episode. Over the next couple years, she'd appear twice more, growing closer to the Bunkers each time—until her storyline takes a dark turn.

Her second appearance comes a year after her first in season seven's "Beverly Rides Again." The mischief starts down at the corner bar where some of Archie's friends pull a series of practical jokes on him. Annoyed, Archie storms home to plot revenge, but is surprised to find Beverly paying a visit. That Beverly recurs is a minor television miracle, considering how rare queer characters still were at that point. For comparison, the same year this episode aired, the show *Family* had a gay teen on a single episode and the regulars talk about him like they just discovered a mutant:

KATE: I think of myself as a fairly sophisticated woman, but . . .
DOUG: You've never been touched by anything like this personally.
KATE: It's something I've almost never thought about.[10]

Family's gay friend appears once, promises to keep in touch, and then never returns. Beverly, on the other hand, is now a recurring part of the Bunkers' lives, and in her friendly banter with Edith we see that the family is starting to develop a more personal relationship with her. And as they become comfortable around her, so can the audience.

But Archie's not quite comfortable yet. Still fixated on the pranks at the bar, he gets the bright idea to set his friend Pinky up with Beverly on a dinner date as a practical joke. This is in keeping with the long-standing "drag as deception" trope, but he encounters unexpected pushback. Edith feels the prank is too mean, and Beverly is simply scandalized—not an easy thing to do to a professional drag queen.

"Mr. Bunker, this is deceiving a total stranger," Beverly gasps. "I can't go along with that!"

But Archie insists, and Beverly reluctantly agrees. When Pinky comes over, he flirts with her a bit and then takes her aside to reveal a twist: he has recognized her as a drag performer from her posters. He's not mad, though—he's amused, he tells her, and wants to go along with Archie's plan in order to give his friend the satisfaction of thinking he's pulled off a prank.

Beverly is skeptical, but after securing Pinky's assurance that his intentions are honorable and he just wants to give his friend Archie a win, she agrees and off they head to a Chinese restaurant adorned with history's most aggressively seventies decor.

Edith, still feeling a bit tense about the whole thing, watches uncomfortably as Pinky snuggles with Beverly. She takes Archie aside and insists that he come clean, and he does—but then Pinky triumphantly sneers that he knew about Archie's ruse all along, and was just biding his time so he could ruin the prank and make Archie feel dumb for failing to pull it off.*

But as Pinky gloats about the failed practical joke, there's one more twist: his girlfriend Doris barges in, sees him with Beverly, and throws a fit. As it turns out, Archie had secretly called her to tip her off about Pinky's date. Beverly takes the opportunity to perform a wig-reveal, Doris goes into hysterics, and Pinky flees, humiliated.

Archie is now beside himself with glee. "This is one of the greatest nights of my life! I finally got even with that guy! I gotta thank you two swell girls!" he declares, kissing Edith and then—before he realizes what he's doing—turning to kiss Beverly with just as much enthusiasm. The episode ends on his stunned expression.

It's an outstanding comedic twist, and a sign that Archie's discomfort around Beverly has waned to the point that he can forget that he even felt it. Beverly is just one of the "swell girls" in his life, and the fact that some of those girls are queer is—at least momentarily, when he's sufficiently distracted—an incidental detail.

Meanwhile in real life, queer people were growing even more present in the lives of Americans, particularly at the ballot box. It's appropriate that this time is marked by the appearance of recurring queer characters on television, as queer politics had become a recurring presence in the news.

---

* Heterosexuals, it must be noted, are exhausting.

As this episode aired, San Francisco camera store owner Harvey Milk had become a fixture of the community—the "Mayor of Castro Street"—and, after being appointed the first openly gay city commissioner in the United States, was contemplating a run for office.[11] In Michigan, University of Michigan senior Kathy Kozachenko was well into her term as the first openly queer elected official in the country.[12] And there were ominous signs of things to come in Miami, where a beauty queen turned anti-gay activist named Anita Bryant was readying a campaign to roll back an equal rights bill.

Impressively, *All in the Family* was able to anticipate a particularly contentious ballot issue one year later, in 1977. It came in season eight's "Cousin Liz," which marks a point at which queer characters became more than just friends—they became a part of the family.

The episode opens with Edith and Archie traveling to the funeral of their cousin Liz, a beautiful woman who—mysteriously to the family—never married, and lived with another woman named Veronica.

At the wake, Veronica takes Edith aside to explain something. They step into another room of the house . . .

EDITH: Was this Liz's room?
VERONICA: Well, this was our room.
EDITH: Oh, you shared the same bedroom.
VERONICA: We shared everything. [Audible gasps from the audience.]

As with Beverly's first appearance, it takes a few attempts to make the situation clear. Veronica deploys euphemisms, all of which sail far over Edith's head . . . until Veronica hits on something that makes sense:

VERONICA: This was . . . more like a marriage.
EDITH: A marriage? Oh, but it couldn't be. I mean, you and Cousin Liz was both g . . . [Her face falls.]

Marriage, it turns out, was the magic word. Edith might not know much about lesbians (and no wonder, because the word is never spoken), but she knows what a marriage is. And she feels terrible that, unlike her and Archie, Veronica and Liz had to keep their relationship secret from the rest of the family. "It must have been terrible," Edith sympathizes, "loving somebody and not being able to talk about it."

A conflict soon arises when Veronica asks if she can keep a tea set that belonged to Liz as a reminder of their twenty-five-year relationship. Edith immediately says yes: "It belongs to you. You're really her next of kin." Again, the word *marriage* has unlocked total understanding in Edith's mind.

But Archie's not so eager to go along with this—the tea set belongs to blood family, he insists—and suggests they take the matter to court. Veronica tenses up. "I can't do that," she says, "because I might lose my job."

Veronica is a teacher, and in 1977 it was common for teachers to be fired simply because they were suspected of being queer.[13] In fact, this episode aired one year before California voted on a measure called the Briggs Initiative that would have barred homosexuals from working as teachers, counselors, and school administrators.

The timing was a coincidence, according to Lear. "I don't recall it being connected to that," he said.[14] But in a fortuitous bit of timing, the episode was rerun a year later—one night before the election. The next day, Briggs went down in a landslide defeat. It was the biggest ballot victory for queer organizers to date, and it didn't hurt that voters had just been introduced to a sympathetic lesbian character with language—"marriage"—that even Edith could understand.

Archie, the clear villain of the episode, threatens to out Veronica if she won't give up the tea set:

ARCHIE: Who the hell wants people like that teachin' our kids? I'm sure God don't. God's sitting in judgment.
EDITH: Well, sure, he is, but he's God. You ain't.

Edith gets a huge round of applause for that comeback. It's rare that she stands up to Archie so assertively, but this is important to her. "She's all alone in the world now," Edith implores. "And she didn't hurt you, so why should you want to hurt her? Archie, I can't believe you'd do anything that mean."

Archie relents (though he steals the sugar tongs when Veronica's not looking), leaving the audience to reflect on the question at the heart of this episode: Should gay people be considered a part of the family? Edith isn't particularly worldly, but she knows what a family is—people who love and support each other—and she unequivocally considers Veronica a part of that arrangement. In the years to come, guiding television audiences toward a similar understanding would emerge as a crucial organizing tactic—a strategy made starkly clear in Beverly LaSalle's third (and heartbreakingly final) appearance in December of 1977.

*

In the season eight episode "Edith's Crisis of Faith: Part 1," Beverly is once again back at the Bunker home, celebrating Christmas and her upcoming show at Carnegie Hall. They all seem to have grown a lot closer over the past year, with Edith compiling a scrapbook of Beverly's appearances. "We're just proud of you," Edith beams. "There've been a lot of celebrities in this house—Sammy Davis Jr., Nina Fleishhacker, whose niece did a TV commercial for bad breath. You're the only one that's like family."

This explicit declaration that Beverly is "like family" is something that many queer people couldn't even hope to hear from their own relations in 1977. Beverly is touched:

BEVERLY: I love you, Edith. To me you're like a sister.
EDITH: Oh Beverly. To me you're like a sister. No, I mean brother.
    Oh, well, both rolled into one.

The Bunkers have a truly warm moment with everyone gathered, happily enjoying each other's company, and then Beverly and Mike walk to the corner to catch a cab. A few minutes later, the family hears sirens and rushes outside. Beverly and Mike were attacked by muggers just steps from the Bunker home. Beverly tackled the muggers, but they were carrying a pipe and started beating her.

In the hospital, Edith learns that Beverly did not survive the attack.

She receives this news with an expression of sheer horror, as if a sister she'd known her whole life had just been killed, and there's a long span of incredible silence as she looks from Archie to a doctor in disbelief.

The next day, the family sits, stunned, and Archie reflects sadly on the loss. "I wish I'd told Beverly what a nice fellow she was," he says.

Edith is even more bereft, especially when Gloria observes that this wasn't just a random mugging—Beverly was beaten to death, she says, "because he was different."

Once again, there's a moment of silence that's deeply unusual for a sitcom. Edith's face shifts from confusion at Gloria's line to an emotion that's hard to identify at first, before becoming something more determined. She was just about to go to church, but she suddenly changes her plans:

EDITH: The way I feel today, I may not go to church ever.
ARCHIE: Now, Edith, I really think somebody from the family
    ought to be there representing us in front of God.
EDITH: [Furiously] Why? What good does it do?

That hard-to-identify emotion, it turns out, was anger. Beverly's loss has changed something fundamental for Edith—her faith in God's love.

This was the first half of a two-parter, ending on Edith's renouncing of her faith with the second half airing in some markets on Christmas Day (happy holidays, everyone). Part two opens with Edith in a deep depression, unable to participate in Christmas. Archie tries to cheer her up, but his words are counterproductive: "This is New York," he says. "Guys like Beverly, they're either getting murdered by strangers or close friends. You see it in the paper every day."

To Archie, the death is part of an abstract problem that happens all the time to "guys like Beverly." He's not wrong; queer people were often the victims of violent crime in the 1970s—and, for that matter, still to this day. Just a few months after this episode aired, a gang of teenagers armed with baseball bats targeted gay men for beatings in Central Park, seriously injuring six.[15]

But Edith isn't thinking about "guys like Beverly," she's only thinking about Beverly. Homophobia was a systemic, society-wide problem, but Edith is experiencing it through her personal connection with one particular victim. The tragedy has placed a human face on a problem that otherwise might have seemed abstract, far away, or like someone else's problem.

That Edith comes to understand the plight of a marginalized group through a personal connection is a common phenomenon. Personal connections often help people understand larger issues in ways they didn't before, spurring them to take action.

For example, just one month before this episode aired, Harvey Milk was elected to the board of supervisors in San Francisco. By that time, Milk had become an integral part of the community; locals knew him not only as an icon of queer empowerment, but on a personal level as a longtime neighbor and friend. That personal connection helped get him elected, thanks to the volunteer work of folks who'd come to know and respect him, and led to the mourning and rage when he was murdered one year later.

In the months following Milk's slaying in 1978, San Francisco experienced waves of grief, with multiple vigils in his memory. And when his killer, Dan White, got the lightest possible sentence, that grief turned to anger and action. Protestors stormed City Hall when the sentence came down, furious that Milk had been denied justice. San Francisco police had raised $100,000 for White's defense, according to the exhaustive account of Milk's life by journalist Randy Shilts,[16] and the community was fed up. That night, they set fire to police cars, tore down the ironwork around City Hall, smashed windows, and rioted.

A group called the Fruit Punch Collective recorded audio of the scene, including a fiery speech by an organizer named Amber Hollibaugh:

It's time we stood up for each other. That's what Harvey meant to us. He wasn't some big leader. He was one of us. I don't think it's wrong for us to feel like we do. I think we should feel like it more often . . . Don't you listen to anybody that tells you you don't need to fight back![17]

The recording culminates in the crowd chanting along with her: "Fight back! Fight back! Fight back! Fight back!"

Following the White Night riots, San Francisco instituted reforms in the police department, Mayor Dianne Feinstein appointed numerous queer people to public office, and Milk's replacement, Harry Britt, got to work on the nation's first domestic partner legislation (which was vetoed by Feinstein but signed by her successor).

This lesson about the power of personal connection had to be relearned a few decades later in 2008, when California faced Proposition 8, a ballot measure that banned marriage equality. The television ads against Prop 8 were, especially at first, completely impersonal. They focused on vague virtues rather than the impact on individuals: "It's wrong to treat people differently under the law," a narrator intones as text slides past. "No on 8. It's unfair. Unnecessary. And wrong."

Those ads didn't work. Prop 8 passed, and California lost marriage equality for years. But four years later, organizers took a very different approach when a marriage measure was up for a vote in Maryland. Smiling individuals turn to the camera and explain why they, personally, support the freedom to marry. "I'm for everyone getting their slice of the wedding cake," one woman says.

"For my dad," says another speaker, and "for his partner, Tom."

While the Prop 8 ads presented an abstract idea of "unfairness," the Maryland ads showed real people. On 2012's election day, Maryland voters approved marriage equality, something that had never happened before in the United States.

The power of personal connection is what helped marriage equality pass in Maryland. It's what changed San Francisco after Milk was killed. And it's what affects Edith—and with any luck, the audience—in the two "Edith's Crisis of Faith" episodes.

Edith's grief seems like it's going to last forever, but then Mike makes a breakthrough. He's the first to realize that she's not just sad—she's angry. He asks her who she's angry at. "I'm mad at God," she tearfully replies.

Mike is an atheist, and it's remarkable that he, out of everyone in the family, finds a way to comfort her:

MIKE: Maybe . . . maybe we're not supposed to understand everything all at once. Maybe we're just supposed to understand things a little bit at a time.

EDITH: Trouble with me is, I don't understand nothing.

MIKE: Oh, Ma, that's not true. You understand plenty. Ma, if there is a God, you're one of the most understanding people he ever made. We need you.

Mike's right. We do need Edith, and contrary to how she feels, she's the most understanding person in the entire episode. She understood before anyone else that Beverly was a person entitled to love, respect, dignity, and place among the family. She may not understand God, but she understands the people around her.

Hearing that they need her, Edith emerges for Christmas dinner and offers a prayer. "Dear God," she says, "E. Bunker here. I'm sorry that I can't understand everything all at once, but I am thankful for Mike . . . and Gloria . . ." and, her face starting to lighten, she proceeds to list every relative, friend, neighbor, and passing acquaintance she can as the family stares hungrily at their food. Fade to black.

About 18 million people watched this episode when it aired, and it's hard to imagine they weren't changed by having grieved along with Edith, coming away with compassion for people who might've seemed like an abstract "other" before.

*

All in the Family wrapped up its run in April of 1979, having spanned almost the entire decade. Across that time, the show's depiction of queer characters evolved from Archie's ill-informed denial of his gay friend Steve in 1971 to accepting Beverly as a cherished member of the family in 1977.

Archie's growth reflects a real-life evolution in the public's awareness of homosexuals across that time, thanks in large part to the steady maturing of the queer liberation movement. The decade begins with boisterous, disruptive zaps—a tactic that didn't go away, but gradually incorporated more focused, calculated efforts executed over a long term.

Election campaigns around the country proved that queer people could not only gather, but they could organize; and as the 1970s came to a close, national activists (a group that barely existed in significant numbers a decade earlier) pulled together one of their most impressive endeavors yet with a colossal march on Washington. In October of 1979, around 100,000 people descended on the nation's capital, armed with a list of specific demands for federal actions, from nondiscrimination laws to protections for queer youth.

"Today in the capital of America, we are all here," declared Alan Young, one of the event organizers, at the march's opening ceremonies. "The almost liberated and the slightly repressed; the butch, the femme and everything in-between . . . Yes, we are all here! We are everywhere! Welcome to the March on Washington for Lesbian and Gay Rights!"[18]

Over the course of three days, attendees clustered into workshops and strategy sessions, marched on the National Mall, and met with around two hundred elected officials. And they did so under a newly unveiled symbol: a brightly colored rainbow flag, designed in 1978 by Gilbert Baker to unify the nation's disconnected queer communities with a banner of pride.

The community had arrived in the seat of American power and in the

American consciousness—not as the mysterious, misunderstood outsiders they once were, but increasingly as members of the American family.

Recalling Lori Shannon's work on the show, Lear said, "She was a lovely human. It had to feel nice to be in a position where you can help a mass audience understand that a Beverly LaSalle can be someone you care about."

ALICE

ALICE: . . . I shoulda known [Jack was gay]. Mel said he was a man's man.

I n the fall of 1976, there was so much queer energy in the air that cultural commentator Nicholas von Hoffman declared it "the year of the fag"—which, to borrow a Marge Simpson line, was "true, but he shouldn't say it."[1]

In theaters, *Sanford and Son*'s Redd Foxx journeyed to Hollywood in the movie *Norman... Is That You?* to meet his son's new roommate, only to suspect something queer about their living arrangement when he spied a lavender window treatment—lavender having a decades-long history as code for queerness. In the movie *The Ritz*, actor Jack Weston was busy hiding from the mob at a gay bathhouse.* The movie *Car Wash* featured *Starsky & Hutch*'s Antonio Fargas as a femme icon who reads a coworker for filth: "Honey, I'm more man than you'll ever be, and more woman than you'll ever get!" And although it was still months away from becoming a surprise cult sensation, *The Rocky Horror Picture Show* had just had its first midnight screening in New York.

---

* Weston had previously guest starred on *All in the Family* as Archie's nemesis, a disgruntled laundromat operator.

Meanwhile, David Bowie had just come out as bisexual in *Playboy*,[2] and Elton John had done the same in *Rolling Stone*.[3]

But the thickest concentration of gay content was to be found during the week of September 28, when America's TV sets experienced a lavender flood unlike anything broadcast television had ever seen.

It began Tuesday night on CBS with an episode of the Aaron Spelling drama *Family*, in which teenager Willie learns that his friend Zeke has been arrested at a gay bar, leading to tense heart-to-hearts between friends and family members.[4]

The next night on CBS's *Alice*, the diner waitress played by Linda Lavin is dismayed when a hunky paramour ends a date by coming out to her as gay.[5]

That was followed by the debut of Norman Lear's *The Nancy Walker Show* in ABC's Thursday night lineup. Walker, who was familiar to audiences as the mother on CBS's *Rhoda*, now played a Los Angeles talent agent with a live-in gay houseboy, nearly a decade before *The Golden Girls* launched with a similar sidekick.[6]

Later on Thursday night, viewers whose dials remained on ABC for the cop-comedy *Barney Miller* were treated to the sight of a police station slumber party featuring two Greenwich Village regulars, a gay couple named Marty and Darryl.[7]

And over all of these programs loomed one conspicuously absent homosexual: a sardonic hairdresser was to appear on the new David Brenner series *Snip*, set to debut Thursday night before it was yanked from NBC's schedule under mysterious circumstances.[8]

*

Television was primed for a period like this. Following *All in the Family*'s success with "Judging Books by Covers," there had been a few scattered gay-themed episodes elsewhere on the dial. A 1974 episode of *Maude* featured Bea Arthur's character eagerly befriending a gay writer (played by future *Soap* star Robert Mandan), prompting whispers and innuendo from family and friends.

"What's all the fuss about?" demands Maude's housekeeper, Mrs. Naugatuck. "Just because a man's homosexual? We think quite highly of them in England. Our government's full of them. The only one we're positive isn't a queen is the Queen!"[9]

That same year on *M*A*S*H*, the company is thrown into a tizzy when a young soldier, George, reveals to Alan Alda's Hawkeye that he's gay:[10]

> GEORGE: Actually, Doc, there were two guys in my unit who got beaten up. One colored . . . and one homosexual.
> HAWKEYE: [After a pause] So you're a Negro.

The episode is oddly prescient. A month after it aired, a Vietnam War veteran named Leonard Matlovich read an interview in which activist Frank Kameny mentioned his plans to challenge the country's ban on openly gay servicemembers, which prompted Matlovich to come out to his commanding officer.[11] That kicked off a years-long battle with the US government; it wasn't until the 1980s that the Air Force offered Matlovich a financial settlement to voluntarily leave service. The military did not end its ban until 2011.

Viewers probably weren't surprised that shows like *Maude* and *M*A*S*H*, which were known for pushing the envelope, were ready to tackle homosexuality. But in an unlikely move, *The Mary Tyler Moore Show* beat them both to the punch, with a 1973 episode in which busybody landlady Phyllis believes her brother, Ben*, is falling in love with her tenant Rhoda, only to discover to her great relief that there's no budding romance because Ben is gay.[12]

That *The Mary Tyler Moore Show* was willing to broach the subject of homosexuality suggests that tolerance for queer characters on television had rapidly shifted. The show was not exactly known for pushing boundaries

---

* Ben is played by actor and director Robert Moore, best known for directing the original off-Broadway run of *The Boys in the Band*.

and had previously rejected a script from *All in the Family* writer Barry Harman in which Mary's boyfriend would have come out as gay.

"We were always very jealous of *The Mary Tyler Moore Show*, because they were doing fluff," said writer Bob Schiller, who worked on several of Norman Lear's shows. When *Maude* was preparing to air a two-parter about abortion, Schiller joked that *The Mary Tyler Moore Show* would probably retaliate: "They're doing a *three*-parter about mayonnaise."[13]

If sitcoms considered "safe" were happily throwing homosexuality into the mix, clearly standards had shifted. Producers were eager to explore. But their creative process was unexpectedly corked for two years thanks in part to Congress, the National Parent Teacher Association, and Linda Blair—yes, the little girl from *The Exorcist*.

*

To understand how America got into this mess—and then got itself out—it's helpful to look at the second episode of the show *Alice*.

Even outside of the context of 1976's gayest week, *Alice* was a strange oddity—a sitcom based on, of all things, a gritty Martin Scorsese film. The original 1974 comedy-drama *Alice Doesn't Live Here Anymore* is about a single mom who flees domestic violence and the broken dreams of her youth, eventually finding love in a greasy spoon diner. Filmed in a contemplative vérité style, the movie featured wrenching, emotional performances by Ellen Burstyn and Kris Kristofferson (and a brief cameo by seven-year-old Laura Dern enjoying an ice cream cone).

Two years later, CBS lifted the single-mom Alice character and diner setting out of the grit and grime and plopped her into a conventional multi-cam studio-audience sitcom, complete with corny jokes, sassy sidekicks, and the grinning catchphrase "Kiss my grits." It was a strange transfiguration of the original work, but only the start of the show's surprises.

The *Alice* pilot aired in late August of 1976, and the series then took an odd month-long hiatus before slipping into its regular Wednesday time slot on September 29 with an episode titled "Alice Gets a Pass."

The story starts with Mel, the owner of the diner, informing the waitresses that his old college friend Jack is coming to town. Jack's a tall, broad-shouldered, seventies-mustached Adonis played by Denny Miller.*

Alice and Jack hit it off and go on what Alice assumes are a few dates. She's happy for the companionship and especially pleased to have a stable masculine figure for her son, Tommy, to look up to. After getting to know Jack, Alice invites him to take Tommy on a fishing trip with Mel, her boss, and he agrees. But trouble emerges when Alice makes a move and Jack rebuffs her:

JACK: I'm gay.
ALICE: You don't mean just . . . jolly?

Jack's candor is a surprise to Alice, and likely to viewers as well—it was only a few years earlier that comings-out were virtually unheard of on television, and a colossal risk in real life. But times were changing, and although Alice receives the news with wide eyes, she manages to keep her language supportive:

ALICE: Well, I don't see why that should matter, I mean, uh,
    you're a person and I'm a person, and . . . [long pause] . . . gay?

All in all, it's a relatively gentle reaction for 1976. (It would be outdone a month later on an episode of *Phyllis*, the *Mary Tyler Moore Show* spinoff, in which Cloris Leachman's titular character worries that her boyfriend has been avoiding physical contact because there's something wrong with her.

---

* A former UCLA basketball player, Miller had played the first blond Tarzan in the lower-than-low-budget *Tarzan, the Ape Man*; sitcom audiences might recognize him as a wayward surfer named Duke on *Gilligan's Island*, or as Carol Brady's high school boyfriend Tank on *The Brady Bunch*. Alternately, younger audiences may know him as the Gorton's Fisherman from some commercials in the nineties.

When he confesses that he's gay, she cheers, "Oh, that's wonderful!"—a reaction any queer person would welcome.[14])

Alice handles Jack's news with a wistful shrug, seemingly more disappointed about her romantic miscalculation than homophobic. After Jack leaves, she muses, "I shoulda known. Mel said he was a man's man."

But then she feels a twinge of fear when she realizes that she'd invited Jack to take her kid on a fishing trip.

In the next scene, Alice and her coworker Flo wrestle with feelings of discomfort around Jack's sexuality. At first, Flo refuses to believe the news:

FLO: Any woman would die to take that hunk of candy home! Why, he spends half his life surrounded by big virile men, in locker rooms, in showers, being tackled by other football players. [Her face starts to fall.] Jumpin' up and down and huggin' each other. [Long pause.] Pattin' each others' butts. [Even longer pause.] If that don't beat all, Jack Newhouse, gay!

They're also not sure if Tommy should accompany Jack and Mel on their fishing trip. On one hand, Flo and Alice have absorbed the "common knowledge" of the time that gay people are somehow dangerous, even if they can't articulate *why* gays are a threat:

ALICE: I'm not sure I want him to go.
FLO: Oh, you mean because Jack is a … [Both arch their eyebrows as the audience laughs.]

But on the other hand, in the short time she's known him, Alice has come to consider Jack a friend. She can see that the presumptions that she carries about gays don't seem to match the guy she's been going out with— or at least, *thought* she was going out with. A brief battle of ambivalence ensues:

ALICE: I'm just overreacting.

FLO: Sure you are.

ALICE: Maybe you're right, I'm just being silly and narrow-minded.

FLO: Of course you are.

ALICE: Of course I am.

FLO: So what are you going to do?

ALICE: Tell Tommy he can't go.

FLO: Good.

But despite her resolve in the moment, Alice can't shake a nagging feeling that in trying to protect her son, she's inadvertently done something wrong.

*

Heading into the commercial break, Alice is torn between conflicting impulses that mirror a crisis that much of America was experiencing in the mid-1970s.

For decades, Americans had held deeply entrenched beliefs that queer people were a sinister threat. (Remember that line from the 1961 film *Boys Beware*: "One never knows when the homosexual is about. He may appear normal, and it may be too late when you discover he is mentally ill.")

The general public attitude toward queer people in the early seventies was reflected quite clearly on the show *Marcus Welby, M.D.* That series featured Robert Young as a kindly, old, paternalistic family doctor who dispensed homespun wisdom and compassionate treatment—but his compassion had its limits when it came to homosexuals. On a 1973 episode titled "The Other Martin Loring," Dr. Welby advises one patient (a married father who confesses feelings of attraction to men) that homosexuality is "a serious illness" that the patient must resist before he can "deserve the respect" of his son. That was bad enough, but then the next year an episode of the same show titled "The Outrage" centers on a male teacher who sexually assaults a fourteen-year-old boy. Gay media activists were furious that the show reinforced the gay child-molester trope, and organized an aggressive invasion of ABC offices in protest.

But in the years that followed the Stonewall uprising in 1969, a new attitude was starting to take hold. Americans were witnessing the first Pride parades, starting with gay liberation marches in Chicago, New York, and San Francisco in 1970s. The American Psychiatric Association voted to delist homosexuality as a mental illness in 1972. A handful of states moved to decriminalize gay sex, and there was an unprecedented push to come out of the closet. After a gay man foiled an assassination attempt against President Ford in 1975, Harvey Milk declared that it was time to "show that gays do heroic things, not just all that ca-ca about molesting children and hanging out in bathrooms."[15]

With gay culture charging out of the closets and into the streets, many straight Americans were encountering openly queer people for the first time in their lives—or at least seeing them openly on television for the first time—and were flummoxed to discover that their long-held fears didn't match reality.

But in 1974, a conservative project emerged that threatened to undo those advances, culminating in a phenomenon known as "the Family Viewing Hour." An attempt to clean up television and protect impressionable youth, it was a colossal fiasco for everyone involved, and set the stage for the conflict Alice would feel about allowing her son to go fishing with a gay friend.

*

The Family Viewing Hour mess started the evening of September 10, 1974, when NBC crossed a line.

That night, the network broadcast a TV movie called *Born Innocent*, starring Linda Blair as a fourteen-year-old runaway who winds up in a detention center. The movie, broadcast at eight o'clock on a Tuesday night in the same timeslot as *Happy Days* and *Good Times*, includes a graphic scene in which Blair's character is sexually assaulted by other girls. The entire sequence is long, explicit, and utterly shocking—viewers see a young girl screaming in bloodcurdling agony while lurid camera angles show her legs pulled apart and leave no doubt about what is being done to her. It is the stuff of nightmares, far more traumatic to watch than the fantasy-horror of Blair's ordeal in *The Exorcist*.

Critics were appalled. "The homosexual rape scene—though homosexuality is a problem of our penal system—could have and should have been omitted," harrumphed critic Noel Holston.[16] But critical disapproval was the least of NBC's worries, because public outrage threatened their entire business.

In recent years, activist groups of varying stripes had started toying with a novel method for applying pressure to broadcast television: challenging the licenses of stations. In the United States, airwaves are considered public property and regulated by the Federal Communications Commission (FCC), which has the right to deny broadcasters access if their programming is not considered "in the public interest." A major test of that regulation had come in 1964, when a group of civil rights organizations pushed for the FCC to pull the license of WLBT in Mississippi. That station's behavior was particularly appalling: it used racist slurs in local newscasts, and cut the feed of national broadcasts that included Black people—even baseball telecasts, according to viewers. A white power group was allowed to run a bookstore in the station's lobby, and station manager Fred Beard railed on air against "Negro propaganda."[17]

It took seven years of petitions and hearings by a community-based coalition, but in 1971, the FCC pulled WLBT's license and gave control to a nonprofit group run by a diverse board of directors. Beard was replaced by station manager William H. Dilday Jr., the first Black person to run an American television station.

Following that success, dozens of stations saw their licenses challenged by a broad array of groups, from the National Organization for Women to the NAACP to the United Church of Christ. Few got much traction, but in 1974 the graphic assault in *Born Innocent* drew an unprecedented level of outrage—more than three thousand calls and letters, according to NBC.[18] A few days after the broadcast, reports emerged that a group of children in San Francisco attempted to re-create the scene, and Congress stepped in to urge an FCC investigation. It was clear that the threat of government intervention, currently directed at local stations, could soon apply to the national networks.

The three major networks, sensing that there was already a public appetite for license challenges, moved fast to prove that they were capable of self-regulation. In 1974, their lobbying organization, the National Association of Broadcasters, announced a new initiative called "the Family Viewing Hour," and pledged that all broadcasts from 8 to 9 PM (on the coasts) would be free of controversial content. No sex, no violence, and no homosexuality.

The Family Viewing Hour went into effect at the start of the fall season in 1975. America's children were safe. Simple, right?

Wrong. It was immediately clear that something wasn't working. Eliminating controversial content meant that certain shows had to keep sliding around on the schedule; a program that was normally fine to air at 8 PM might need to jump over to 9 PM for a week and then back to its original slot depending on content. In the fall of 1975, figuring out when to watch your favorite show was suddenly extremely confusing.

There was also inconsistency when it came to enforcing the policy, and each network's censors repeatedly sparred over what sort of content crossed the line. CBS, for example, maintained that *All in the Family* should remain in its current timeslot, but pushed ABC to move its police procedural *The Rookies* to later in the evening. At one industry meeting, ABC's chief censor Alfred Schneider reportedly blew up at his CBS counterpart Tom Swafford, hollering, "Well, if you are not going to move the goddamn program *All in the Family*, we are not going to move the goddamn *Rookies*."[19] (Schneider later claimed that his language had not been so colorful.[20])

And aside from the logistical headache, the Family Viewing Hour was—there's no other way to put it—incredibly boring. There were vanishingly few new shows that year, and what few series premiered tended to not last long. You likely do not have strong fond memories, for example, of *McCoy*, featuring Tony Curtis as a con man with a heart of gold.*

Another problem: the new content policy tied the hands of creators who wanted their shows to reflect the rapidly shifting new reality of American life. In California, where much of the nation's television programming was created, homosexuality had been decriminalized that year—but you'd never know it looking at the season's scripted programming, from which queer themes had been almost entirely purged.

When *All in the Family* was bumped out of its comfortable time slot, the frustrated cast took to performing a parody version of their theme song for studio audiences. The skit, which was taped but never aired, began with the actors gathering around the piano with Jean Stapleton announcing "the 1975 version of 'These Are the Days,'" with lyrics like "single girls can take a pill / Robert can propose to Bill." That was followed by a muttered aside from the whole cast, "After nine o'clock," and an annoyed groan from Carroll O'Connor, "Eghhh." It's hard to say how much of his groan is from an in-character Archie versus O'Connor's own exasperation.

Meanwhile, to the great displeasure of television producers, non-televised media was free to have a gay old time. At movie theaters, audiences could enjoy cutting-edge fare like *The Naked Civil Servant*, a 1975 biopic about celebrated British dandy Quentin Crisp, in which John Hurt declares to a gang of ruffians, "You cannot touch me now. I am one of the stately homos of England." That same year, *Rocky Horror* debuted (though it struggled to find an audience at first), Al Pacino played a queer bank robber in *Dog Day Afternoon*, and New York bathhouse culture made a splash in *Saturday Night at the Baths*.

It was also the year of *A Chorus Line* on Broadway, a colossal hit that featured multiple gay characters; and less successfully, a jaw-dropping musical

---

* In fact, one of the only successful new shows of 1975 was *Barney Miller*, which managed to both evade and infuriate network censors on the topic of homosexuality.

titled *Let My People Come* that included a coming-out ballad straightforwardly titled "I'm Gay."

And on top of all that, there was one more problem: viewers hated the Family Viewing Hour. Ratings that season plunged.

"Of this season's new shows, a lot—seventeen perhaps—will have bit the dust by mid-year," Columbia Pictures television president John Mitchell told the *New York Times*. "This will be the highest percentage ever. No one can tell me the Family Hour was not responsible."[21]

In trying to protect themselves from the threat of public outcry over controversial content, the networks had invented a solution that created a suite of entirely new problems. The Family Viewing Hour had become a colossal source of frustration.

But in late 1975, the networks spotted a way out of their dilemma.

Exasperated by the logistical headaches, the censorship, the low ratings, and the tantalizing storylines that they simply couldn't touch, a coalition of industry groups filed suit against CBS, claiming that because it was prompted by FCC action, the Family Viewing Hour represented undue government interference with First Amendment rights.

Among those filing the suit were Norman Lear, *M*A*S*H* producer Larry Gelbart, *Barney Miller* creator Danny Arnold, and *The Mary Tyler Moore Show* producer Allan Burns. The policy "drastically curtailed the free flow of ideas and expressions on television and is stifling the creativity of many artists," wrote spokesperson Michael H. Franklin.[22]

Speaking to the *New York Times*, Norman Lear declared, "The Family Viewing Hour is a deceit," and pointed out that as a policy, it made no sense: "Nine on the coasts is eight in the Midwest," he said. "Why are the networks abandoning the little ones in the heart of the Bible Belt?"

The case proceeded rapidly through the courts, with a ruling expected in the fall of 1976. Observers noted that the lawsuit might provide the networks with a convenient release from the headache they'd created for themselves: if the Family Viewing Hour was ruled unconstitutional, they could claim that at least they'd *tried* to clean up their programming, but ultimately it was out of their hands.

As the fall 1976 television season neared, it appeared as though ABC, CBS, and NBC were all placing bets on whether the Family Viewing Hour would last.

NBC, whose TV movie kicked off the outcry that led to the Family Hour, held back on allowing any gay content at first. The network had originally planned on launching a show called *Snip*, which featured a gay hairdresser. But at the last moment they postponed the debut—first by a week, then by a few months, and then indefinitely. To this day, *Snip* has never aired in the United States.[23]

But after holding back for all of the previous year, ABC and CBS went all in on queer content in the initial episodes of the 1976 fall season, resulting in those remarkably gay opening weeks of television. On the ABC show *Family*, a teenager discovers that one of his friends is gay. On *The Nancy Walker Show*, a recurring gay character played by Ken Olfson* appeared in the premiere episode. On *Barney Miller*, a show set at a Greenwich Village police station, two gay characters lend a hand around the office, and wind up making the best coffee the cops have ever tasted:

NICK: What did you do to the coffee?
DARRYL: Well, it was nothing special. It just takes a . . . unique talent.
NICK: I was afraid it was something like that.

Not to be outdone, the next week *The Bob Newhart Show* on CBS added a recurring gay character to the therapy group, reflecting the

---

* Olfson said in interviews that he didn't like labels but that he'd had bisexual experiences. He also noted that one of his early roles was a singing raisin in a cornflakes commercial. "I was wet all day."

recent de-listing of homosexuality as a mental illness. "You've had a rough time," Bob Newhart's character consoles his patient* after a difficult coming-out experience. "Would you care for coffee, tea, fruit?" He winces. "Coffee?"[24]

And then there's the second episode of *Alice*, which of all the shows in the new 1976 season does the best job of capturing the cultural whiplash that so many Americans had experienced over the past decade—shifting from a lifelong assumption that gays are a threat to discovering that they might actually be very pleasant company.

*

When *Alice* comes back from commercial break, we see the consequences of Alice telling Tommy that he can't join Jack on the upcoming fishing trip. Tommy's unhappy and confused by the about-face; Alice is feeling miserable and guilty; Jack is pissed by the betrayal of someone he thought was a friend. He comes by the diner to clear the air between them:

> JACK: Why won't you let Tommy go? Is it because I'm gay?
> ALICE: [Looking guilty.] Yes.

As Alice frantically tries to keep up with customer orders, Jack lends a hand in the kitchen.† As they prepare meals, Alice explains her reasoning:

> ALICE: Part of being a parent is protecting your child. And I'd
> just rather that Tommy didn't go at this time.

It certainly sounds reasonable that a parent would want to protect their child, but Jack asks her to consider what that has to do with calling off the

---

* The patient, Mr. Plager, is played by Howard Hesseman, better known as Johnny Fever on *WKRP in Cincinnati*.

† Which seems a little unsanitary, but then again, he *is* the Gorton's Fisherman.

trip. After all, Alice trusted Jack when she thought he was straight. And even though Jack's a relatively new acquaintance, her boss, Mel, will be going on the trip too. As Jack points out:

JACK: If I were straight and you had a twelve-year-old daughter,
     would you trust me with her?
ALICE: [Hesitant] Yes, I suppose I would.
JACK: There's no difference, Alice.

That puts things in a new perspective. Alice sees that she's been treating Jack differently not because he'd done anything wrong, but simply because of an old assumption about gay people. Deep down, she knows that Jack isn't a threat, but she treated him like he is.

To his credit, Jack doesn't push her too hard to change her mind, and doesn't accuse her of being a bigot:

JACK: I don't agree with your decision about Tommy but I under-
     stand your right to make it and I respect that.
ALICE: Thanks.

But he doesn't have to push. As he's leaving, she stops him:

ALICE: Take Tommy with you.
JACK: Are you sure?
ALICE: Yeah, I'm sure . . . When I told Tommy he couldn't go, I
     just felt awful. Especially after the way he looked at me, and
     then the way *you* looked at me, and the way *I* look at me.

Alice knows her gut reaction was wrong, and choosing to prevent her kid from spending time with a friend was just making everyone unhappy for no reason . . . just like the networks' self-defeating choice to impose a Family Viewing Hour that served no one. Jack, Mel, and Tommy wind up having a fine fishing trip—after returning, Tommy guiltily confesses that he had a sip of beer—and all's well.

*

As the dust settled from the gayest week in television history, critics were a bit shell-shocked. "Homosexuality on TV: Just a Passing Fad?" asked the *Baltimore Sun*.[25] "Homosexuals on Television: Should They Be Included?" mused the *Atlanta Constitution*.[26]

"Imagine," an irate mother told an *Atlanta Constitution* reporter. "My son sat and watched all three shows and he kept asking me, 'Mama, what's a gay?'"

Others marveled at how far the country had come in such a short time: "How encouraging that homosexuals can be portrayed on TV not only as well-adjusted people, but as people so well-adjusted they make everyone else look like neurotic wrecks," wrote one critic. "Homosexuals may be the first over-adjusted group in history."[27]

The most aggressive reaction came from commentator Nicholas von Hoffman, who unleashed an article that was both wildly offensive and oddly prescient. "Is network television about to kill off the bitchy, old-time, outrageous fruit and replace him with a newtype homo?" he wrote. "Perhaps the furry basso-profundo police sergeant who lives next door?"[28] In fact, *Barney Miller* would introduce a gay officer a few years later. "Public television," von Hoffman went on, "will probably import a BBC drama in which the audience sees America's first televised homosexual kiss." Sure enough, in 1993, PBS would indeed air America's first prime-time gay kiss on *Tales of the City*, coproduced with the UK's Channel Four.

Von Hoffman's other observations did not age quite so well. He summarized the cultural shift as having highlighted "the importance of faggotry in our national social life." It's at least a memorable line, if not one you'd trot out in polite company.

Meanwhile, a few weeks after all these shows aired, Judge Warren J.

Ferguson of the US District Court for the Central District of California ruled that the Family Viewing Hour was, in fact, unconstitutional.[29] Because the FCC had pressured the networks so heavily into adopting it, the Family Viewing Hour was a violation of the First Amendment, and thus overturned.[30,*]

Just like that, the Family Viewing Hour was gone for good.

*

There's a sweet little coda at the end of the episode of *Alice*. Tommy's returned from the fishing trip in good spirits, and Alice has an awkward-mom moment in which she tells him why she was so concerned about the trip. "Tommy, Jack Newhouse is a homosexual," he says, her tone serious.

Tommy is unfazed. "The way kids talk, I thought you could always tell," he shrugs. "I don't care, though."

In the end, it's no surprise that the fishing trip was unremarkable—the fear that it was ever a cause for concern was something Alice had concocted in her own mind. But Tommy, a product of the modern seventies, carries fewer hang-ups than his mother.

In the same way that Alice fretted needlessly about Jack being gay, the Family Viewing Hour treated homosexual characters as though they were a threat to impressionable youngsters. But just as there was no reason to stop Tommy from going fishing, preventing kids from seeing queer characters on TV protected nobody, because those characters were never a threat to begin with. Banning them simply made everyone miserable for a year, from the showrunners to the network executives to the viewers.

It's fortunate that Judge Ferguson ruled as he did. If the Family Viewing Hour had been upheld, there's no telling how long the prohibition on homosexual storylines would have lasted.

But on at least one show, there was a backup plan to circumvent network

---

* Ferguson's impact on American television is incalculable: in 1979, he wrote the ruling that legalized the sale of VCRs in the United States.

censorship. A risky plan B was brewing behind the scenes of *Barney Miller*, with the show's producer gambling his career on an unlikely alliance with a gay activist and taking on one of the most powerful arbiters of morality and taste in showbiz.

BARNEY MILLER

BARNEY: [Reading from a newspaper] "Supreme Court upholds anti-gay statute."
DARRYL: Nine old men who dress up in black robes and they say we're peculiar.

There was probably no better place on Earth to enjoy being gay in the 1970s than Greenwich Village. Following the Stonewall uprising in June of 1969, the Village was cemented as the epicenter of American queer culture, and New York's Lower West Side overflowed with political protests, groundbreaking theater and art, and jubilant sex.

This was the setting of *Barney Miller*, an innovative sitcom that fundamentally changed how sitcoms were made.

When producer Danny Arnold created the show, he strove to capture the reality of life in the gayest neighborhood in the world, including the often-antagonistic relationship between police and the neighborhood's residents. Arnold saw to it that the show featured a lot of firsts for queer representation on TV: one of TV's first recurring gay characters; one the first recurring gay couples; one of the first gay immigrants; and even one of the first gay sleepovers.

But each of these firsts presented overwhelming challenges. The seventies was a time when television was under pressure from Congress to clean up its act, and networks had decided to scrub gay content from the airwaves. To make *Barney Miller* happen, Arnold had to gamble his career, his livelihood, and even his home in order to put gay characters on TV.

Fortunately, he had a secret weapon up his sleeve, in the form of a gay activist enlisted to help defeat one of Hollywood's most powerful censors.

*

A former Marine who served in the South Pacific, Danny Arnold started his career in showbiz as an actor with some small-time summer stock shows and as a vaudeville stand-up comic. After his brief military service, he moved to LA and appeared in scattered bit parts in a few comedies, then found more success behind the camera as a writer.[1] In the early 1960s, he approached Screen Gems—the TV wing of Columbia Pictures—about adapting the naval comedy film *The Wackiest Ship in the Army* into a television show. Screen Gems felt the concept was only half-baked, and while Arnold continued to polish it, they asked him to pitch in on a new project about a closeted witch hiding in suburbia with her husband.

Arnold spent a year producing the first season of *Bewitched*, then got his chance to produce *The Wackiest Ship in the Army*. After that flopped, Arnold was ready to try something a little more grounded in reality. What he came up with was *Barney Miller*, a workplace sitcom about a bunch of gritty-but-lovable cops working in a run-down New York police station: the stalwart captain, Barney (Hal Linden); staff himbo Detective Stan "Wojo" Wojciehowicz (Max Gail); deadpan Detective Nick Yemana (Jack Soo); grizzled veteran cop Phil Fish (Abe Vigoda); and smooth-talking Detective Ron Harris (Ron Glass). It was a stellar cast with decades of acting experience between them, and Arnold planned to use the strong ensemble to tackle contemporary real-world issues.

"The show was not a gimmick show," he told one interviewer. "It was not about somebody dying and coming back as a ball of butter or a radio."[2]

He pitched the show to ABC in 1974, and they bought it—but just barely. The network was so skeptical about the concept that they only ordered two episodes,* so Arnold knew that he'd need to knock their socks off.

*

Setting the show in Greenwich Village was a stroke of genius—or madness. The Village had long been a center of bohemian life in New York, and over the last few decades it had become a sort of Main Street for the city's growing queer population, or as the 1948 book *New York: Confidential!* referred to them, "long-haired men, short-haired women, and those not sure exactly what they are."[3]

This was the neighborhood where, just five years earlier, a police raid had touched off the modern gay liberation movement. Police raids were a frequent hazard at gay bars; at the time, it was illegal to serve alcohol to a known homosexual. Raids were frequent and generally resulted in a relatively orderly parade of arrests, along with a few ruined lives when the identities of the patrons leaked.

It was a hot June night in 1969 when police stormed the Stonewall Inn, expecting the patrons to meekly submit to arrest as they had countless times before. But this time was different. According to many accounts, as police lined up the patrons and loaded them into waiting wagons, a restless, angry crowd gathered. Cops pulled one woman out of the bar—widely said to be Stormé DeLarverie, a popular lesbian singer, bouncer, and neighborhood presence—who was bleeding from the head, and as they shoved her toward the police wagons, she turned and called out to the crowd, "Why don't you guys do something?"[4]

Witnesses later describe that as the moment when the crowd became

---

* Similar to the meager four-episode order that NBC would give *Seinfeld*'s first season fifteen years later.

a violent mob. Bystanders started pushing over police vehicles, slashing tires, and throwing beer cans. There was no leader, no planning, no organization—just the boiling-over of a rage that had been seething for years. For the next few nights, police and locals battled for control of the streets—and the locals won. Not only were the cops consistently pushed back, but in the days that followed, it was clear that it would no longer be possible for police to terrorize Greenwich Village. And the old culture of fearful closeting was giving way to a new spirit, one that would soon be captured in a word new to the homophile movement: Pride.

"The word is out," wrote witness Ronnie Di Brienza. "Christopher Street shall be liberated. The fags have had it with oppression."[5]

This wasn't the first violent queer response to police brutality. But it was the one that was cemented in national memory as the turning point from the quiet, timid organizing of the past to a more raucous, rebellious attitude. And Greenwich Village was the point of origin.

*

By setting his show in this neighborhood, Danny Arnold all but ensured that it would have to acknowledge queerness at some point—much to ABC's dismay.

Sure enough, the show's second episode, aired in January of 1975, opens on a gay character named Marty Morrison—a thief caught snatching purses, now being booked while his victim looks on:

MARTY: I've thrown away better purses than that.
PURSE OWNER: Maniac!
MARTY: You love this attention, don't you?[6]

Marty's clearly a regular at the station. He has a friendly relationship with the police, including Captain Barney Miller. In fact, he mentions, he once tried to become a cop:

BARNEY: They turned you down?

MARTY: Of course they turned me down. It's ridiculous. What's wrong with a gay cop? There are gay robbers.

It's worth noting that there's some audience laughter at the line, "What's wrong with a gay cop?" The idea of a gay police officer seemed so ridiculous at the time that it was just assumed to be the punchline of a joke.

But this is more than just a joke—it's an example of how the show lifted storylines from real life. At the same time that this episode was being filmed, two legislators from New York had just introduced the first nationwide bill to ban employment discrimination on the basis of sexual orientation. The Equality Act of 1974 was sponsored by Representatives Bella Abzug and Ed Koch (who would later become mayor of New York), and it would have banned discrimination on the basis of sexual orientation nationwide.[7] It had virtually no chance of succeeding, and in fact died in committee almost immediately, but the point was not to pass it on a first try. The bill existed to start a snowball rolling at the top of a very long slope, to start a conversation about issues that had for decades been ignored. That conversation would play out in Congress, in newspapers, in casual conversations—and for the millions of people watching TV that night, in words exchanged between Barney and Marty.

From its earliest episodes, *Barney Miller* was already using its platform to introduce what was, to many viewers at the time, a brand-new concept.

Marty is not an overtly political person. His main function in the episode is to hang around the station and make funny quips:

PURSE OWNER: You're just lucky the police got you before my husband did.

MARTY: Same to you.

But as a rare example of an assertive, out gay man on television, Marty's mere existence is political, even when he's not talking politics. He's funny, confident, smart—and unabashedly gay, with no ambiguity or winking. Locked in a cell with another criminal, he says:

MARTY: What did you do?
HOLD-UP MAN: I held up a candy store.
MARTY: [Suggestively] I have candy at my place.

Behind the scenes, Marty was met with discomfort at ABC. Openly queer characters were still relatively new to primetime, and the networks had just been put through the wringer after some particularly bad portrayals of gay characters on other shows had prompted protesters to gain access to executive offices and stage a sit-in until their grievances were heard. ABC was not eager to repeat that experience, and when network bosses first saw the script for the Marty episode, it looked like they might not allow it to air.

But Danny Arnold was ready. He had a secret weapon—a man named Newt Dieter.

Dieter was a clinical psychologist who worked with an organization called the Gay Media Task Force (GMTF). The task force formed just two years earlier in LA, an offshoot of another organization called the National Gay Task Force, and sought to improve the depiction of queer characters on TV.

Arnold knew that a handful of shows had started running scripts past the GMTF before shooting to make sure there wasn't anything that would cause another protest, so he called Dieter in to take a look at the Marty character.[8]

Dieter's opinion was that while Marty did conform to some stereotypes, he was still far less offensive than what viewers had seen on *Marcus Welby, M.D.* and *Police Woman*. Dieter didn't think Marty was a problem and gave the episode a thumbs up, and with his blessing the episode was allowed to air. A few weeks later, ABC felt confident enough to allow Marty back for a second appearance in an episode titled "The Guest."

The story of this episode is that the precinct must protect a mafia informant who is convinced the mob is trying to kill him.* Meanwhile, Marty's arrested for stealing luggage, and as usual he gets all the good jokes:

> BARNEY: When are you going to learn you can't take things that belong to other people?
> MARTY: Why would I take something that belonged to me?

Marty's fairly incidental to the plot this time—his role is mostly to stand around making quips, and actor Jack DeLeon does a great job of wringing laughs from the audience with just a glance. When Barney tells him, "I won't book you, but I'm gonna have to hold you," Marty's look of interest elicits a major laugh.

Still, by the time season one ended in the spring of 1975, Marty had achieved something that almost never happened on TV: by appearing in multiple episodes, he'd become one of television's earliest recurring gay characters.

There'd been a few others before him—on the shows *The Corner Bar* and Norman Lear's *Hot L Baltimore*—but those were both, bless their hearts, huge flops that almost nobody watched. Marty was among the first on a show that actually gained a following.

Yet queer audiences didn't initially celebrate this trailblazing new character. As it turns out, Newt Dieter misjudged. Even though Marty was better than characters who had appeared on other shows, gay audiences were still miffed that the gay character was a career criminal, and they objected to his mincing poses and his shallowness.[9]

The Gay Media Task Force got an earful from gay viewers, and fortunately Dieter and Arnold were both receptive to the feedback. After Marty's episodes aired, the two of them went back to the drawing board to try to come up with a solution.

---

* The informant, incidentally, is played by Herb Edelman, who would go on to play Stan on *The Golden Girls*—he just has terrible luck with Italians.

It wasn't a simple problem to solve: on one hand, Dieter felt that Marty wasn't unrealistic—there are indeed many effeminate, flamboyant gay men, and he didn't want to lose the character altogether.

But on the other hand, because Marty was the only gay character on the show, it reinforced a popular misconception that *all* gay men are effeminate and also amoral criminals out to seduce straight men. That trope had a way of showing up over and over on TV, and if it was the only depiction viewers ever saw, then it would just deepen the stereotype in the public's mind.

So Dieter and Arnold hatched a plan: What if they kept Marty, but with a couple of strategic changes? As they got to work on the show's second season, the writers started cooking up a bunch of big, bold tweaks to the character, and by the summer of 1975, they were ready to go into production on a script for the fall season.

But then a new problem came up: a man named Alfred Schneider.

*

Schneider was ABC's chief censor from 1960 to 1990, and he had more veto power than nearly any other person in showbiz. His role at ABC emerged from the quiz show scandals of the 1950s, when producers were revealed to have coached contestants to provide right or wrong answers for the sake of drama. Facing public outrage, television executives had been hauled before Congress to miserably explain themselves, an experience none of them were eager to repeat. To prevent future scandals, the networks created Standards & Practices (S&P) departments that had wide-ranging authority to block any programming that might run afoul of the law—or simply offend.[10]

"One of my first mandates from an unhappy Leonard Goldenson, president of ABC," wrote Schneider in his memoir, "was to see that he never again suffer the embarrassment of having to defend himself before a congressional investigating committee."

Sometimes, the S&P department's work was clearly beneficial, such as when they pumped the brakes on dialogue that contained slurs or reinforced derogatory stereotypes.

But they could also be overcautious, sometimes preferring to veto scripts that merely acknowledged the existence of minorities rather than run the risk of offending them. Since the dawn of television, that had been the default stance—to keep queer characters off the air, straightwashing them out of existence. Even as networks flirted with more daring programming in the early 1970s, Schneider would temper scenes in absurd attempts to "balance" the shows' tolerance with homophobia.

For example, in the 1972 made-for-TV movie *That Certain Summer*, actor Hal Holbrook plays a man named Doug in a relationship with a man named Gary, played by Martin Sheen, and at one point Doug has a frank talk with his teenage son about homosexuality. In the original script, Holbrook's character delivers a brief three-sentence monologue:

DOUG: You probably heard about it in the streets or in school. But
     that's just one side—put-downs and jokes. [Pause] Nick, Gary
     and I have a kind of marriage.

It's a tender moment, one that gently guides the audience to reconsider whatever prejudices they might carry. But Schneider and his S&P colleagues wrote additional lines and ordered them to be inserted into that pause. Here's what aired:

DOUG: You probably heard about it in the streets or in school. But
     that's just one side—put-downs and jokes. A lot of people—
     most people, I guess—think it's wrong. They say it's a sick-
     ness . . . They say it's something that has to be cured. Maybe
     they're right, I don't know . . . I do know that it isn't easy; if I
     had a choice it's not something I'd pick for myself. But it's the
     only way I can live. Nick, Gary and I have a kind of marriage.

This new dialogue completely changes the impact of the "marriage" revelation by placing after a long, apologetic ramble that positions homosexuality as something loathsome and unwanted—and by extension, Doug and Gary's relationship as undesirable too. But this was often the best scenario that audiences could hope for in the early 1970s—it was either this or nothing. Explaining his edits, Schneider wrote, "The production would have to be cleared by the stations and supported by advertisers to get on the air."

Just as *Barney Miller* was preparing to air in January of 1975, Standards & Practices departments at all three networks got a supercharge of authority in the form of the Family Viewing Hour. With the networks determined to tamp down on controversial programming, Danny Arnold had already butted heads with Schneider over early episodes of *Barney Miller*. One script had a line about a character who was a sex worker, and Schneider insisted that Arnold remove it. But Arnold refused to budge. As actor Hal Linden recalled, "He goes to the network and says, 'I'm shooting it the way I wrote it. It's up to you if you put it on the air. But if you don't, I'm not going to make any more.'"[11]

This was a huge gamble. Arnold had believed so strongly in his show that he mortgaged his house to pay for production. The cast and crew believed in it too, working long hours—sometimes all the way through the night, long after the studio audience had been dismissed—to make sure every moment came out just right. Arnold was sure that audiences would fall in love with the show if the network would just get out of his way. "I knew that the success of the show would depend upon allowing the audience to get to know these characters," he later recalled.[12]

ABC, on the other hand, was doubtful about the show's chances of success, and the network could easily have replied, "That suits us fine." But in a twist of good fortune—for *Barney Miller*, at least—ABC was hurting for programming that year. They'd lost popular series like *The Partridge Family*, *The Brady Bunch*, and *Love, American Style*, and they'd finally taken a few struggling shows off life support like the Paul Lynde–helmed *Temperatures Rising*. The network's new shows that year were struggling, such as the too-smart-for-TV *Hot L Baltimore*, Sonny Bono's post-Cher *Sonny Comedy Re-*

vue, and a cop show called *Nakia* that was centered on a Native American deputy in New Mexico.*

ABC needed grist for the schedule, and Schneider was overruled on the line about the sex worker. *Barney Miller* survived its first season—but just barely, ending in sixty-eighth place out of the eighty-four network series tracked by Nielsen that year.[13] Across all three networks, it was the lowest-rated show to get renewed.

Going into season two, everyone knew they were in a precarious position. Despite all their hard work, despite all the late nights, despite the very special cast, their low ratings and clash with Standards & Practices meant that ABC wouldn't need much more provocation to cancel the show.

As production on the second season started in the summer of 1975, Schneider—still determined to enforce Family Viewing Hour policies—had *Barney Miller* in his crosshairs and started ordering numerous changes. When shooting began in August, he came down to monitor the set with his staff one afternoon. According to Arnold, when Schneider showed up Arnold told him, "You and your staff are making it very tough on me."

Schneider reportedly replied, "Danny, I'm not going to take any shit from you." (He later denied swearing.)

This exchange played out in front of the entire cast and crew, all of whom had been working tirelessly to keep the show from getting yanked from the schedule. Now, one of the most powerful people at the network was talking openly in front of them about how the show and their jobs could get wiped out. Arnold asked if they could go someplace more private, and Schneider said no: "There's nothing that I have to say to you that I can't say in front of my staff or in front of anybody else."

To which Arnold replied, "Okay, then you can go fuck yourself." He added, "This is my staff and my show . . . if you want to talk to me like a gentleman, I'll talk to you. If not, go screw off."

---

* Also that season: a short-lived trucker show called *The Texas Wheelers* starring a pretty-faced newcomer named Mark Hamill.

"War was declared," Schneider later wrote of that day, adding that they "almost came to blows."

Taking this hardline stance was another huge gamble on Arnold's part. All he had was a brand-new show with no established stars that was pretty low in the ratings. Schneider, on the other hand, had a huge amount of power, and following that confrontation the two men stopped speaking to each other. Schneider intensified his crackdown and ordered Arnold to remove the words *damn* and *hell* from scripts. He forced them write the sex worker character off the show.

In the end, Arnold had to go along with most of those changes. There was too much at stake, and Schneider was too powerful to challenge.

But there were some issues he was willing to fight for, and one of them was fixing the depiction of the Marty character. Arnold, a notoriously self-punishing perfectionist, knew that they could do better, and he was determined to make it happen despite Schneider's interference. ABC had already rejected the gay script that he wanted to shoot for season two, but without the network's knowledge, Arnold ordered the cast and crew to go ahead and tape the episode anyway. He paid for it out of pocket—about $100,000 of his own money, which adjusted for inflation would have been a little over half a million dollars today. Then, with the episode in the can, he sent it to ABC, sat back, and waited to see what would happen. If ABC rejected it, not only would he be out all that money, but there was a real possibility that he could lose his job and his show.

During the run of *Barney Miller*, Arnold gave an interview that hinted at his motivation. "We're doing a tremendous disservice to the American people, to kids, if we keep telling them that life is *The Brady Bunch*," he said. "It's really our job to tell them that life has to do with issues, has to do with problems, has to do with sex, has to do with a lot of things that they're going to come into contact with when they get out into the world."

He recalled a conversation he'd had with a member of the crew one night while they were shooting a scene with Marty: "The whole problem is going to arise when some kid turns to his parents and says, 'Mommy, what is gay?'" the crewmember had said. "What better place to have that question asked than in the home? And what better person to ask than a parent?"[14]

*

What Arnold didn't know was what was happening behind the scenes at all three networks. In late September of 1975, Schneider met with censors from NBC and CBS to talk about how the Family Viewing Hour was working out for all of them. At that meeting, they privately admitted that it had been a disaster. None of the network censors had any consistent standard for what constituted offensive material. They confessed to each other that they were all just guessing about what to take out or what to leave in, and that there was no consistency from network to network.

Schneider accused his counterparts at NBC and CBS of not censoring enough, but they told him that he was censoring too much—they wanted to allow more controversial content back on the air, which would put ABC at a competitive disadvantage. By the end of the meeting, Schneider had started to change his mind, and he told them, "Maybe I've been too tough."

Schneider left the meeting, and took a look at the gay episode that Arnold had shot with his own money. Two days later, word came back: the episode could air as is.

Because Arnold had stuck to his principles, the episode survived even as queer content was purged everywhere else on the schedule. *Barney Miller* was the only ABC show to air anything queer in the Family Viewing Hour block for the entire year.

When the episode, titled "Discovery," aired in 1975, viewers saw Marty swing open the station door with a new character standing by his side: a tall man named Darryl Driscoll, draped in a flowing pink sweater. The two of them confer in hushed tones, Darryl peering nervously through the doorway:

DARRYL: I don't like it here!
MARTY: Will you stop being silly?

DARRYL: [Nervously] Po-*lice*.

MARTY: Come on.

DARRYL: I don't want to go through with it! [MARTY swishes
   into the room and is met with a long audience laugh. DARRYL
   hangs back.] This is enemy territory.

MARTY: Don't be ridiculous. These are my friends.

This is the start of the fix that Danny Arnold and Newt Dieter concocted. The first change is the introduction of a new character, Darryl—Marty's partner, though that relationship isn't established until later. And the second is that, unlike in season one, the gays haven't been arrested. They're not criminals. They're here to report a crime. Marty no longer considers the cops to be adversaries; they're "friends."

Darryl and Marty take Barney aside and explains that a few days earlier, a cop accosted Darryl as he was coming out of a gay bar. Darryl, still nervous, begins to feel more comfortable speaking up.

BARNEY: What charge?

DARRYL: Being unique.

BARNEY: Is that all?

MARTY: He was coming out of The Velvet Den when he was
   busted.

BARNEY: Drunk?

MARTY: No, I was ... enthusiastic.

The cop, Marty says, demanded a $50 bribe, or he'd beat Darryl up and arrest him for being gay. Getting a shakedown from a cop (or someone posing as a cop) was an all-too-familiar scam at the time, sometimes referred to as a "fruit hustle." But that's not the sort of department Barney runs, and he's furious to hear that one of his colleagues might be harassing the neighbors. He immediately wants to find out who's responsible:

BARNEY: What'd he look like?

MARTY: He was ugly.

BARNEY: Tall ugly or short ugly?

DARRYL: When you're ugly, what's the difference?

Barney has a hunch that it wasn't a cop at all, just a scammer dressed as one. But to be sure, he has Marty and Darryl look through photos of all the cops in the 12th Precinct.

As before, the gays get all the best jokes:

DARRYL: I hope it doesn't take too long. I have a lecture at noon.

BARNEY: You go to school?

DARRYL: No, I'm having lunch with my mother.

But in addition to the solid gags, the writers used the opportunity to give us a deeper understanding of Marty and Darryl than we got in season one. In this episode's B-plot, a man named Mr. Buckholtz is being held in a cell after threatening to jump off the Washington Arch.* Marty goes over to console him:

MARTY: It's none of my business, Mr. Buckholtz, but take it from someone who knows: suicide is not the answer.

MR. BUCKHOLTZ: Oh, I wasn't going to jump, I was just looking around.

MARTY: I know, I've seen that view myself.

It's a quiet, kind, sympathetic moment—a genuine display of kindness from Marty, the apparently-reformed purse-snatcher, and an insight into

---

* A Greenwich Village gathering point, the Arch was the location of the first Pride rally in 1970.

what must have been his unhappy past. Mr. Buckholtz asks how he overcame his feelings of hopelessness. Marty's answer is poetic:

> MARTY: I was standing on the railing of the Brooklyn Bridge, and this car came by and they had the radio on. And Doris Day was singing "Que Sera, Sera." And I thought, "You know? She's right."

The song he's talking about, "Que Sera, Sera (Whatever Will Be Will Be)," was for decades a staple of gay culture (and still is, if you go to the right bars). It's sung in the voice of a young woman who wonders what the future holds, and who comes to terms with not knowing: "Whatever will be, will be / The future's not ours to see."

The song was made famous by singer-actress Doris Day, a gay icon who would go on to star in numerous rom-coms with our old friend Rock Hudson. Day's repertoire would also have been familiar to gay audiences of the time thanks to one of her other famous songs, "Secret Love" from the movie *Calamity Jane*, which refers to hidden affections with lyrics like, "Once I had a secret love / That lived within the heart of me."

It's no wonder that "Que Sera, Sera"—a song sung by a gay icon who clearly knew a thing or two about the discomfort of concealed affections, with lyrics about learning to embrace an uncertain future—might've brought Marty some peace of mind. His dialogue provides a surprisingly tender moment that humanizes the character, and signals to gay viewers that this show understands them.

Meanwhile, as Darryl pours through the photos, a plainclothes cop named Forbes hauls in a suspect. Forbes says that he caught a man trying to pull a fruit hustle scam, and Darryl instantly recognizes him:

> DARRYL: That's the man! I told you he was ugly.
> MARTY: You were being kind!

Forbes explains that the suspect grabbed him as he was coming out of a gay bar:

BARNEY: Where'd you pick him up?
FORBES: Outside Gogie's.
WOJO: The gay bar on Second Avenue?
FORBES: That's right. I just walked out and he grabbed me.
WOJO: [Smirking] He thought you were gay? A detective sergeant
    in the New York police force?
FORBES: Que sera, sera. [Big audience laugh, followed by
    applause.]

It's clear why Danny Arnold felt this episode was worth sticking his neck out and fighting for it. Not only is it a great, funny story with a fantastic twist at the end, but it significantly improves on the gay storylines of the first season. Marty's no longer a criminal; he gets compassionate dialogue, a sympathetic backstory, and a relationship—all while getting to be as fun and flamboyant as ever. The presence of Darryl is an innovative touch as well, since there had been virtually no gay couples, recurring or otherwise, on television before this.

And then there's the reveal of Detective Sergeant Forbes, a handsome hunk who bucks TV's usual gay-trope stereotypes and shows the audience that a gay cop isn't so ridiculous after all.

This 1975 episode was met much more warmly than Marty's initial appearances, and the success of this episode led to storylines that deepened Marty and Darryl's relationship, and added even more groundbreaking gay characters.

*

Now that he was freed from the worst of the censors' interference, Arnold could bring Marty and Darryl back, and tackle a host of other contemporary gay issues. By 1975, there was no shortage of topics to choose from, as queer liberation had rapidly accelerated: gay rights groups had exploded in number across the United States; numerous cities and towns around the country passed laws decriminalizing homosexuality; Leonard Matlovich had become a celebrity for challenging the military's ban on open service; Kathy Kozachenko became the first openly queer elected official in the country; and San Francisco's Harvey Milk was about to follow her lead.

Revolution was in the air, and its heart was Greenwich Village, where this phase of the struggle had kicked off in 1969.

Barney Miller brought Marty and Darryl back the next season in a 1976 two-parter called "Quarantine." Once again, Darryl peers distrustfully into the room before entering:

DARRYL: I don't like this place.
MARTY: Well, he helped us the last time, didn't he?
DARRYL: Yes, but he didn't enjoy it.

Marty and Darryl are thinking about moving to California, due to a recent Supreme Court ruling:

BARNEY: [Reading from a newspaper] "Supreme Court upholds anti-gay statute."
DARRYL: Nine old men who dress up in black robes and they say *we're* peculiar.

This is likely a reference to a 1976 Supreme Court ruling that upheld Virginia's statute banning "crimes against nature." While the text of the law prohibited anal or oral sex by any individual, in practice police used it to harass queer people and shut down bars that served them. In 1975, two men filed a lawsuit against the state over the statute with help from the National Gay Task Force—the organization that had created Newt Dieter's Gay Media Task Force—and Philip Hirschkop, the attorney who successfully overturned Virginia's ban on interracial marriage a decade earlier in *Loving v. Virginia*.[15]

Hirschkop's argument, in part, was that the Due Process and Equal Protection clauses of the Fourteenth Amendment protect personal privacy and that the Virginia law overstepped constitutional bounds. In fact, the Supreme Court of the United States would eventually agree with him—but not until many decades later, when ruling on marriage equality in 2015. In 1976, the Supreme Court allowed the law to stand by upholding a lower court ruling that criminalizing homosexuality "is appropriate in the promotion of morality and decency."[16]

Marty and Darryl explain that they've decided to pack up and move to San Francisco, where such laws can't touch them:

MARTY: The gay community is prominently represented in industry, business, city government . . . police force.
DARRYL: Just like everywhere else.

But they can't move yet. Marty's still on parole for shoplifting, and he wants Barney to write a character reference to his parole officer. Barney is incredulous:

BARNEY: Marty, I've had you arrested six times.
MARTY: [Sheepishly] I need someone who's known me for two years.

While they're in Barney's office, a suspect outside collapses. A doctor comes to examine the suspect, and concludes that the man might have smallpox. If so, everyone in the station may have been infected, and so they're ordered to quarantine there together. It's a storyline that feels uncomfortably current in a COVID-era rewatch, especially when a few characters are tempted to ignore the orders or label it a hoax.

After some debate, the group begrudgingly accepts the doctor's orders.

Until the man who collapsed can get tested, they're all confined to the station, and at first, things seem tense. As night falls, Wojo doesn't want to let the gay couple sleep on cots next to each other. Barney tries to calm him:

> WOJO: If it ain't gonna bother you, it ain't gonna bother me.
> BARNEY: It ain't gonna bother me.
> WOJO: It's gonna bother me.

But the show once again finds opportunities to give more depth to Marty and Darryl. They start talking to a cop named Inspector Luger, who's particularly homophobic and doesn't approve of them:

> MARTY: Love and affection between two human beings is nothing to be ashamed of, inspector.
> LUGER: Of course not. But you two, you're carrying it too far, don't you understand?
> DARRYL: It isn't *that* much further. [LUGER looks astonished.]

And as the hours wear on, the regulars find themselves unexpectedly connecting with Darryl and Marty—especially after they make coffee for everyone:

> NICK: These cups look different.
> MARTY: I scrubbed off all the mold and mildew.
> NICK: I thought it was a pattern.

They're actually getting to be friends by the time the test results come back from the hospital. It turns out that the man had chicken pox, which in the 1970s most people caught once and were then immune. Everyone's free to leave—and Barney says he'll be happy to write that character reference for Marty:

BARNEY: They probably won't even listen to me.

MARTY: They would if you got emotional about it.

*

Two years on from Marty's first introduction, Newt Dieter's guidance can be seen paying off. *Barney Miller* used his recommendations to make gay characters more diverse and complex—still as funny as in those first few episodes, but now also deeper. And crucially, the show was able to use them to broach topics that had never been discussed on television before, spurring conversation that could spill off the screen and into real life and back again.

The next year, the show broadened its depictions of gay characters even further in a 1977 episode about a Russian singer, named Fyoder Jininski, who wants to defect to the United States.[17] Barney tells him he can only be granted asylum if his reasons for wanting it are not frivolous, and Fyoder asks what "frivolous" means:

BARNEY: Well, let's say you were in love with an American girl. Frivolous.

FYODER: Me? No, I'm not frivolous.

WOJO: Of course you're not.

FYODER: I'm homosexual.

This might be a reference to the real-life story of Gennady Smakov, a gay Soviet writer who claimed asylum in the United States in 1975 (just as the future president Vladimir Putin was entering the KGB). Conditions for queer people in the Soviet Union were extremely harsh; citizens accused of homosexuality could be sentenced to years of hard labor.[18]

"To the bureaucratic leaders, gay people seem totally bizarre, beyond understanding," Smakov told *The Advocate* in 1977. "Worse, they are viewed as threats to the system. Why? Because homosexuality is considered a sign of one's intrinsic freedom and that, of course, is dangerous."[19]

Hardly anyone in the United States was talking about the Soviet Union's treatment of homosexuals at this time, and it's astonishing to see a sitcom tackle the topic.

In 1979, the show broke new ground again, with a character named Officer Zatelli. He'd sporadically appeared on the show for a couple of years, and then in a season-six episode he confides in Barney that he's gay. "I had to trust *somebody*, sir," he says, looking desperate.

Zatelli asks Barney to keep his sexuality a secret, and the episode ends with him still closeted to everyone else—but that's not the end of his storyline.

That same season, Marty and Darryl return to the station while Zatelli is present. The couple immediately bumps into Wojo, who'd always been a little uncomfortable around them:

WOJO: [Awkwardly] You're looking good.
DARRYL: [Also awkward.] Thanks. You look good yourself.
[A pause.]
MARTY: Can I get in on this?

Wojo's not wrong about Darryl's appearance, which has evolved significantly since he first appeared. It's early 1980 now, and Darryl's no longer dressed like a flamboyant gay 1970s hippie. Now he's got tidier hair, a nice overcoat, and a business suit. His look's shifted to what would be considered successful by eighties standards, which is to say, he looks like he has money. That was a fairly unusual way for gay characters to be depicted at the time—aside from Steven Carrington on *Dynasty*, gay characters tended not to dabble in executive realness. But Darryl looks like he'd fit in more on Wall Street than Christopher Street, and even gets a little dig in at the trope of the homosexual decorator:

MARTY: [Looking around the station] My, you've certainly done some lovely things with this room since the last time . . .

DARRYL: Could we stop perpetuating the stereotype for a moment and get on with this?

They've come because they need help. Darryl, it turns out, was once married to a woman named Eleanor, and they have a son named Jason. A court granted them joint custody of Jason, but lately Eleanor's been refusing to let Darryl see him:

DARRYL: Jason is my only son.

BARNEY: Mr. Driscoll, I . . .

DARRYL: Captain, my chances of having another are incredibly slim.

This is another ripped-from-the-headlines moment. At the time, it was extremely difficult for queer parents to assert custody of their children; courts had gone so far as to remove kids from loving same-sex parents and place them in foster care simply because other children might make fun of them for having gay or lesbian parents.[20] (We'll take a closer look at this phenomenon in the chapter about *Soap*.)

At first, Barney says, he can't help. Even though a court has ruled that Darryl's entitled to custody and Eleanor is violating the terms, he'll have to go to court to get it ironed out—something that everyone in the room knows will be difficult, expensive, and unlikely to succeed.

But Darryl's tired of dealing with a custody system that, at the time, would have been quite hostile to him. So Darryl takes matters into his own hands, and goes to his son's school to pick him up—or at least, he tries to:

WOJO: The gym teacher stopped them.

MARTY: She didn't need to be so rough.

The ex-wife, Eleanor, comes down to the station, furious, and the mood is awkward when she encounters Marty for what is, apparently, the first time:

MARTY: I've heard a lot about you.
ELEANOR: [To DARRYL] *That* is the best you could do?
MARTY: I was hoping we could be friends.

Eleanor wants to press kidnapping charges, but she says she'll drop the issue if Darryl breaks off all contact with Jason:

ELEANOR: I don't want him exposed to a degrading and unnatural lifestyle.
MARTY: You haven't even been over!

The episode turns when Eleanor tries to appeal to the cops on a basis on which she thinks they'll all agree. She lets loose with a furious, bigoted rant while the station regulars gather around—including the still-mostly-closeted Zatelli:

ELEANOR: You deal with these people all the time. You know
how they are. The things that they do, right?
ZATELLI: *I'm* gay!

Everyone seems shocked by Zatelli's outburst, including him. But he couldn't keep quiet in the face of Eleanor's bigotry and her assumption that not only is there no such thing as a gay cop, but that all cops would be disgusted by gay people.

Now that it's clear that the police might not be as sympathetic as she thought, Eleanor starts to backtrack. She says that she never actually minded that Darryl's gay, and she's really just jealous that he's the more fun parent:

ELEANOR: Taking him to the ballet, to Broadway shows, the
best restaurants in town!
DARRYL: What's the matter with that?
ELEANOR: You're making me look bad!

At this point, the episode loses a bit of its steam. It's an oddly abrupt turn-around for a character who was calling Darryl "degrading and unnatural" a few seconds earlier. It's hard to imagine that she meant those harsh comments to refer to Broadway shows—*Cats* was still a year away from opening.

But whatever her true motivation might be, the show was breaking another barrier by depicting a gay dad as *too* good at being a dad. Remember, we started out with Marty as a sassy background purse-snatcher. Now he and his partner are fine upstanding co-parents.

Darryl resolves the conundrum by promising to let Eleanor be the cool parent from time to time, and that's good enough for her. They head their separate ways, with a hint at future encounters:

ELEANOR: Goodbye, Mr. Morrison.
MARTY: Let's do it again soon!

Though the premise of two gay dads and a sharp-tongued ex-wife would have made an excellent spinoff sitcom, viewers wouldn't see Marty and Darryl again for another two years, in one of the last scenes of the series finale. In the final episode of *Barney Miller*, the station is shut down, and a core group of the show's most notable characters gather to say goodbye. Marty and Darryl are among them:

DARRYL: We just wanted to stop by and say thanks . . . to all of
you, for what you've done.

It's meaningful that of all the characters who appeared on the show across eight seasons, Marty and Darryl were among those that Danny

Arnold included in this final going-away scene. Not only did they have a long multi-season arc across the span of the series, but they provided a gateway into issues that had never been broached on a network sitcom. Marty and Darryl were greater than the sum of their parts—they were funny guest characters, sure, but they also provided an opportunity for the show to stand up to censors and distinguish itself as being unafraid to reflect a reality of American life that had always been overlooked or erased.

It's fitting that the show to push open the door to further gay protagonists was set in the very neighborhood where the real-life revolution had its roots.

SOAP

MR. WISSER: *Are you a practicing homosexual?*
JODIE: *I don't have to practice. I'm very good at it.*

This is the story of two sisters, Jessica Tate and Mary Campbell—the main characters of the controversial sitcom *Soap*.

When ABC's *Soap* debuted in September of 1977, there had never been anything like it. A half-hour comedy with a continuing weekly story about the world's most dramatic family, it tackled taboo topics like adultery, religion, and race. Nothing was off-limits for this show, which talked frankly about sex, murders, cults, nymphomaniacs, ninjas, aliens, and a demon baby.

But one of the most daring elements: it was one of the first American sitcoms to have a gay character in the main cast, which touched off a huge fight before the first episode even aired.

Two diametrically opposed groups faced off together against ABC. On one side of the cultural clash were gay activists, afraid the show would paint a target on gay people in real life. On the other: arch conservatives who wanted total control of the airwaves. In the leadup to the show's premiere, there was only one thing on which these groups could agree: *Soap* could never be allowed to air.

*

The fuss began in the fall of 1976, when ABC announced that it was developing a new primetime sitcom that would be a satire of soap operas, exaggerating the stock characters and storylines of soaps and throwing in edgy, controversial topics mixed with studio-audience comedy. In the past, there had been a handful of shows that satirized soap operas (*Mary Hartman, Mary Hartman*) or tackled edgy topics (*All in the Family*), but this one was poised to push the envelope further than any of those other shows had.

The executive producers were Paul Witt and Tony Thomas, and they had been working on other people's shows for a few years. Their credits included *Occasional Wife* (a one-season flop produced by *Bewitched*'s Harry Ackerman in 1966), *Here Come the Brides* (a Western about mail-order brides in 1968), and *Satan's Triangle* (a 1975 Bermuda Triangle horror flick starring a slumming-it Kim Novak). These projects weren't exactly failures, but the movies tended not to garner brilliant reviews, and the shows usually didn't last more than a season or two.

Tiring of working on other people's airwave-filler, Witt and Thomas started looking for a show of their own that would make a name for them. That's when they met an up-and-coming writer who would catapult all of them to success.

Susan Harris hadn't planned on a television career. She was generally bored by TV, and in later interviews she confessed that the only two shows she ever liked were *The Muppet Show* and *60 Minutes*.[1] A self-described high school cheerleader turned tortured poet, she'd majored in English, met an actor, and moved across the country to settle in Sherman Oaks. Her marriage lasted long enough to produce a kid (Sam Harris, himself now a famous philosopher, writer, and online influencer) before her husband walked out. Searching for some means to support herself and her toddler, she happened to be flipping channels from one crummy show to another when it dawned on her: "I could do that."

A friend helped her sell her first script for $4,500 (for *Then Came Bronson*, a short-lived 1969 series about a motorcycling philosopher), which was followed by scripts for *The Partridge Family* and *Love, American Style*. Her big breaks came from episodes of *All in the Family* and *Maude*—in particular, the controversial two-parter in which Bea Arthur's character, Maude, gets an abortion.

This was a tough time for a woman to make a career as a writer on TV, but Harris was tough too. She told one reporter that the first time she met Norman Lear on *All in the Family*, he sized her up and said, "Nobody can look like you and write." She told him, "That's an appropriate remark for a man doing a show about a bigot."[2]

Throughout the first half of the seventies, Harris distinguished herself as a writer with a knack for finding humor in challenging topics and for making funny stories poignant. Her work brought her in touch with Thomas and Witt, and the three soon found that they worked well together. They would sit around Harris's kitchen table, keeping an eye on her son while spitballing ideas for shows they might make.

In 1975, it seemed like they'd finally got their shot at success with a sitcom called *Fay*, about a divorced woman making a life for herself in San Francisco—sort of a *Mary Tyler Moore Show* clone but with a sharper edge. The show earned positive reviews, but NBC programmed it against *The Waltons* on CBS, at the time one of television's most popular shows. NBC executives told the cast and crew of *Fay* not to worry, and arranged for the star, Lee Grant, to appear on *The Tonight Show Starring Johnny Carson* to promote the series. But the same day she was scheduled to appear, everyone showed up to work to discover *Fay*'s sets being dismantled. NBC programmer Marvin Antonowsky had canceled it after just three weeks, explaining that the main character was irredeemably unsympathetic because she was a divorced woman.

Grant went ahead with the *Carson* appearance and used the opportunity to tear into the NBC executives on the air. Harris was even more furious and stormed an executive meeting to curse out Antonowsky. Newspaper accounts hinted at her using hyphenated expletives of ten and twelve letters in the outburst, inviting readers to imagine what she might've said like a filthy crossword puzzle. Her rant became the stuff of legend around NBC's Burbank offices, and when the dust had settled, Witt, Thomas, and Harris went back to the drawing board to come up with something new for another network, ABC.

*

At the time, soap operas were wildly popular, watched by 70 million Americans every day. The gang started to wonder: What if they took the proven-popular format of soaps, with their ongoing storylines; tackled hot-button topics like another hit, *All in the Family*; and wrapped it all up in Harris's flair for comedy and poignancy?

Harris loved the idea, especially since it was a way to slip more serious messages onto television.

"The first job was always to entertain," she said years later in a rare interview. "Then I was looking for something more, something to say, to express myself." The sitcom, she found, was a convenient means to that end: "Comedy is a less threatening way to deliver messages to audiences."[3]

Blissfully unaware of what lay ahead, ABC loved the idea of a soap opera parody, and work got underway with an expected premiere in fall of 1977. Witt, Thomas, and Harris started cooking up a multi-season story about two sisters with complicated families, embroiled in infidelity, crime, and forbidden sex.

"Start to finish, everything was different about this show," said Marsha Posner Williams, who started out on *Soap* as a production secretary and worked her way up to associate producer. "I couldn't believe what I was seeing and hearing and reading at the time."[4]

But soon, things got complicated. A reporter from *Newsweek* named Harry Waters got wind of the controversial new series that ABC was planning and published an exposé labeling *Soap* as "impure." Waters leaked the most salacious details from the first few episodes: a promiscuous woman would seduce a priest in church, he wrote; a gay man would date a pro football player; all the characters were having sex with each other. Some of this was true and some was exaggerated, but readers were outraged. Pearls were clutched over the sexual elements, over the religious elements, over the gay elements—you name it, someone was offended by it, and the spring of 1977 saw countless articles and newsletters and community group meetings about what to do about the show.

Nobody had even seen the show at this point. It wasn't scheduled to air for months. But various groups had decided that *Soap* was public enemy number one. As one minister said in response to the *Newsweek* article, "We don't have to see the show to know it's indecent."[5]

One of the loudest opponents of the show was a man named Donald Wildmon. Until a few years earlier, he'd been an obscure Mississippi preacher, author of a few self-help books, and pastor of a church with about seventy-five members. In his autobiography, he wrote that he was "bored" with such a small congregation, and felt like "a monkey in a cage."[6]

That feeling ended one night in 1976, when Wildmon was watching television and had a brainstorm. It was the middle of the Family Viewing Hour debacle, and Wildmon realized he could piggyback off that to get publicity for himself. He quit his job as pastor, created a new group called the National Federation for Decency, and began publicizing a national "turn off the television" week in July of 1977 to protest what he declared was excessive sex and violence on the airwaves. *Soap* came along just as this was happening, and it was a golden opportunity for him. The show had inadvertently given the former pastor a target to attack, and a way to get famous.

Wildmon started courting newspapers to denounce the show—which, again, nobody had seen—and, through his professional network, organized churches to oppose it. Soon *Soap* had been condemned by the National Council of Churches, the National Council of Catholic Bishops, numerous Catholic dioceses around the country, the Christian Life Commission of the Southern Baptist Convention, the United Church of Christ, and more.[7] Meanwhile, Wildmon's religion-backed "Clean Up Soap" coalition sent out forty-five thousand packets containing stickers for adherents to put on their TV sets, reminding them not to watch dirty shows.

But conservatives weren't the only ones up in arms about *Soap*. On the other side of the aisle, gay groups were worried about reports that the show's family would include a gay son. And they had good reason to be nervous.

For the last few years, public sentiment toward queer people had slowly been improving. The first Pride parades had taken place in 1970 and were expanding to new cities every year; homosexuality was no longer officially considered a mental illness thanks to a 1973 vote by the American Psychological Association;[8] a handful of towns had passed first-in-the nation civil rights laws that made it illegal to fire or evict someone for being gay.

But *Soap* had gay organizers worried. At the time, TV shows had a way of painting queer characters in a negative light—the recent episodes of *Marcus Welby, M.D.* were still very much on everyone's mind. If *Soap* leaned on offensive tropes with a gay man in the main cast, activists were afraid that the show would cement negative attitudes in the public's mind, just as sentiment was starting to improve.

They were particularly sensitive because of a bruising political fight earlier that year. In January of 1977, Miami had passed a nondiscrimination law that protected queer people in jobs and housing. Conservatives were furious, and a beauty queen and Florida orange spokesmodel named Anita Bryant spearheaded a campaign to overturn the law. For months, Bryant gave interviews and ran TV commercials accusing queer people of being indecent, a public menace, and a particular threat to children.

"In San Francisco, when *they* take to the streets," intones one of her ads, showing a Pride event, "it's a parade of homosexuals. Men hugging other men! Cavorting with little boys!"

And her campaign worked—in June of 1977, Bryant convinced voters to overturn Miami's civil rights law. Victorious, Bryant promised to bring more anti-gay campaigns to towns across the country at what just happened to be the exact same time that *Soap* was about to premiere.

Gay activists were terrified that *Soap* would play right into Bryant's hands, further entrenching negative views about gay people on a massive national scale and jeopardizing civil rights nationwide.

Ronald Gold, an organizer with the National Gay Task Force, said, "In light of the Anita Bryant campaign this kind of thing is political murder."[9]

ABC was getting nervous about a potential backlash to the show. They brought in gay media consultant Newt Dieter, who had a track record of helping shows like *Barney Miller* avoid similar pitfalls, and invited various gay groups to meetings in New York.*

Dieter told ABC that there was indeed a problem with *Soap*'s gay character. He was too passive, Dieter said, and should be more assertive—a militant gay liberationist who didn't take abuse and harassment, but answered back to his bullies and always came out on top. If they made that change, Dieter said, gay audiences would be satisfied.

One of Dieter's colleagues was a little less gentle. Media activist Ginny Vida told the network, "Unless changes are made in the portrayal of the gay son on the series . . . you're going to have the gay community down your corporate necks in a way you've never experienced."[10]

The timing for all this couldn't have been worse for ABC. Executives had a brewing public relations nightmare on their hands, just as their PR department was about to embark on a labor strike that summer. They had to respond to the public outcry—but how?

First, the network ordered a lockdown of the cast and crew, barring everyone from doing interviews.

Next, they screened a test pilot of the show for local station managers in May of 1977, hoping to calm the affiliate stations' fears of local protests. But that effort backfired. *The Chicago Tribune*'s TV critic reported that after the screening, word around the industry was that the pilot was "sex-drenched," "kinky," and "the most over-sexed program ever on TV."

After seeing the pilot, one station manager said, "We'll probably get a

---

* One of those groups, calling itself the International Union of Gay Athletes, claimed to represent 450 members around the world; years later, a *TV Guide* reporter uncovered the truth that the entire organization existed only on paper, and consisted of fewer than a dozen crafty activists.

bomb threat a week."[11] This was no idle fear. In the 1970s, bombings were a lot more common than they are now. There had been a wave of bomb attacks by groups like the Weather Underground, and the Unabomber had sent his first explosive device that spring. Violent protest was a real concern.

Protests began in earnest, right outside *Soap*'s production offices.

"All of us who had offices that faced the street had to keep our curtains closed because there were protesters," recalled then-secretary Marsha Posner Williams. "We were afraid someone was going to throw a brick through our windows."

So ABC tried again. In July, the head of the network, Fred Silverman, delivered a video message to all the local ABC stations. He told them that the reaction was overblown, and that once people saw the show, they'd see it was no big deal. But just to be safe, they'd reshoot certain scenes to tone down the controversial content.

ABC also leaked their internal censors' notes to show how much offensive content they'd take out. The reshoots and edits would remove slurs like "fruitcake" and blasphemous phrases like "oh my God." Fellatio jokes were cut, as were racist comments, and a reference to transgender tennis star Renée Richards. There were notes to desexualize certain jokes, like "have the secretary dump the coffee somewhere other than her boss's lap." And: "On page 5, delete '. . . the slut.'"[12]

Williams recalled Witt, Thomas, and Harris wrangling with censors over exactly what would change, haggling over language like they were bargaining in a marketplace: "'Look, we'll trade you two hells for one damn'; that's what they did."[13]

Eventually, *Soap* made enough changes that some of the protestors started to calm down—but then Fred Silverman stepped back into controversy. On a call, he told station managers, "Jodie, the homosexual man, is going to meet a girl and find out there are other values worth considering."

That was welcome news to Donald Wildmon and his fellow conservatives, who saw that they had successfully pressured ABC into giving them what they wanted. But gay groups were livid. Silverman seemed to be saying that *Soap* would show Jodie getting cured of homosexuality—playing into a far-right talking point that being gay is a choice.

Gay groups resumed their threat of a boycott. Ginny Vida at the National Gay Task Force sent ABC a letter explaining just how deeply the network had messed up, concluding, "We are experts on what is offensive to gay people; you are not."[14]

Time was running out before the scheduled premiere. ABC's best chance at avoiding a crisis was convincing all the various angry groups to hold off on their boycotts until the reshot, reedited show premiered and everyone could judge it for themselves. ABC ran ads asking the public not to judge the show, showing people exiting a test screening with generally favorable reactions.

Behind the scenes, nobody knew if the fixes would be enough to satisfy everyone who had objected. And as the September premiere approached, it felt like a tense standoff, with conservatives on one side, gays on the other, and ABC caught in the middle along with Witt, Thomas, and Harris.

One of the few people optimistic about the show's chances was ABC's on-staff psychic, Beverly Dean. Harris visited her in the leadup to the pilot, and was told that *Soap* would be a hit. "As a writer, I'll try just about anything once," Harris said.[15]

*

Finally the day of the premiere came. It was the culmination of all the work that Harris and the rest of the creative team had put in, and of all the fighting between various groups waiting to see how much influence they'd managed to wield. By this point, most of the sponsors had fled; the only ones that stuck around were a watch company and Vlasic pickles. Nineteen stations refused to carry the pilot, and sixty-four waited until the middle of the night to put it on the air.

The pilot began with a parental warning, something that was extremely rare for the time. A deep-voiced narrator* warned viewers, "*Soap* is

---

* Ernie Anderson, also known as horror-movie host Ghoulardi.

a continuing adult character comedy. Certain dialogue and situations may not be appropriate for all members of the family."

And with that, America finally got to see what all the fuss was about.

The pilot introduces the Tates, a rich family in which the father, Chester, is cheating on his wife, Jessica. Jessica's sleeping with her tennis coach, one of their daughters is also sleeping with the coach, and the other daughter is so prudish she's never seen herself naked. Jessica's sister, Mary Campbell, is married to a man who, unbeknownst to anyone else, killed her first husband; Mary has one son who's trying to get out of the mob, another son who's gay, and a long-lost stepson who turns out to be . . . the tennis coach mixed up with the Tate women.

It's a lot to take in. No wonder each episode had a recap at the start and end of every episode.

Critics weren't impressed. Not that "suggestive, sexy, amoral, or even that funny," said one.

"A prolonged dirty joke," said the *LA Times*.

"It's rude, it's vulgar," and too similar to *Welcome Back, Kotter*, opined *The Boston Globe*.

But viewers loved it. Eighteen million tuned in, and ratings stayed high over the next few weeks. The show was daring, bold, funny, and as boundary-breaking as the pre-premiere buzz had suggested. Nearly a decade before *The Golden Girls*, *Soap* would feature scenes in which women sat around a kitchen table, eating cake and talking openly with each other about sex:

EUNICE: I don't think you're depressed, Ma. I think you're horny.
JESSICA: [Befuddled] What is horny?
EUNICE: It's what you feel like when you're not having any sex.

"Who says that back in the seventies?" Marsha Posner Williams laughed. "We did! And I'm so proud of it."[16]

And strangely enough, after the premiere, both conservative groups and gay groups claimed victory. Conservatives said that ABC had scaled back the raunchy content, just like they'd demanded. Gay groups said what they'd seen of the gay character wasn't as offensive as they'd feared. And both said they'd hold off on any more protesting—for now. One wrong step, though, and boycotts from either side could be back on at a moment's notice.

For the time being, the show was off to a cautiously promising start.

But then there was a new wrinkle involving Jodie, the gay character, played by an up-and-coming young comedian named Billy Crystal.

*

Today, you might know Crystal for playing Mike Wazowski in *Monsters, Inc.*, for hosting the Oscars, for a lusty diner scene in *When Harry Met Sally*, or for holding the record to this day for the fastest win on the game show *Pyramid*.

But in the fall of 1977, Crystal was just a little-known stand-up comic (and occasional substitute teacher) who was not at all a household name. As a teenager, he followed his family into showbiz: his father was a music executive, his uncle Milt Gabler founded Commodore Records, and his mother even voiced Minnie Mouse in the Macy's Thanksgiving Day Parade.*

Through his early twenties, Crystal clawed his way through live comedy shows, sometimes surviving by the skin of his teeth in less-than-friendly venues (at one show, a disgruntled patron fired off a gun during his set). But by the mid-1970s, he'd married his high school sweetheart, Janice, and realized he needed to settle down and support his family—so he decided to give Hollywood a shot. By a stroke of incredible luck, Crystal happened to be performing at a comedy club when Michael Eisner, then a VP of programming at ABC, was in the audience, and soon Crystal was signed to a development deal at the network.

The role of Jodie on *Soap* was one of the first he was offered, and he was intrigued by the possibilities.

---

* When they were young, the Crystal kids were occasionally babysat by friend-of-the-family Billie Holiday.

"If we did it right, we could make a change in the way that gay people were looked at on television," he recalled thinking in an interview years later. "And maybe if that worked ... it's a very positive thing for the world."[17]

But he was also nervous about this being the first role in which many people would see him. Playing a gay character was a risky move in 1977, and he was worried about getting typecast—especially since he'd just played an ambiguously gay flight attendant in a made-for-TV schlock film titled *SST: Death Flight*.

As he mulled over the offer, he thought to himself, "Is this how I want my career to start? ... I didn't want to go down in the annals of TV history as the bionic fairy."*

Before he made up his mind about taking the role of Jodie, Crystal met with Susan Harris over the course of several weeks to talk about how he'd play the character. He wanted to make sure Jodie wouldn't be a one-note joke or offensive stereotype, and Harris assured him there was a lot of potential for the character to be much deeper.

"And I so trusted the creative group," he later recalled, "that I said, 'OK. I'll do it.'"

But as tapings began, the first few episodes had him worried. Characters would direct slurs and abuse at Jodie, and the character was written to just smile and take it. "Go away from me, fruit," sneers his stepfather, Burt, played by Richard Mulligan. The family's butler, Benson, played by Robert Guillaume, calls Jodie "tinkerbell," and his stepbrother, played by Jay Johnson, mutters about "the sissy." (Well, technically, that last insult comes from Bob, a wooden dummy puppeteered by Johnson's character—*Soap* was nothing if not quirky.)

As an actor, Crystal was also unhappy that the character had what he considered very little depth. Jodie played into easy stereotypes like constantly

---

* Ironically, one of Crystal's next roles after *Soap* was a Joan Rivers comedy titled *Rabbit Test*, in which he played a pregnant man, followed by a World War II movie with the coincidental title *Enola Gay*.

primping in mirrors and wearing one of his mother's dresses. Crystal felt like the show was setting the gay character up as, in his words, "a buffoon."

"What Susan wrote initially was more of a stereotype," he said. "And I was uncomfortable with it."

As they filmed the initial episodes, Crystal could hear the audience laughing not with the character, but derisively at heartfelt lines about one man loving another.

"I could hear them laughing," he recalled. "I wanted to go, 'What's your problem?'"

The reaction from viewers out in the world was even worse. Crystal started getting harassed in public; at one point, he was at an airport and a bunch of teenagers started following him around, yelling, "There's the fairy." He often had slurs shouted his way, and when he went to meetings at ABC, he said he "could feel people deal with [him] differently."

In one interview, Crystal said that the last straw was how people would walk up to him at parties and whisper, "Hey, you aren't what they say you are, are you?" He said, "I wanted to shout at them, 'Yeah, and what if I am?' I made up my mind that something had to be done."[18]

So he went to Harris, who was writing every episode of the show, and told her about what he was experiencing—and what he wanted to change. His suggestions were similar to those of Newt Dieter: he wanted to deepen the character, make him more than a one-off gay joke, and try to get the audience on Jodie's side instead of making fun of him.

"I wanted Jodie to come to grips with his homosexuality the way the majority of gay people have come to grips with their homosexuality," he said. "They don't see it as a problem, and I didn't want Jodie to see it that way either."

Harris had faced stereotypes too, as someone who was dismissed as a writer because she was a woman. And to her credit, she listened to Crystal's ideas and took action. There's a major shift in Jodie's portrayal early in the first season, starting with a scene where Jodie tries to come out to his macho older brother Danny, who refuses to believe him:

JODIE: Danny, it's no joke. I'm gay.

DANNY: [Laughing it off] You never quit, do you?

At first, Danny tries to deal with it by pretending it's not true, brushing his brother off as he packs for a trip:

JODIE: Face facts, will you, Danny? I'm a homosexual. It's the truth. I'm gay.

DANNY: [Looking uncomfortable] Hand me those pants.

But then Danny shifts over the course of the scene, dropping the denial and confessing his true feelings:

JODIE: Danny—

DANNY: You are not gay. You are not gay. I don't want you to be gay and you're not, so shut up and hand me those shirts.

The scene culminates in a tense moment where it seems like Danny might reject his gay brother, but then Jodie makes an important point:

JODIE: Hey, I'm still the Jodie who plays tennis with you. I'm still the Jodie who bowls with you. I'm still the Jodie who laughs with you. I'm still the Jodie who counts on you.

DANNY: You're probably not gay.

JODIE: I am! And it shouldn't make any difference. And if it does, and you don't love me now because of it, then you've never loved me at all.

There had seldom been anything like this on TV before—a scene about how a gay character could still be the same person his family had always loved:

DANNY: I was afraid that if I ever heard it, I . . . couldn't look at
   you again.
JODIE: Well, can you?
DANNY: [Slowly turning to face him, then smiling] Yeah.
JODIE: Friends?
DANNY: Are you kiddin'? [They embrace.]

This had a big impact on viewers. "The storyline of Jodie resulted in us
getting letters from parents that said, 'I get it now, about my child, thank
you for opening my eyes,'" recalled Williams. "That made it all worth-
while . . . I was so proud that we were responsible for that."

*

From there, Jodie's storyline runs into some bumps in the road. Jodie's boyfriend is Dennis, a famous and closeted football player. Times being what
they are, Jodie and Dennis keep their relationship secret, because it would
destroy Dennis's career if people knew he was dating a man.
   Jodie comes up with a solution:

JODIE: A sex change operation.
DENNIS: A sex change operation? Which one of us?

This is where things get a little confusing from a modern vantage point,
because in one scene, the dialogue suggests that Jodie only wants to live as a
woman so that he can marry Dennis: "Listen, Dennis, I'm becoming a girl
for you," he says.
   But in other scenes, transitioning is something Jodie's always wanted:
"I've always felt like a woman," he tells his mother.
   And in still other scenes, Jodie continues to identify as a gay man.

JODIE: You hate me because I'm gay, right?
BURT: I guess if you need a reason, that's a good one.

It seems as though *Soap* was falling into a common misconception of the time about gender (which describes how an individual identifies) and sexual orientation (which describes their attraction to other people). In the 1970s, there wasn't a widespread understanding of the difference between the two; and there certainly wasn't the standardized terminology that we have today.

So is Jodie a gay man? A trans woman? Gay and trans? Neither? It's hard to answer that definitively. The character is the result of a misunderstanding of those experiences, written by a straight, cisgender woman and performed by a straight, cisgender man. In cases like these, the best option may be for audience members to interpret the character in whatever way they prefer, while acknowledging that others may see Jodie differently.

If nothing else, Jodie is a sympathetic character who is some flavor of queer, even if that flavor is a bit nebulous:

JODIE: Just think of me as a person, that's all. I mean, that's what
    I am. I'm a person sitting here. Burt, look at me. I'm a person.
BURT: [Begrudgingly turns.]
JODIE: Who happens to like men.
BURT: Eeeesh!

Queer storylines were still very much a work in progress in the late seventies. But this was at least a baseline, a place to start. And to *Soap*'s credit, Jodie's character gets significantly deeper in the next storyline. Halfway through season one, Jodie goes to a hospital to get that "sex change operation." At first, it seems like the scenario is going to be played for laughs, especially when Jodie meets his roommate, Barney, who's there for a heart operation:

JODIE: I'm in for a sex change.
BARNEY: Why do you want to change sex? If I remember cor-
    rectly, it was pretty terrific.

While he's waiting for surgery, Dennis comes to visit. He confesses that he's planning to marry an actress—not because he loves her, but as a safeguard against gay rumors, similar to Rock Hudson's brief marriage in real life. He doesn't want Jodie in his life anymore.

DENNIS: Jodie, I'm sorry.
JODIE: No, I love it. The homosexual and the starlet are getting married. You'll kill each other fighting over the electric rollers.

Jodie's pretty upset. Audiences normally think of Billy Crystal for his light comedic roles, but his performance here of a broken heart is quite moving. He slowly plucks the petals off a flower in his hospital room, repeating "I'm fine" to himself as he blinks back tears.

Then the scene takes a dark turn. After Dennis walks out, Jodie doesn't want to go ahead with the operation. In fact, he doesn't want to go on living. "It would make life a lot easier for me," he tells himself. "Mom. Burt. Anita Bryant."

He finds an unattended cart of pills and takes them all, then lies down, ready to die. And that's when Barney, his hospital roommate, finds him.

Barney doesn't know about the pills, but he overheard the breakup. He sits down next to his friend, and tells him a story about how he was once married to a woman he loved, and when she died, he thought he'd never be happy again. A few years went by, and one day Barney met another woman who made him happy. Not in the same way, a different kind of happy, but it still felt amazing. "And one day," he tells Jodie, "I laughed."

Then after ten happy years, she passed away too. Once again, Barney thought he'd never be happy again. "Once was wonderful," he says. "Twice, incredible. A third time . . . would be asking for a miracle."

But then he says that he doesn't really believe that. If he believed it, he wouldn't be in the hospital getting his heart fixed. There's always going to be another chance to be happy. "I know you don't feel terrific right now," he says. "But wait, Jodie . . . Someday I guarantee you're gonna hear somebody laughing, and you're gonna turn around, and it'll be you."

Jodie closes his eyes, and that's the end of the episode.

The next week, Jodie's family gets the news about his overdose, and they rush to the hospital. They burst into Jodie's room, frantic, and discover that he's going to be okay. More than okay, in fact; he tells them, "I want to live."

This storyline marks a major turnaround for the Jodie character, giving him a depth that was unprecedented for a queer sitcom character and a newfound sympathetic side that nobody saw coming.

And that was only the beginning of the changes for Jodie.

*

Later that season, Jodie meets a woman named Carol who's hellbent on making him straight. This was the storyline that the head of ABC had alluded to, and the one that gay groups were worried would end with Jodie being "cured" of homosexuality.

At first, Jodie resists her advances, but Carol keeps pressing Jodie for a date. After a lot of cajoling, eventually he gives in and they have sex. The next morning, he's furious . . .

JODIE: . . . because of what I did last night.
CAROL: Well, I did it too, but I'm not angry.
JODIE: But I'm gay.
CAROL: That's debatable.

At this point, it seems like Jodie might be bisexual. But this is another moment that the show kind of fumbles, because that's never even floated as a possibility. The word *bisexual* never comes up. It's just a big mystery how Jodie could have relationships with both men and women. "What does this make me?" he asks himself. "Imagine how confused my hormones are."

It's not like bisexuality was unknown in the late seventies. Elton John had talked about being bisexual a year earlier, and David Bowie before that. *Taxi* had an episode with a bisexual character just two years later. It's hard to say why *Soap* doesn't raise bisexuality as a possibility, but Jodie steadfastly maintains that he's a homosexual. Especially when talking to Carol.

But when season two opens, Carol's got some news for him. She's pregnant.

This starts a new storyline for Jodie that would come to be the defining arc of his character and reflects a new understanding of gay issues in real life. A gay dad seems normal enough today, but in the late 1970s, the concept was shocking. Even Jodie is stunned at first:

JODIE: But we only slept together once.
CAROL: That'll do it.

But he's committed to raising the baby with Carol. He even plans to marry her, but Carol skips town. Jody tracks her down in Texas at her mother's house, though he's not exactly welcome. "We don't have homos in Texas," Carol's mother says. "At least, not live ones."

That is a chilling line. Jodie's taking a big risk by pursuing a relationship with Carol, and he's doing it because he's trying to do the right thing. But that's not going to be easy:

CAROL: I don't want you to be the baby's father.
JODIE: What?
CAROL: Someday I hope to marry. And whoever I marry will be
    the baby's father.

A year ago, the Jodie character was just a punchline. Now, just like Newt Dieter had recommended, Jodie has become a complex, assertive gay character. He's living openly and honestly, and he's determined to parent that way too:

JODIE: Carol, it's a mistake. It's a gigantic mistake, because it's a
lie. And a lie will always catch up with you later. And when it
does, Carol, when my child wants his father, I'll be there.

A few episodes after this confrontation, Carol gives birth to a girl she
names Wendy, and then immediately abandons the baby. Carol's mother
drops Wendy off with Jodie, and it's clear that he's a devoted, loving father,
from the first moment he holds her:

JODIE: It was so much easier when I didn't know anything about
you. Because now that I've seen you, and now that I've held you,
I never want to let you go.

Given the commonly held belief of the time that gays were a threat
to kids, this was a remarkable depiction. Not only is Jodie presented as
a gay man successfully raising a daughter, but the show is taking a bold
stance that it's possible for a gay dad to be a better parent than a straight
mom. Even more remarkable is the next phase of the story in which Jodie
co-parents with his friend Alice, a lesbian. Two gay parents! Or in the ver-
nacular of the time:

JODIE: I'm still a homo.
CAROL'S MOTHER: But you're with a girl.
ALICE: We're both homos.

But Jodie's qualities as a parent were about to be put to the test with his
biggest challenge yet—and another milestone for queer people both on TV
and in real life.

Midway through season three, Carol returns. She has a new boyfriend,
and they want to take Wendy away. Jodie refuses to give the baby up, and
Carol declares that she'll take Jodie to court for custody.

Even though Carol abandoned Wendy and Jodie raised her, every viewer would know that he'd have almost no chance of retaining custody in the cultural climate of the late seventies. When this *Soap* storyline began, no US court had ever granted custody to a gay parent. Just a few years earlier, Anita Bryant's whole campaign was about "saving children" from gay people. In California, Harvey Milk had just barely defeated the Briggs initiative, a bill to prohibit people suspected of being gay from working in schools. And just a year earlier, an episode of *Alice* had hinged on whether it was safe for a kid to spend time around a gay friend of the family.

A mid-seventies poll from NBC found that 57 percent of Americans believed homosexuality was a mental illness and 52 percent believed it was immoral. As late as 1997, a Pew survey that found only 6 percent of Americans thought that gays and lesbians raising kids was a "good thing." Pew surveys wouldn't find majority support for same-sex parental adoption until around 2010.

On *Soap*, the case goes to court, and when Carol takes the stand, she lies. She fabricates claims that "a group of homosexuals" threatened her if she came back for Wendy, playing into the prejudices about gay people being dangerous. Even though it's not true, Jodie knows that the court will believe sinister lies about a gay man before they'll believe the truth. He takes the stand, heartbroken, and has one last speech before, he knows, he'll lose his daughter:

JODIE: I've proven, at least to myself, what kind of father I am. And whether Wendy lives with me or not, at least she'll know that I've always wanted her and I'll always be there for her.

That's the cliffhanger where season three ends—with Jodie not knowing if he'd ever see his daughter again.

*

This storyline was particularly relevant because of something that had just happened in real life. A few months before the start of *Soap*'s third season, two lesbian moms in Washington became the first same-sex couple in US history to win a custody battle.

Sandy Schuster and Madeleine Isaacson met one day in 1970 at a Pentecostal church outside Seattle. The two women were both married—unhappily—to men, parenting six children between them with little support from their husbands, and quickly became close friends and confidantes. Soon, Isaacson realized that for the first time in her life, she was experiencing romantic feelings for another woman, and on a church trip to Oregon she told Schuster, "I have some very different feelings welling up within me."[19]

In an interview with *People* magazine, Schuster recalled, "I darn near drove off the road." She felt the same way.

Their relationship deepened, and one night in 1971, Isaacson recalled, "We just threw the diaper pail and the sleeping bags and our clothes into the van and took off," taking their kids with them. Their husbands pursued, attempting to gain custody of the children, and nearly a decade of legal wrangling followed. Courts initially ruled that the two women could keep their children, but only if they agreed to stop living with each other. That was followed by numerous rounds of challenges, and then finally in May of 1979 the case was finally resolved in their favor.

"The mothers have shown stability, integrity, and openness," the court ruled, "despite their homosexuality."

It wasn't exactly the most ringing endorsement from the legal system, but at least it was a win—which was rare for the time. A spokesperson for the Lesbian Mothers' National Defense Fund estimated that in the late seventies and early eighties, "when lesbianism becomes an issue in custody cases, it becomes the only issue, and a woman has only a 15 to 20 percent chance of getting custody." Still, she said, "when we started four years ago, the chances of winning were 1 percent."[20]

The legal tide was finally starting to turn, and Americans could see this new reality playing out for the first time on *Soap*.

But nobody knew whether Jodie's case was going to work out in his favor, until season four premiered on November 14, 1980.

At first it doesn't look good for him. The judge is prepared to rule in Carol's favor: "An infant needs the kind of care that can be given by a mother," she says, echoing a frequent (and unfounded) assumption made by courts in real life.

But then the judge drops a bombshell. The night before, she says, Carol's mother called to confess that she and Carol had lied on the stand in order to discredit Jodie as a father. "Therefore, I have decided to break with normal tradition," the judge continues, "and award custody of the infant, Wendy, to her father, Jodie Dallas."

At that line, the studio audience—all die-hard fans of the show who clamored every week for tickets to live tapings—burst into wild applause. And they weren't the only ones relieved by this win. In the leadup to *Soap*'s fourth season, ABC ran a poll for viewers to weigh in on how they thought the judge should rule. Viewers supported Jodie by a margin of three to one.

"America in this poll wanted Jodie to have the baby," Billy Crystal recalled years later, "and I thought that was a victory. That was the big thing. They trusted a gay man with a child."

This was the culmination of years of work—on the part of gay activists like Newt Dieter and Ginny Vida, who pushed the show to humanize the gay character; on the part of Crystal, who insisted that the character be greater than a collection of stereotypes; and on the part of Susan Harris, who had given the character unprecedented depth.

Not only was Jodie finally reunited with his daughter, free to raise her openly and honestly as a gay dad, but he could do it with the support of an overwhelming majority of the audience.

As Harris put it in a later interview, "Billy Crystal took a brutally difficult role, a dangerous part, a character that is the butt of jokes in this country, and made him warm and lovable and funny. Billy made Jodie Dallas someone people root for."[21]

"That," Crystal said, "is the great payoff for the series . . . I was really proud of what we did on that show."

It was an extremely satisfying conclusion to a years-long arc.

*

And then *Soap* got a little silly.

In its fourth season, *Soap* started veering into stories that were more about gimmicks than characters. There was a storyline about an alien abduction; the family gets swept up in a South American revolution; Wendy is kidnapped by ninjas; Jodie gets hypnotized into living as a ninety-year-old man (essentially an opportunity for him to pivot to a persona that audiences loved in his live stand-up shows).

After that great payoff for the Jodie character, season four was mostly a collection of wacky premises.

Meanwhile, there was more trouble on the horizon. Conservative groups led by Donald Wildmon had continued applying pressure to advertisers as *Soap* went on. According to one ABC executive, the show lost $3 million a year because the network had to sell ad time at a steep discount. And by season four, almost all the sponsors had fled. At this point, Harris said in later interviews, the only sponsor still with the show was the pickle company.

"The controversy never ended in four years," Marsha Posner Williams recalled.

"The last year, we went on without sponsorship," said Crystal. "Because the show was so controversial."

Things were about to get even worse. Wildmon was planning a new round of protests, now with the backing of evangelical influencer Jerry Falwell. Falwell was a huge religious force whose support had helped Ronald Reagan win the presidency, with Election Day falling just a few days before the airing of Jodie's custody win. Emboldened to embark on further cultural crusades, Falwell pledged to form a coalition with Wildmon, pledging $2 million and a mailing list of four and a half million families to support Wildmon's boycott efforts.[22]

They had an early victory over the summer of 1981 when Owen Butler, the chairman of Procter & Gamble, told reporters, "We think the coalition is expressing very important and broadly held views about gratuitous sex, violence and profanity. I can assure you that we are listening very carefully to what they say."[23] Procter & Gamble was the single biggest advertiser on television, spending around $250 million on commercials—equivalent to nearly a billion dollars today. When the company announced they would drop ads from fifty different programs they deemed inappropriate, shows that were seen as daring suddenly looked like colossal liabilities to the networks.

*

Season four of *Soap* ends with a dramatic cliffhanger, the main character in front of a firing squad. Nobody will ever know what happens next, because ABC pulled the plug on *Soap*.

Even with the decline in advertisers, the cancellation was still a surprise for the writers. They had thoughts about where *Soap* could go, but they'd never get to put them on screen.

Instead, Susan Harris, Tony Thomas, and Paul Witt focused on *Benson*, a spinoff of *Soap* featuring Robert Guillaume, and tried to generate momentum for some new shows. But their efforts yielded a string of flops: in 1980, there was *I'm a Big Girl Now*, which was canceled after a year. Then came *It Takes Two* in 1982, a comedy in which Richard Crenna and Patty Duke Astin played a married couple (with a teenage daughter played by Helen Hunt), which also got canceled after its first year. That was followed by *Hail to the Chief* in 1985, in which Duke played the first woman president of the United States. As with *Soap*, the show featured a gay character in the main cast, this time as a Secret Service agent whose family rejected him for his homosexuality:

SECRET SERVICE AGENT RANDY: When my father found
    out when I was in college, he never again could look at me.
PRESIDENT JULIA MANSFIELD: Even now?
RANDY: Now particularly. He's dead.

That show lasted just seven episodes.

This was a difficult time for Witt, Thomas, and Harris, who kept trying to make new shows work—and writing gay characters where they could—but couldn't seem to find anything that clicked.*

Nevertheless, across the eighties and into the nineties, gay characters started appearing on more and more shows, from *The Love Boat* to *Night Court* to *Cagney & Lacey*, and with complex, recurring characters on broadcast dramas like *Dynasty* and cable sitcoms like *Brothers*. Conservative control over the airwaves was beginning to wane,† and from the perspective of several decades later, what was once the most controversial show on TV now seems fairly tame.

Still, said Billy Crystal, "I'm proud we did this character when the *Will & Grace* actors were in elementary school. As flawed as some of the moments were . . . we did something important."

And Harris's best work was still to come.

---

* Until the fall of 1985, when they embarked on their most unlikely project yet—a sitcom about four elderly women sharing a home in Miami.

† After Donald Wildmon convinced Procter & Gamble to drop their ads in 1981, his next target was an upcoming NBC show called *Love, Sidney*, which starred Tony Randall as a gay man. Wildmon announced a boycott of NBC's parent company, RCA, but during the period of the boycott, company profits went up. Wildmon's campaign seemed to have no effect whatsoever, and his credibility was effectively shot. He would be increasingly marginalized in the years to come, a punch line who was largely laughed at for protesting Hallmark's same-sex greeting cards, and for accusing American Girl dolls of promoting lesbianism.

CHEERS

DIANE: Carla, you're not prejudiced against gays, are you?
CARLA: I'm not exactly crazy about 'em. I mean, I get enough competition from women.

In the early 1980s, NBC was in trouble. The network was last place in ratings by a large margin, and its shows were regarded as a joke not just within the television industry, but by NBC employees themselves.

President Fred Silverman, who had recently defected from ABC, struggled to turn the network around but mainly floundered from one disaster to another. There were mortifyingly unloved shows like 1979's *Hello, Larry*; a catastrophically unfunny season of *Saturday Night Live* during which Al Franken begged the network, on air, to put the show out of its misery; *Supertrain*, a lavish *Love Boat* knockoff that nearly bankrupted the network in 1979; and the loss of one of NBC's most lucrative broadcast events when the United States boycotted the 1980 Olympics—which was hardly Silverman's fault, but it didn't help.

Hoping to turn NBC's fortunes around, Silverman launched a new corporate slogan, "We're Proud," which came with an extensive advertising campaign and upbeat jingle. Sample lyrics: "In a special way / we're gonna light your nights / and fill your days."

Jaded NBC staffers found the song creatively inspiring, but not in the way Silverman had hoped. They hired the same studio singers to record a parody version called "We're Loud," with the lyrics "We're gonna screw around / and run this network in the ground" and "The peacock's dead / so thank you, Fred."

Desperate, executives wooed a team they hoped might reverse the network's fortunes. Jim Burrows, along with Les and Glen Charles, were credited as having significantly contributed to the success of CBS's *The Mary Tyler Moore Show* and *The Bob Newhart Show*, and ABC's *Taxi*. They weren't particularly interested in jumping over to NBC, but the struggling network coughed up a deal they couldn't refuse: a guaranteed thirteen-episode run.

Burrows, the Charles brothers, and a gaggle of NBC executives convened for a meeting over breakfast, where they hashed out their idea for a show inspired by sports-themed Miller Lite commercials.[1]

Cheers debuted in late 1982, set in an informal Boston bar run by former baseball champ Sam Malone (played by Ted Danson, who'd appeared as a gay hairdresser a few years earlier on *Taxi*) and populated by quirky characters: brainy Diane (Shelley Long, pre–*Troop Beverly Hills*), tough-talking Carla (Rhea Perlman), well-meaning Coach (Nick Colasanto), sad-sack Norm (George Wendt), and know-it-all mailman Cliff (John Ratzenberger, who'd recently appeared as a gay bathhouse birthday boy in the movie *The Ritz*).

Like most NBC shows of the time, it was an immediate flop.

Cheers's ratings in its first few months were abysmal. It wasn't helped by a bewildering NBC ad campaign in which a woman turns to the camera to insist that even though the show wasn't on ABC or CBS, it was still pretty good, really it was.

"If you watch the first four or five episodes, you'll see we were all experimenting a little bit with what the show was going to be," said writer Ken Levine in an interview with the Television Academy Foundation.[2]

As the fledgling show struggled to find a direction, it took a bold leap as one of the few sitcoms in the early eighties to have any acknowledgment of homosexuality. In the show's second episode, a distraught father named Leo wanders into the bar, upset that his son is gay and looking for a sympathetic ear. Initially, Coach suggests that Leo throw his son out of the house—not a particularly warm piece of advice, but telling of mainstream attitudes at the time.[3]

But then there's a twist: Coach's suggestion makes Leo realize that he can't throw his son out, because he loves him too much:

LEO: I see what you're saying.
COACH: You do? What?
LEO: If I can't accept the kid the way he is, I'll lose him.
COACH: Boy, that's good.

It suddenly pivots to become a surprisingly touching scene—a parent realizing that their love for their kid is more important than the homophobia they've internalized their whole life. But it's worth noting that the gay character exists completely off screen, spoken about rather than speaking for himself. In something of a pattern for the show over the next decade, queer people don't get to bring their problems to the bar to be solved; instead, *they* are the problems that need solving.

*

The next time homosexuality wanders into the bar, it's far more overt, in the late-season-one episode "The Boys in the Bar."

The episode begins with reporters convening on the bar for a book release party. "How can that be in a place where no one can read?" Diane wonders.

As it turns out, Sam's college friend Tom just published an autobiography, and Sam's hosting a book release party for him. Sam is excited for everyone to read it—even though, he confesses to Diane, he hasn't read it yet himself. "Didn't want to wear out your lips?" she says.

If Sam *had* read the book, titled *Catcher's Mask*, he might've discovered that it's a coming-out story. That may be a reference to the real-life athlete Glenn Burke, the country's first openly gay pro baseball player.* He played with the Los Angeles Dodgers and Oakland A's in the late seventies and competed in the 1982 Gay Games just a few months before this episode aired.

The reporters' pointed questions at the press conference lead Sam to realize what's going on, and his initial reaction is to literally run away, hiding in a back room of the bar and cycling through "I can't believe it's not heterosexual" cliches: "He should have told me," Sam sputters to Diane, then reflects, "I should have known. I remember sitting at a piano bar with him and he requested a show tune."

Sensing Sam's discomfort, Tom prepares to leave—but seeing him go, Sam realizes what he's done, and in front of the news cameras, tells his friend to stay. It's a bold gesture, given the times:

TOM: I appreciate this, Sam. I really do.
SAM: Well, you didn't dump me when I had a drinking problem.
TOM: Uh, sure I did, you were just passed out at the time.

Joking aside, after the ugliness of his initial shock, Sam quickly pivots to become a good friend. He's an extension of the bar—or maybe the bar's an extension of him—and the theme song tells you what kind of person and setting this is: a place where everybody knows your name, where everyone's troubles are the same. In other words, a place where everyone's equal and everyone's welcome.

But the regulars aren't on board. The next evening, Norm takes Sam aside with a warning. He explains that after another nearby watering hole let gays hang out there, it turned into a gay bar, and Norm's scared that the same thing could happen to Cheers:

---

* Burke is credited with being the inventor of the high five during a game in 1977, which means that all high fives are gay.

> NORM: All the regulars left, Sammy. Out went the oars and moose heads and in came plants and ferns. Ferns!

The reference to ferns might not make much sense today, but back then, for some reason, gay bars and ferns went hand in hand. They're visible all over the background of a 1977 episode of *Maude* set at a gay bar, and there are what look like fake ferns in the background of the 1971 movie *Some of My Best Friends Are . . .**

As the regulars wring their hands about Cheers turning gay, Diane drops a bombshell. Not only do gay people come to Cheers all the time, she says, but there are two gay men in the bar at that moment. Norm doesn't believe her:

> NORM: Looks like a straight crowd to me. Too ugly to be gay . . .
> Too ugly to be *out*.

But Diane maintains that there are, indeed, queers in their midst, and that she's even spoken to them. Now on high alert, the gang spots a few unfamiliar faces at a nearby table—and their suspicions are further roused when the strangers order light beers and greet a friend with a hug. Diane rolls her eyes at the simmering homophobia:

> DIANE: Come on, I've seen you guys hug.
> NORM: Yeah, but we hate it.

The regulars start rumbling angrily about the presence of possible queer people across the bar, and a few insist that Sam throw them out.

The behavior of the *Cheers* patrons is harsh, but not unrealistic given the

---

* Coincidentally, both projects star Rue McClanahan, whose *Golden Girls* bedroom would reveal her to be quite the fan of a bold floral.

times. The premise spelled out by the show's theme song is that it's a place where everyone is welcome, but in this episode those words are being put to the test—as Diane points out when the regulars announce their plan to abandon the bar if Sam doesn't kick out the gay patrons:

> DIANE: You've gone out of your way to make a bar where custom-
> ers can feel like they belong, part of a family. And now they're
> walking out on you.

Under pressure from his homophobic clientele, Sam uncomfortably makes his way to the men who are the target of the crowd's displeasure. He's prepared to ask them to leave, but then they recognize him from the news coverage about his friend, Tom, and they remember that Sam stood by him:

> PATRON 1: We read the article in the newspaper.
> SAM: Oh right.
> PATRON 1: That took a lot of guts.
> PATRON 2: It really did.
> SAM: Yeah. Um . . . Coach, get these guys a beer on the house.

In that moment, Sam realizes that if he gives in to the mob, he's not only betraying Tom, but betraying his own values about what he wants Cheers to be.

The regulars are furious, but this time he has the nerve to stand up to them:

> NORM: Okay, Sam, you know what kind of bar this could turn
> into.
> SAM: It's not going to turn into the kind of bar that I have to
> throw people out of.
> DIANE: That was the noblest preposition you've ever dangled.

But there's one twist left. Turns out, those guys weren't gay. The gay patrons, Diane reveals, were actually mingling with the regulars the whole time:

DIANE: They, along with myself, have had a wonderful time watching you make complete idiots of yourselves . . . the guys I was talking about are still here. Right guys?

THE ACTUAL GAYS: Right. [They lean in and kiss NORM.]

NORM: [Considering the kisses] Better than Vera.

This episode was a big risk for low-rated season-one *Cheers*—and for NBC, which was still teetering on the verge of collapse. But this episode was well-received by viewers and critics; the show's ratings began to climb in summer reruns, and "The Boys in the Bar" earned an Emmy nomination for outstanding writing and won a Writers Guild Award for best screenplay. *Cheers* marked a turning point for NBC, the start of a new era of programming that by the end of the eighties would transform it into a comedy juggernaut with programs like *The Cosby Show* and *The Golden Girls*, and—after a slow build—mega-hits like *Seinfeld*.

This one episode alone didn't save the show, or NBC, but it certainly helped.

The message is, on balance, favorable to queer people—our hero rejects bigotry, and everyone learns a lesson about tolerance—but it's important to note that the gay characters once again aren't so much characters as plot devices. The crisis of the episode rests squarely with the straights: What's to be done about this homosexual headache? Although gays are, in the end, tolerated, they exist primarily to be a complication in the lives of the main cast. They're outsiders, barely present, and when they make themselves known, it throws the bar into chaos.

This was a frequent context for queer characters in the eighties.

Obviously, gay people exist everywhere, even in bars—sometimes especially in bars—but as queer characters blossomed on sitcoms in the late

1970s and early 1980s, many shows engaged in a strange sleight of hand in which gay characters became strange phantoms. On many shows, they were either shoved off camera, turned out not to have been gay at all, or saw their very existence denied.

For example, since its premiere in 1977, the entire premise of *Three's Company* was that the gay guy is, secretly, not really gay. On a 1978 episode of *WKRP in Cincinnati*, a false rumor that news director Les Nessman is gay must be debunked before he jumps off a ledge. On the 1979 pilot episode of *The Facts of Life*, Jo thinks she might be a lesbian because she likes sports, but Mrs. Garrett convinces her that in time, she'll straighten out. A 1980 episode of *The Love Boat* hinges on a misunderstanding about a honeymooning gay couple that turns out to be two straight friends. A 1984 episode of *Murder, She Wrote* features a drag queen who turns out to be straight; and in a 1984 episode of *Kate & Allie*, the straight characters lie about being lesbians to get a discount on rent.

To be fair, there were also some genuinely strong queer characters around this time, like Beverly LaSalle on *All in the Family*, Edie Stokes on *The Jeffersons*, and a surprisingly dignified gay man on an episode of *Night Court*. An ostensibly queer character was part of the core cast of *Dynasty* starting in 1981 (though his sexuality varies over the run of the series, taking until the 1991 reunion special to settle decisively on gay). But from the late seventies to the early nineties, queer characters often had a way of existing just beyond the scan lines of the television screen—hinted at, absent, or revealed to have been straight all along.

This phenomenon occurs repeatedly on *Cheers*. On a 1984 episode titled, perhaps appropriately, "Fairy Tales Can Come True," the gang wonders if Cliff might be gay because they've never seen him with a woman. Coach breaks in with a speech that's *almost* very affirming:

COACH: I can't believe what I'm hearing. You can't tell a gay guy
by his appearance. We had an outfielder on the Red Sox, Duke
Roberts. I mean, he never got married, he never went with

girls, he even wore those fancy Italian shoes, and he lived with
a guy who was a florist. And Duke wasn't gay.

SAM: Yes, he was, Coach.

COACH: He was? Do you think he'd like to meet Cliffy?

The sentiment is sweet, but Duke's yet another gay character who exists completely off-screen, and he's assumed to be straight. In the world of *Cheers*—and, indeed, on many shows of the time—queer people barely seem to exist.

*

That brings us to the 1988 episode "Norm, Is That You?" There's already a touch of lavender in the episode title, a reference to the 1976 film *Norman... Is That You?* in which a father played by Redd Foxx refuses to believe that his son is gay. The movie is laden with some hilariously specific tropes about what signifies homosexuality, as described in the trailer: "Norman used to be the all-American boy. Now he has purple drapes . . . flowered underwear . . . and a roommate . . . named Garson."

And of course, times being what they are, the film includes a scene where a gay person is told he's not gay: "You don't walk like one," huffs Redd Foxx as the boy's father, "you don't talk like one. I say you're *not* one!"

It's an unexpected basis for an episode of *Cheers*, but like the film, the "Norm, Is That You?" episode hinges on a misunderstanding about someone's sexuality. The setup is that snooty intellectual married couple Frasier Crane (Kelsey Grammer) and Lilith Sternin-Crane (Bebe Neuwirth) are decorating their apartment, but their pompous interior designer's ideas are all terrible.* After the Cranes fire the designer, they discover that Norm has a surprising eye for interior decor, something that for him has always been a secret source of shame. "I spent my whole damn life trying to cover up the

---

* The designer is played by B.J. Turner, who played a person of ambiguous gender on an episode of *Night Court*.

fact that I have a great sense of color and I always know where to put the ottoman," he laments.

Cajoled into helping his friends, Norm does such a good job decorating the Cranes' apartment that they recommend him to their yuppie friends Robert and Kim.*

Frasier prepares Norm for the meeting with these new clients by explaining that they have some preconceptions about what a decorator should be: "They're narrow-minded, trend-sucking dilettantes who insist that their chefs be French, their mechanics be German, and their designers be . . ." he cocks his wrist, ". . . stylish."

Norm allows them to think he's gay, but things get complicated when they swing by Cheers and he has to jump back and forth between his gay deception and straight life like it's the climax of *Mrs. Doubtfire*. He ropes Sam into posing as his boyfriend, but the deception falls apart (as they always do in the last five minutes of a sitcom farce), and Norm begrudgingly delivers a speech in which he reveals his terrible heterosexual secret.

By today's standards, the "coming out as straight" joke feels hacky and overdone, but since few people had come out as *anything* on television in 1988, it was at least somewhat novel to hear this sort of language:

NORM: It's time that I came out of the closet. I'm straight.
ROBERT: Impossible.
NORM: No, no, ever since I was a little boy I've known I prefer
    girls.

Off their aghast reaction, Norm concludes, "I think you should judge people for what they do, not for . . . *who* they do."

It's a fine place for Norm to land, and it's pleasant that the show suggests that it's wrong to pre-judge people on the basis of their perceived

---

* Kim is played by Jane Sibbett, who would go on to portray the lesbian ex-wife Carol on *Friends*.

sexuality. But on the other hand, it's just the slightest bit galling that the line comes from a straight person protesting their oppression, as if saying, "Won't someone think of the plight of the poor beleaguered heterosexual?"

Those thoughtful words about the harms of prejudice would probably resonate a bit more crisply if they weren't coming from a show that hadn't given openly queer characters more than a few words of dialogue in, at this point, seven seasons.

*

For a gay character to enter Cheers and say more than a few words, viewers would have to wait another four years for the 1992 episode "Rebecca's Lover...Not." (*Wayne's World* had just come out that year and everyone was doing "not" jokes.)

This episode is a milestone not just for *Cheers*, but for television in general because of the actor playing the gay character: Harvey Fierstein. Maybe you know him as the brother from *Mrs. Doubtfire*, or Edna from *Hairspray* on Broadway, or Yao in *Mulan*—or as the first openly gay actor to play a gay lead on a sitcom (on the 1994 blink-and-you've-missed it series *Daddy's Girls*).

In "Rebecca's Lover . . . Not," Fierstein guest stars as Mark, the high school boyfriend of Kirstie Alley's character Rebecca. They met in Drama Club, the story goes, and haven't seen each other in years. What Rebecca doesn't know is that in the intervening years, Mark has come out. But Rebecca, clueless, plans to pick up where they left off. *Cheers* finally gets a gay character, but he exists to be a heterosexual love interest.

That Fierstein is playing a character who could even be mistaken for heterosexual is a little absurd, and not just because their characters are supposed to have met in Drama Club. It's important to note just how significant a queer figure he was—essentially gay theater royalty.

Fierstein started out in the New York theater scene in the 1970s, acting in Andy Warhol's *Pork* among other countercultural productions. Success came when he wrote his first play, *Torch Song Trilogy*, a three-part exploration of the lives and loves of a gay man, from dating to parenting to coping with the death of a partner. It wasn't the world's first gay-focused play, but after a four-year climb from off-off-Broadway to off-Broadway in 1978 and then Broadway in 1982, it was the first that broke through to mainstream audiences. The cast included a very young Matthew Broderick and a slightly less young Estelle Getty.

The great innovation of Fierstein's *Torch Song Trilogy* was that it exposed mainstream audiences to the realities of gay lives. It wasn't sensationalized or a caricature presented by heterosexuals, but a real portrait of same-sex love and loss. This was a time when queer people were gaining more public visibility than ever, thanks to the triumphs of queer liberation and the tragedy of the emerging HIV epidemic; and after years of misleading portrayals of queers in the media, many people—even Broadway audiences—had no idea what a homosexual person's life was like.

This cluelessness was, at times, exhausting: in a 1983 *20/20* interview with his friend Barbara Walters, the exasperation on Fierstein's face was clear when Walters asked, "What's it like to be a homosexual?"

In his memoir, Fierstein wrote that his internal reaction to the question was, "Who the fuck is this woman and what did she do with my friend Barbara?"[4] After a pause, he sighed, and explained that he is, in fact, just a person.

"Love, commitment, family belong to all people," he told her. "Those are not heterosexual experiences and those are not heterosexual words—those are human words."

It's *Torch Song Trilogy*'s humanity that contributed to its success. The main character, as played by Arnold, laments his loneliness, bristles at the meddling of his mother, and struggles to maintain his grasp on a family of his own making. Thanks to Fierstein's play—and 1988 film adaptation—thousands if not millions of people saw a queer person living a queer life, with an undercurrent of emotion that was universally recognizable and relatable.

After *Torch Song Trilogy*, Fierstein wrote the book for *La Cage aux Folles*,* a musical based on the same French play that would be adapted into the film *The Birdcage*, followed by various hit roles on stage and screen.†

And that's Harvey Fierstein: an actor and playwright who, while the regulars at Cheers were wringing their hands with concern at the mere existence of gay people, was winning Tonys for showing the world that not only do gay people exist, but they're everywhere. Unabashed, unashamed, he told Barbara Walters, "I've never heard of a family without a gay member in it."

*

Now back to the episode. Rebecca's planning a fun night out with Mark, assuming it's a date, and everyone at the bar lets her go through with it because humiliating Rebecca had become a competitive sport in the last few seasons of the show.

Mark stops by her apartment, and she's ready to seduce him with a sexy nightie. He is, indeed, transfixed: "Is it silk?" Mark demands, grabbing her and spinning her around to peek at the label. "Rayon! I don't believe it! So what do you do, put it in the delicate cycle and then spin? We have to talk."

Rebecca, impatient, gives up on subtlety:

REBECCA: You know perfectly well that the point of this nightie
is not laundry instructions. The point of this nightie is to ...
MARK: To what?
REBECCA: You know, a man and a woman ...
MARK: [Looking around] Where?

---

* *La Cage's* big act-one finale, "I Am What I Am," is one of Broadway's great showstoppers, an anthem in which a drag queen proudly declares himself and refuses to be shamed.

† Of note: Fierstein originated the role of *Hairspray's* Edna Turnblad, a character originally created by Divine for the John Waters film; when Fierstein stepped out of that role, he was replaced by, of all people, George Wendt—Norm from *Cheers*.

And then he utters words that nobody, in all of ten years and 243 episodes, had ever had an opportunity to say on *Cheers*:

MARK: Rebecca, you know I'm gay, don't you?
REBECCA: [Flustered] Why... of course I do! Why do you think
    I feel so comfortable wearing this in front of you? I mean, this
    is my housecoat! I know it's sexy, but I paint in it.

They're both a little embarrassed, but as old friends they quickly relax into their regular rapport, sitting back on Rebecca's couch in an affectionate hug. They spread a blanket spread over their laps, and then Mark looks suddenly startled...

MARK: What are you doing?
REBECCA: Looking for the remote control.
MARK: It's on the coffee table.
REBECCA: You can't blame me for trying.

The unintentional joke here is that *Cheers* finally has a gay character—one—but *still* attempts to deny his queerness (not to mention suggesting that Rebecca has sexually assaulted her friend, a "joke" that would certainly be received very differently today). That's a shame, because with this episode *Cheers* is close to discovering a character archetype several years ahead of its time: a straight woman's platonic gay best friend and former romantic interest.

That's a trope that, these days, is so overexposed it's become self-parodying. But in 1992, it was a relationship that had barely been explored on screens. Movies would cautiously explore the straight woman/gay man relationship over the next few years in *Reality Bites*, *My Best Friend's Wedding*, *The Object of My Affection*, and *As Good as It Gets*; then television would finally catch up with *Will & Grace*. *Cheers* and Fierstein got there before all of them, but the show doesn't seem to notice the potential—like most gay guests of the time, Mark never returns.

Meanwhile, for much of the early nineties, sitcoms would continue to push back against the continuing existence of queer people. Halfway between this episode of *Cheers* and the premiere of *Will & Grace*, episodes of *Seinfeld* would depict homosexuality as a misunderstanding (in the infamous "not that there's anything wrong with that" episode), or as a changeable affliction in a 1995 episode where Elaine tries to "convert" a gay man:

> JERRY: You're thinking *conversion?*
> ELAINE: Well, it did occur to me.
> JERRY: Are you that desperate?
> ELAINE: [Thinking it over] Yes, I am.[5]

But her efforts at conversion are such a failure that the episode essentially concludes that it's not worth trying. Television was finally reaching a point of acknowledging that gay people exist and have lives beyond serving as a crisis of the week. Now, the straight characters were going to have to—as the protest slogan goes—get used to it.

THE GOLDEN GIRLS

BLANCHE: *Jean has the hots for Rose? I don't believe it. I do not believe it.*

DOROTHY: *I was pretty surprised myself.*

BLANCHE: *Well, I'll bet. To think Jean would prefer Rose over me? That's ridiculous!*

Picture it: Saturday night, 1986, at the most popular gay bar in town. The clock strikes nine, the music stops, and everyone turns their attention to the TV monitors for the highlight of the evening: *The Golden Girls*, one of the luckiest accidents in television history.

It all began on September 17, 1984, when NBC broadcast a one-hour special to promote their upcoming fall season. It was, to put it mildly, a mostly dismal lineup. The network was in the throes of a chaotic transition from the near-bankruptcy of the late seventies into the eventual juggernaut of Must See TV in the nineties, but their mid-eighties slate was a truly insane chimera. Though they'd eked out a few hits like the cop-dramas *Hill Street Blues* and *Knight Rider*, the network was also home to justifiably forgotten sitcoms like *Jennifer Slept Here*,* the dismal Jim Carrey vehicle *The Duck Factory*,† and *Mr. Smith*.‡

On NBC's September special, wedged between celebrity banter about a young show called *Cheers* that was still floundering for its audience and an inexplicable NBC-themed dance number, out came a pair of actors from two of NBC's few successful shows: gravel-voiced Selma Diamond from *Night Court*, and Doris Roberts (who would go on to play the mom on *Everybody Loves Raymond*) from *Remington Steele*.

They'd been brought out to introduce the action-drama *Miami Vice*. But as a little goof, Diamond feigns that she mistakenly believes the title refers to a Miami retirement community:

> DIAMOND: We're here to introduce a show that takes place in the most wonderful resort in the world, Miami. A land of Coppertone and corned beef. Mink coats. Cha-cha lessons. *The Jackie Gleason Show*.
>
> ROBERTS: It's been canceled.
>
> DIAMOND: Canceled?
>
> ROBERTS: Better him than us. [Tepid audience laughter; Doris shrugs resignedly.]
>
> DIAMOND: This is a show about sitting on the beach . . .
>
> ROBERTS: No no no, Selma, honey, no no. This show is not called *Miami Nice*. This is called *Miami Vice*.
>
> DIAMOND: Doris . . . don't do this to me.

The material is stilted, and the actresses seem to know it and long to break free—at one point, they smirk at each other and, in cross talk, play-

---

* A horny teen is haunted by the ghost of a beautiful actress.

† A serialized story about a low-budget cartoon studio. The show was rendered completely baffling when NBC aired the episodes out of order.

‡ A talking orangutan becomes a high-powered Washington, DC, political consultant.

fully throw out what seem like a few improvised lines ("I'm in no condition for fooling around," Diamond deadpans as Roberts cracks up and pats her scene partner's cheek) before introducing "the gorgeous Don Johnson and the gorgeous Philip Michael Thomas." The *Miami Vice* hunks saunter out onto the stage to find Diamond and Roberts both lustily grabbing for them. They introduce a clip from the show, and after it rolls, Diamond laments, "Can you believe I didn't see *one* of my friends?"

Cut to commercial.

Ordinarily, that would have been the end of it. But sitting in the audience was NBC's thirty-five-year-old entertainment president Brandon Tartikoff, and he couldn't help noticing how funny the two actresses were, joking about retirement activities and craving younger men. They were the bright spot of the evening, and as the night wore on, Tartikoff and his colleagues started to wonder: Could that one-off *Miami Nice* joke—a show about single Florida retirees—be so crazy it just might work?

There were a couple factors working in the concept's favor. For one thing, Miami was a particularly trendy city in the early eighties, so it was an attractive setting for a TV show. For another, Tartikoff had been looking for a way to create a TV adaptation of the 1953 movie *How to Marry a Millionaire*, in which Marilyn Monroe, Lauren Bacall, and Betty Grable play plain-talking New York gals searching for love (sort of a *Sex and the City* precursor).

One more factor: the previous year, the overwhelming success of *The Cosby Show* had proven that there was a huge and underutilized talent pool of Black actors whom television had been ignoring for decades. Executives started to wonder if the same might be true of actresses of a certain age.

But at that point, the entire concept was, essentially, "What if we made a show about horny retired singles in Miami?" Tartikoff needed someone who could develop it into a series, and to find a better name than the working title of *Miami Nice* (or the even worse second choice, *Ladies Day*).[1]

That was when they called in a familiar name: Susan Harris. After the rapid demise of her shows *I'm a Big Girl Now*, *It Takes Two*, and *Hail to the*

Chief, she was eager to land a project that would recapture the glory of *Soap* and *Benson*, or at least survive to the end of its first season. But the project that Tartikoff was proposing seemed like a long shot.

"Are you sure you want to put this on the air?" Harris asked executives at one point.

"If you write it," development executive Warren Littlefield told her, "we'll have to, because you're wonderful."*

But as confident as Littlefield was in Harris's writing, the success of the project would depend on far more than her ability to craft a brilliant script. For a show that centered entirely on the interpersonal chemistry of four close friendships, it was vital that they find the right cast.

*

Casting *The Golden Girls* was a laborious process that nearly went off the rails multiple times. And although it certainly wasn't intentional, by a strange quadruple-coincidence, all four actresses that they cast had a history of participating in particularly queer projects.

The team got lucky early on when sixty-year-old Estelle Getty walked into an audition. Born in Manhattan's Lower East Side in 1923, Getty had decided to become an actress early in life because of her love of vaudeville, but success had been elusive. For most of her career, she worked as a secretary by day and appeared in tiny off-off-off-Broadway shows at night. Among the highlights—well, lowlights really—was a 1972 show called *The Divorce of Judy and Jane* about a lesbian couple ending their relationship. Getty played a tough-talking librarian known as Uncle Maxie, and the *New York Times*'s reviewer ripped the show to shreds, calling it "impertinent."[2]

She'd finally found fame in the early eighties with Harvey Fierstein's *Torch Song Trilogy*, in which she played the mother of a drag queen. After that success, her agent persuaded her to come to Los Angeles for a handful of auditions, and one of those was for *The Golden Girls*'s eighty-year-old

---

* He would repeat the same assurance, about a decade later, to the creators of *Will & Grace*.

THE GOLDEN GIRLS * 139

Sophia. From the moment Getty walked in, carrying a bamboo purse she'd found at a thrift shop, she nailed the role.

The rest of the cast was a little more challenging.

For the roles of sweet, innocent Rose and lusty Blanche, producers had their eyes on Betty White and Rue McClanahan. By strange coincidence, just as with Getty, both actresses' careers had a history of queer themes. White had recently appeared on *Love, Sidney*, an NBC sitcom that starred Tony Randall as a gay man. McClanahan's stage debut was in an Erie Play-house production of *Inherit the Wind*, a play about the Scopes Monkey Trial, with a mostly gay group of actors; of the cast, she wrote in her memoirs, "the chimp was the first male to show any interest in me since I got there." Later, she'd turn heads in the 1971 no-budget fagsploitation film *Some of My Best Friends Are...*, playing Lita, a self-described "hag" in a long mink coat. And in 1978, she played the mother of Leonard Matlovich in a made-for-TV dramatization of the challenge to the military's ban on gay servicemembers.[3]

The producers of *The Golden Girls* loved White and McClanahan, but something seemed off about their casting. At first, they'd slotted White in the Blanche role and cast McClanahan as Rose, and while they were cer-tainly capable actresses, the chemistry just didn't gel.

The problem was identified by their first-choice actress for the part of tough-talking Dorothy. Susan Harris had her heart set on Bea Arthur for that part; the two women had worked together on *Maude*'s abortion-themed two-parter, and Arthur had a deadpan, no-nonsense attitude that suited the Dor-othy character. In fact, before establishing a career as an actress known for playing take-no-prisoners women, Arthur was a truck driver in the Marines.*

But Arthur was totally disinterested in *The Golden Girls*. She explained that she'd already seen McClanahan in a soft-hearted role as Vivian on *Maude*, and White as man-hungry Sue Ann Nivens on *The Mary Tyler Moore Show*, and she wasn't inclined to commit to a show where they'd just be doing more of the same.

---

* One officer wrote that Arthur was a good worker... "if she has her own way."

As luck would have it, she wasn't alone. Veteran director Jay Sandrich, who'd been brought on to helm the pilot, noticed during casting that McClanahan and White both seemed miscast, and asked them to try switching parts. McClanahan was only too delighted by the suggestion, as she had secretly hoped to play Blanche all along, and White was game to give it a shot. When word got back to Arthur that they'd both be playing against type, her interest was piqued. "Now THAT," she later recalled saying, "is very interesting."[4] She agreed to take the part of Dorothy.

Like Getty, McClanahan, and White, Arthur's résumé had copious flecks of lavender. *Maude* was notoriously unflinching in its approach to social issues, and ran two episodes centered around gay topics: one in which Arthur's character accidentally offends a gay man when she laughs a little too hard at the thought of ever being romantically attracted to him, and another in which she aggressively campaigns to save a gay bar from being shut down by her homophobic neighbor (whose name, coincidentally, is Arthur):

ARTHUR: Do you approve of homosexuals?

MAUDE: Arthur, it doesn't matter whether I approve or disapprove. They are human beings. They exist. It's like asking me if
I approve of dwarves.

ARTHUR: That's different; there's no such thing as gay dwarves.

MAUDE: Come on, Arthur, you've read *Snow White*.[5]

With the core cast now in place, rehearsals began immediately with Bea Arthur as acerbic Dorothy; Estelle Getty as her wisecracking mother, Sophia; Betty White as oblivious Rose; Rue McClanahan as sex-driven Blanche; and Charles Levin as Coco.

Wait... who's Coco?

He's the girls' gay houseboy, of course. Susan Harris often included gay characters on her shows, and Coco was sort of a continuation of Jodie from *Soap*. Levin had played a gay sex worker on *Hill Street Blues*, and the plan was for his character to serve as the show's younger voice. In the pilot, he's present in the kitchen for Dorothy to complain to when no one else is around; he offers a quippy remark now and then; and there's a hint at some friction with Sophia.

But as Jeffrey Jones,* another actor considered for the part, observed at his audition, the character seemed unnecessary. As they rehearsed the pilot, it became clear that Jones was right. There just wasn't room for a fifth housemate. Harris made the tough call to mostly cut Coco from the series so they could focus on the dynamic between the women—but it wouldn't be the last time gay characters would visit the house.

*

The Golden Girls debuted on September 14, 1985, with a straightforward introductory story. Blanche, who owns the house, has been seeing a gentleman for a while; when he asks her to marry him, the girls (and Coco) support her, but privately they worry about what that means for their living arrangements:

> ROSE: What if she marries him? What will happen to us? This house is hers.
> DOROTHY: Well, then we'll move.
> ROSE: We can't afford to buy a house. What do we have for collateral? A gay cook?

In the end, it turns out that Blanche's beau is already married, and he's arrested and taken away just minutes before the wedding.† After the

---

* Also known as the principal in *Ferris Bueller's Day Off*.

† And if you enjoy playing Six Degrees of Queer Separation, the policeman who breaks the news to Blanche is played by Meshach Taylor, who played Anthony on *Designing Women* and Hollywood Montrose in *Mannequin*, which starred Estelle Getty; he also appeared in *Mannequin: On the Move*, which was written by Ken Levine, writer of *Cheers*'s "The Boys in the Bar" episode.

wedding is called off, Blanche is heartbroken, but after a few days, she comes to a realization:

> BLANCHE: At first I wanted to give up, to die, truly. Only time I ever felt worse was when George died. But then I had the kids with me and I pulled through it. This time, I thought, "This is my last chance, my last hope for happiness." I just thought I'd never feel good again.
>
> SOPHIA: How long is this story? I'm eighty. I have to plan.
>
> BLANCHE: Then this morning I woke up and I was in the shower, shampooing my hair, and I heard humming. I thought there was someone in there with me. No, it was me. I was humming. And humming means I'm feeling good. And then I realized I was feeling good because of you. You made the difference. You're my family, and you make me happy to be alive.

Not only is this speech quite similar to the one that Harris wrote for Barney to deliver to Jodie on *Soap*, it also gets to the heart of why *The Golden Girls* resonated with gay viewers. At a time when family-focused sitcoms had been returning to a fifties-era template of traditional nuclear units—mom, dad, kids—this was a nontraditional arrangement with only one biological connection among them. It's a group of women who came together in friendship, grew close, and came to support each other in an arrangement familiar to many queer people, especially at a time when they were often rejected by parents and had to find support elsewhere.

The episode ends with everyone going out to lunch, except for Sophia:

> SOPHIA: I got a date tonight.
>
> DOROTHY: Huh? With whom?
>
> SOPHIA: The fancy man and I are going to the dog track.
>
> BLANCHE: Your mother bets?
>
> DOROTHY: No, she rides. She's a dog jockey.

Maybe that's why Coco disappears after the pilot: Sophia left him at the track.

The Golden Girls was the number one show during its debut week. Of everyone watching television that night in the United States, about a quarter of all sets were tuned to the premiere—not bad for a show based on a throwaway joke from a network promo. Clearly, they'd hit on something good.

Following the pilot, the show quickly picked up a gay following that grew over season one. Gay bars made *Golden Girls* viewing parties a regular event every Saturday night, something that delighted season one writer Stan Zimmerman: "In West Hollywood, they would stop everything on Saturday at nine o'clock and on the video bar screens they would show *The Golden Girls*, and I'd go there—because I wanted a free drink," he recalled.

"Gay men like old ladies . . . I don't know why," Betty White said at a panel event, years later. "The gay bars would stop the music at nine o'clock, the show would come on, they'd all watch the show, and at nine thirty they'd turn it off and start the dancing again. We felt very honored."

But despite the show's gay aura, it was clear that not everyone in Hollywood was completely accepting.

"We had to be in the closet as writers on season one," said Zimmerman. He was just breaking into the industry in 1985, and back then a young writer could easily have been fired if he came out to the wrong person. There was already reason to suspect Zimmerman might be gay; one of his first writing credits was on *Brothers*, a Showtime sitcom about a gay man's relationship with his siblings. If word got around that a writer was gay, it could mean the end of their career.

But as it turns out, Zimmerman had someone looking out for him on the inside. Early in rehearsals, he said, Estelle Getty beckoned to him and his writing partner behind the scenes. "She was like, 'Come here,'" Zimmerman said. "Took us behind the set and was like, 'You're one of us.' And I was like, 'Jewish?' . . . And she was like, 'No, gay.' She considered herself part of the community before the word *ally* was even there. She was like the pioneer of allies because she had done *Torch Song Trilogy* on Broadway."[6]

Getty promised that she'd look out for Zimmerman and any other gay members of the crew. Knowing that Getty had his back, Zimmerman was able to write for the show with an added sense of security, and by the end of the first season, he'd picked up a Writers Guild Award and established his place in the industry.

*

After Coco's vanishing act, the show avoided gay issues throughout season one—a fact that disappointed another up-and-coming young television writer named Jeffrey Duteil. Duteil's career was on the rise, with an episode of *The Jeffersons* and a segment for *The Love Boat* that involved a closeted character coming out to a longtime friend. Like many gay men, he loved *The Golden Girls* but lamented the disappearance of the gay houseboy. But he also saw an opportunity: one night as he watched the credits roll, he spotted the name Winifred Hervey, a producer with whom he'd worked on an episode of *The New Odd Couple*.

Duteil had already been tinkering with a script for *The Golden Girls*, and when he saw a familiar name, he figured sending it to Hervey was worth a shot. This was the longest of long shots—television shows virtually never accept unsolicited ideas, let alone entire scripts. But as luck would have it, the producers had been looking for just such a story, and Duteil's script landed on Hervey's desk at precisely the right moment. She called him in, bought the script, and the episode went into production.

"Isn't It Romantic?" has Dorothy's old college friend Jean coming to visit after the death of her partner, Pat. Jean is played by Lois Nettleton, a frequent guest player across several decades: you may recognize her as the program director who flirts with Lou Grant on *The Mary Tyler Moore Show*, or the mother who catches George Costanza eating an eclair out of the garbage on *Seinfeld*. In 1973, she'd played a lesbian doctor on the show *Medical Center*, delivering an impassioned speech: "Lesbians are not a bunch of harridans consumed by hatred of the opposite sex," she declares, before absurdly qualifying, "Oh, some are, but it's too bad for them."[7]

On *The Golden Girls*, the Jean character provides an opportunity for the gals to ruminate on what exactly a lesbian is. Only Dorothy and Sophia are aware of Jean's sexuality, which at first they consider somewhat taboo:

DOROTHY: Do you think I should tell Rose and Blanche?
SOPHIA: Jean is a nice person. She happens to like girls instead of guys. Some people like cats instead of dogs. Frankly, I'd rather live with a lesbian than a cat. [A beat.] Unless a lesbian sheds. That I don't know.

Dorothy feels a little unclear about how one handles a lesbian friend, but fortunately Sophia cuts to the chase when Jean arrives:

DOROTHY: Jean . . . I don't know how to phrase this.
SOPHIA: The lesbian thing. Do you keep it under your hat, or what?

Though the question is blunt, it serves an interesting purpose. Jean responds calmly, seemingly glad to have been asked rather than being outed behind her back. By having Dorothy give her the option of choosing whether to disclose, the episode is providing a little teachable moment to viewers about how to talk to openly queer friends, and what questions to ask them. It also shows viewers how queer people make decisions about when they should come out:

JEAN: Dorothy, I'm not embarrassed or ashamed of who I am. You know your friends better than I do. If you think they can handle it, I'd prefer to tell them.*

---

* Jean's line was originally, "If you think your friends are sophisticated enough to handle it," which makes the joke work much better; but Warren Ashley, one of NBC's censors, made the writers change it for fear that homophobes would take offense at being called unsophisticated.

ROSE: [Entering with a tray of desserts] Here we are. Ice cream
   clowns with hats for everybody!
JEAN: [To Dorothy] It'll be our little secret.

With Jean's arrival and cautious approach to disclosure, it's clear that
this is an episode about secrets, the closet, and outing. The first act hinges
on the fact that even the most informed characters have very little knowledge of lesbians, and the others simply assume that everyone they meet is
straight.

Over the course of her visit, Jean spends more and more time with
Rose, and eventually takes Dorothy aside. "I haven't met anyone as good
and decent as Rose since Pat died," she says, looking worried. "And I think
I'm falling in love."

A commercial break saves Dorothy from having to respond, and then
next time we see her it's nighttime and she's having a heart-to-heart with
her mother:

SOPHIA: I'll tell you the truth, Dorothy. If one of my kids was
   gay, I wouldn't love him one bit less. I would wish him all the
   happiness in the world.
DOROTHY: That's because you're the greatest mother in the
   world. And I love you.
SOPHIA: Fine. Now keep your fat mouth shut so I can get some
   sleep.

This sentiment is strikingly similar to Getty's comments a year earlier
to Zimmerman behind the set, a very progressive attitude for 1986. Once
again, the episode is teaching viewers how to react to a gay friend or family
member: love them, be nice, don't reject them. It's an emphatic, unmistak-
able statement of support—but now Getty gets to express it on camera.

Blanche hears the two characters talking and pops her head into the
bedroom. When they tell her Jean's a lesbian, there's a moment of confusion:

DOROTHY: You aren't surprised?

BLANCHE: Of course not. I've never known any personally, but isn't Danny Thomas one?

DOROTHY: Not Lebanese, Blanche. Lesbian.

BLANCHE: [Considering] Lesbian. Lesbian ... *lesbian?*

Whether or not television star Danny Thomas was a lesbian we'll never know. But we do know that his son, Tony Thomas, was one of the producers of *The Golden Girls*, making this a cute little in-joke—along with being one of the most-quoted lines of the entire series.

Once the confusion is cleared up and Blanche learns that Jean's developed an affection for Rose, she's shocked:

BLANCHE: Jean has the hots for Rose? I don't believe it. I do not believe it.

DOROTHY: I was pretty surprised myself.

BLANCHE: Well, I'll bet. To think Jean would prefer Rose over me? That's ridiculous!

Meanwhile, Rose and Jean have been growing closer, but Rose has no idea how Jean feels about her. When she hears that Jean's planning to spend the night on the sofa, Rose insists on sharing her bed—and before joining her, Jean tries to let her know what's going on. Rose is already under the covers at this point, her eyes closed, with Jean sitting nearby:

JEAN: I like you very much, Rose.

ROSE: I like you too, Jean.

JEAN: I think you're very special.

ROSE: I think you're special, too.

JEAN: What I really want to say is, I ... I'm quite fond of you.

ROSE: I'm fond of you, too. [ROSE's eyes open wide, then she clamps them shut and starts fake-snoring.]

Then, in a bit of action that was not in Jeffrey Duteil's original script, Jean moves to a sofa on the other side of the room, bedding down to make it clear to audiences that the two women did not share a bed.

The next morning, Rose is upset that no one told her about Jean:

DOROTHY: Honey, I didn't even know if you'd know what a lesbian was.
ROSE: I could have looked it up!

Ironically, of all the cast, Betty White was probably the one who least needed a lesbian education, because in real life she was a loving mother to a lesbian stepdaughter named Sarah, a karate instructor in Chicago. In fact, their close relationship once led the *National Enquirer* to label Betty "pride of the lesbians."[8] It's a touch ironic that the episode shows the characters learning about lesbians for what seems like the first time, when in real life the actresses had spent so much time around queer people—and the character who seems the most naïve was played by an actress with a lesbian child.

Her secret out, Jean decides she should leave first thing in the morning. But first Rose kindly offers her a cup of coffee and a chance to talk:

JEAN: It's just that this last year has been so difficult for me. Pat was the person I planned to spend the rest of my life with. And when she died, I just felt so terribly alone. Empty. I thought I could never care for anyone again. Until I met you. I just got very confused. I hope I didn't make you feel uncomfortable.

Once again, the episode is demystifying the life of the lesbian, showing viewers that queers are nice, relatable people who—just like the main characters of the show—fall in love, form families, and mourn their partners' passing. They're not scary or the taboo Dorothy seemed to fear before Jean arrived.

Rose's response is a model of empathy:

ROSE: Well, I have to admit, I don't understand these kinds of
feelings. But if I did understand, if I were, you know, like you,
I'd be very flattered and proud that you thought of me that way.

It's a beautiful piece of dialogue. Jean essentially made a pass at Rose,
and instead of giving in to panic or fear, Rose offers her understanding. The
two women hug, just in time for Sophia to reenter:

JEAN: This isn't what it looks like.
SOPHIA: I know, I was listening at the door.
ROSE: Why were you listening at the door?
SOPHIA: Because I'm not tall enough to see through the win-
dow. [DOROTHY and BLANCHE sheepishly appear at the
kitchen window. Roll credits.]

When this episode came out, there were vanishingly few queer characters on TV, much less characters befriending and defending them. The
Golden Girls was way ahead of most other sitcoms of the time, sticking its
neck out by broaching a topic that could have alienated many viewers.

But instead of turning viewers off, this was the fourth-most-watched
show the week that it aired, with 24 million households tuning in. When
awards season came around, the episode won an Emmy and a Directors
Guild Award for outstanding direction, Betty White and Lois Nettleton
were both nominated for Emmys, and Jeffrey Duteil was nominated for
outstanding writing for his script. "Isn't It Romantic?" was held up as a
positive example of quality writing, the industry's way of saying, "Good job.
Keep doing this."

And that's just what they did.

Two years later, in the season four episode "Scared Straight,"
Blanche's brother, Clayton, comes to town (played by Monte Markham,
in real life an old friend of Betty White's). Rose is eager to put out the
welcome mat:

BLANCHE: We don't have a welcome mat.

ROSE: What about the one Dorothy says is at the foot of your bed?

The moment he arrives, Blanche announces she's done a little match-making on his behalf, to which Clayton responds with some weariness. "Not again," he groans, but Blanche bundles him off to a concert in the park with one of her female friends.

The date doesn't go well, and as Rose is out for a stroll, she comes across Clayton sitting alone. They sit together for a moment and admire the scenery, and Rose notices that Clayton's admiring one particular part of the scenery more than others:

ROSE: [Laughing] That's a man and you're a man! You're both men! [She stops laughing.] Clayton, you're that thing that everyone said Olga Larsen's nephew was 'cause he wore paisley clogs and gave out puff pastry on Halloween.

Clayton patiently confirms that he's gay, and it's impressive that he's willing to be so forthcoming. This episode aired in 1988, a particularly dark point in the HIV epidemic when there was tremendous stigma and ignorance around gay men. At this time, many Americans thought that they could get a deadly disease simply by being near gay people. This same year, California voters considered a ballot measure that would have required doctors to keep lists of people who test positive for HIV, and to report those names to a central database, possibly leading to forcible quarantines.[9] Violence against gay people was widespread and tolerated by those in positions of power; earlier that same year, a judge in Texas reduced the sentence of a murderer because his victims were gay.[10]

Considering the climate, it's quite brave of Clayton to come out to Rose. He isn't sure he can muster the courage to do the same with Blanche, but Rose believes in the goodness of her friend:

ROSE: I know Blanche. I mean, she'd be upset, but not for long.
And just think how it would help you two in the long run.
CLAYTON: . . . You're absolutely right. I've got to tell her tonight.
But it's not gonna be easy. I mean, I still haven't told Blanche I
was the one who stole the Montgomery Clift poster off her wall
when she left for college.*

Rose brings Clayton home and prompts him to come out, but he stumbles a bit on his first attempt—afraid of what Blanche will say, his nerves get the better of him and he instead announces that he slept with Rose. That it's so difficult for him to tell his sister the truth isn't a surprise; in 1988, there were very few examples for a queer person to follow unless they were lucky enough to catch Jodie coming out to his brother on *Soap*. The words "I'm gay" were virtually never spoken out loud on television.

In fact, the lack of coming-out role models is what led psychologist Robert Eichberg and activist Jean O'Leary to begin planning the first National Coming Out Day, which took place on October 11, 1988, just a few weeks before this episode aired.

"Most people think they don't know anyone gay or lesbian," Eichberg told the *New York Times* in 1993. "In fact, everybody does. It is imperative that we come out and let people know who we are and disabuse them of their fears and stereotypes."[11]

National Coming Out Day was a powerful new way to demonstrate that queer people are a part of everyone's life and family, and to show Americans that anti-LGBTQ+ attitudes hurt people they care about. In media, coming-out storylines did double-duty: they provided an opportunity for closeted people to observe examples of how to come out, and for straight family and friends to see the right—and wrong—ways of responding.

---

* Though Clift's homosexuality was an open secret among Hollywood friends, it wasn't publicly acknowledged until 2000 when Elizabeth Taylor spoke about their friendship.

By placing this storyline on the air, *The Golden Girls* prompted millions of people to consider the dynamics of coming out. That it happened with the encouragement of sweet, pure-hearted Rose suggests that there's nothing rude or tawdry about discussing such matters. If Rose can support a gay friend, America, maybe you can too.

Clayton takes another swing at it, and this time he gets the words out—but Blanche doesn't take the news as well as Rose had hoped:

> CLAYTON: I'm gay, Blanche.
>
> BLANCHE: Oh, Clayton, please, be serious. You're just saying that so I won't set you up with any more women.
>
> CLAYTON: No, Blanche.
>
> BLANCHE: Well, then you're saying it 'cause you're trying to get back at me for something.
>
> CLAYTON: Blanche . . .
>
> BLANCHE: Clay, I know you too well for this. After all, I know it can't be true. You're my brother.

Blanche's sentiment echoes Danny's on *Soap*, nearly a decade earlier—a sibling worried that their brother isn't the person they thought he was. "I just feel like I don't know you anymore," Blanche laments.

According to McClanahan, this was a hard role to play—she later told Jim Colucci, author of *Golden Girls Forever*, "I'm not homophobic, and Blanche was, somewhat." Blanche refuses to accept what Clayton is telling her, and so he walks out. She catches up with him at a bar, where they have a heart-to-heart:

> CLAYTON: I'm the same person I always was.
>
> BLANCHE: No, you're not. You used to be just like me.
>
> CLAYTON: What? Great-looking?
>
> BLANCHE: Yes.
>
> CLAYTON: Charming?

BLANCHE: Yes.

CLAYTON: Irresistible to men?

BLANCHE: My God, Clayton, you ARE me.

Blanche's eyes finally begin to open. Clayton was right that things might change between them if he came out. But it never occurred to him that they might change for the better—that they might understand each other in a way they'd been missing out on for years. Blanche carries a lot of traditional Southern values, and that includes a conservatism when it comes to sex (which is a bit rich considering how much of it she has), but there's another value at work here: love for her family, and wanting to look out for her brother.

"I'll get used to this," Blanche promises him. "I will."

Blanche would have plenty of opportunities to get used to it over the next few years. In fact, just a few episodes later, on Valentine's Day, she finds herself in a bar, where she meets a young man nervously preparing to propose.[12] Delighted, Blanche tells the man about how her husband proposed to her, and gives him a little pep talk.

"We may be from different generations, but some things never change," she tells him. "Love is love, period."

Her speech helps him overcome his jitters, just in time for his date—another man—to arrive.

A gay proposal was a bold storyline for any sitcom to tackle at this point. Almost nobody was talking about marriage equality in the late 1980s; only a few years earlier, a Harvard law student named Evan Wolfson submitted his thesis about "samesex [sic] marriage,"[13] and it was met with total disbelief. Gay marriage wouldn't enter mainstream national conversation for several more years and wouldn't be legalized nationwide for another fifteen. But The Golden Girls anticipated not just the marriage equality movement, but even one of its more popular slogans—love is love.

Another topic on which The Golden Girls demonstrated impressive boldness was HIV, a subject most shows avoided altogether. In a season five episode titled "72 Hours," Rose learns that she might have been exposed to HIV due to a blood transfusion.* She gets tested but has to wait three days for the results. In that time, the girls have some frank talks about AIDS, and Rose becomes convinced that her friends won't want to be near her if she tests positive.

In 1990, when the episode aired, treatment options were still comparatively rudimentary, and over a hundred thousand Americans had died from HIV-related complications. It would still be five more years before the roll-out of antiretroviral drugs made HIV a more manageable condition. But in the early nineties, an HIV diagnosis was still regarded by many as a death sentence, and the show doesn't shy away from showing how upset Rose is about not knowing her status:

BLANCHE: Now now, Rose, take it easy.

ROSE: Why does everyone keep saying that? I don't feel like taking it easy. I might have AIDS, and it scares the hell out of me. And yet every time I open my mouth to talk about it, somebody says, "There, there, Rose. Take it easy."

BLANCHE: I'm sorry, honey.

ROSE: Why me, Blanche? I'm tired of pretending I feel okay so you won't say "take it easy." And I'm tired of you saying "take it easy" 'cause you're afraid I'm gonna fall apart.

But we also see how the household unites to help her through this stressful time. "We are the only family Rose has here, so we've got to help her through whatever she's going through," Dorothy says, and the others all agree.

Behind the scenes, this episode was personal for many of the people who worked on it, especially Estelle Getty. During her time in *Torch Song Trilogy*, she'd built extensive friendships with gay men, and one by one she'd

---

* The transfusion took place before all blood donations were tested for HIV, as they are today.

seen them come down with a mysterious disease, fall ill, and pass away in a matter of months. These men were more than just colleagues for her; they were like family.

From the earliest days of the epidemic, she was desperate to help, writer Stan Zimmerman recalled. "When she was on Broadway with *Torch Song Trilogy* and AIDS started to happen . . . she brought chicken soup, thinking that was going to cure the cast members that were falling ill," he said. "Finally they had to say, 'No, Estelle, these men are going to die. There's no saving these guys.' So I think in her heart she just wanted to help and do anything she could."

When the "72 Hours" episode was shot, Getty's nephew Steven Scher was living with HIV back east in North Carolina. Over the next few months, his health started to suffer, and Getty arranged for him to move to LA so she could help take care of him. She also used her high profile to host fundraisers and educate the public about the virus.

"God bless her, she took her stardom at such an elder age and ran with it," Zimmerman said. "She wasn't going to just sit at home."

The episode was also personal for Peter Beyt, one of the editors who worked on the show. His partner was HIV positive, and in addition to caring for the love of his life, Beyt was dealing with overwhelming shame. As he worked on the episode, he recalled one line from Blanche that stopped him in his tracks:

ROSE: This isn't supposed to happen to people like me. You must have gone to bed with hundreds of men. All I had was one innocent operation.

BLANCHE: Hey! Wait a minute. Are you saying this should be me and not you?

ROSE: No. No, I'm just saying that I am a good person. Hell, I'm a goody two-shoes.

BLANCHE: AIDS is not a bad person's disease, Rose. It is not God punishing people for their sins.

Beyt told writer Jim Colucci that Blanche's line made him break down in tears in the editing booth. When he regained his composure, Beyt said, all the guilt he'd been carrying started to melt away. It was a message that a lot of people needed to hear, and *The Golden Girls* was able to broadcast it, way out in front of most other television shows of the time.

*

One of the show's boldest episodes came in season six, when Clayton returns for the episode "Sister of the Bride," originally aired on January 12, 1991. Two years earlier, we saw Blanche's brother learn to be honest about who he is and overcome his fear of rejection. Now, it was finally time for Blanche to do the same.

Once again, Clayton has flown in to stay with the girls for a few days—but this time, he's brought someone with him.

CLAYTON: This is Doug. He's my friend. My very special friend.
BLANCHE: Well, any friend of Clay's is a friend of . . . [She freezes.]

Doug is Clayton's partner, and Blanche is desperately afraid of anyone finding out about them. When she realizes that she already offered the guests her bedroom for their stay, she panics:

BLANCHE: Are you crazy? What will the neighbors think if they see two men in my bedroom?
SOPHIA: They'll think it's Tuesday.

Her anxiety goes through the roof when Clayton makes an announcement:

CLAYTON: Blanche, we're getting married.
ROSE: Well, that's impossible, Clayton, brothers can't marry sisters. [A beat.] Oh, that's right, you're from the South.

Once Dorothy clears up the confusion, Rose responds with an understanding "Oh," followed by an alarmed "Oh!" and then a befuddled "Oh?"

At the time that this episode aired, "Oh. Oh! Oh?" encapsulated how many Americans felt about legal recognition of same-sex relationships. Just a few weeks before this episode aired, three Hawaiian couples had filed a lawsuit that marked the start of the strategy that would, over a decade later, achieve full federal marriage equality. Though there had been lawsuits prior to this, the Hawaii suit was the first to be taken seriously, and for a time it looked as though it might actually result in federal recognition of marriage equality by the mid-nineties—if a couple was able to marry in Hawaii, then it meant that any couple might be able to fly in, get married, and then fly back to their home state expecting to be recognized.

Conservative politicians smelled red meat for their base, and quickly crafted a law that became known as the Defense of Marriage Act in 1996, which banned federal recognition of same-sex relationships. It wasn't overturned until 2013, which was also when polls first showed a majority of Americans supporting marriage equality.

But the attitude in the house is generally supportive, except for Blanche. While she frets over Clayton's marriage plans, Rose is the voice of reason and compassion:

ROSE: Blanche, I don't understand you. You can't very well say you've accepted Clayton unless you accept the fact that he dates.

DOROTHY: Rose is right. And besides, Blanche, in this day and age, you should be thrilled that he's in a monogamous relationship.

But Blanche just can't get used to the idea. "Oh, what are people going to say?" she laments, and when Clayton and Doug come to a fancy banquet with the girls, she does everything she can to hide the fact that they're a couple. In effect, she does her best to force them back into the closet:

CLAYTON: I'm Clayton, Blanche's brother. And this is Doug, he's my . . .

BLANCHE: Fire! Fire! Everybody out!

It wasn't long ago that Clayton was in a similar position, going to great lengths to hide who he was for fear of rejection. But in the two years between his appearances, he's moved on, and to his credit, he won't stand for any recloseting from his sister. After Blanche tries to silence him, he's furious:

CLAYTON: What did you mean when you told me you could accept me being gay? Did you mean it was okay as long as I was celibate? Okay as long as I don't fall in love? Doug is a part of the family now, my family, and if you don't like it, you don't have to be a part of my family.

With that, Clayton and Doug stand up and leave. Telling Blanche that he's prepared to cut her from his life may seem harsh, but in many circumstances it's the right thing to do. If Blanche can't accept her brother, if she doesn't want him to fall in love, he's better off living his life without her trying to force him into a lie. This episode serves a message of queer empowerment to viewers, telling all the Claytons watching that they're entitled to take comfort and pride in whomever they love.

It looks like the gulf between the siblings might be insurmountable, but then Sophia comes to the rescue. She has a late-night heart-to-heart with Blanche, and asks a question that completely changes Blanche's perspective:

BLANCHE: Oh, I can accept the fact that he's gay. But why does he have to slip a ring on this guy's finger so the whole world will know?

SOPHIA: Why did you marry George?

BLANCHE: We loved each other. We wanted to make a lifetime
commitment, wanted everybody to know.

SOPHIA: That's what Doug and Clayton want too. Everyone
wants someone to grow old with. And shouldn't everyone have
that chance?

BLANCHE: Sophia, I think I see what you're getting at.

SOPHIA: I don't think you do. Blanche, will you marry me?

This short exchange—less than a minute long—explains marriage
equality to a general audience more effectively than most of the next two
decades' worth of advocacy for the freedom to marry. And it aired at a
pivotal moment, just as the country was starting to take marriage equality
seriously. For decades, most Americans had been accustomed to laughing
off the idea of two men getting married as impossibly absurd. But not for
much longer.

Blanche finds Clayton and launches into another difficult heart-to-heart:

BLANCHE: Well, Clay, this is very difficult for me. I still can't
say I understand, but I'll try to respect your decision to do it. I
want you to be happy.

CLAYTON: I am happy, Blanche.

BLANCHE: I know.

CLAYTON: So, are you telling me you are ready to have a brand-
new brother-in-law?

BLANCHE: I suppose I am. [To DOUG] Now, look here. Now,
he's not perfect. Has a stubborn streak and a bad temper.

DOUG: And he snores.

BLANCHE: [Looks stricken for a moment, then smiles.] That'll
just be our little secret.

Put yourself in the position of a queer person watching this episode on
its first airing: Your relatives might have rejected you for being queer, or

refused to recognize your partner, or denigrated your relationships. To see a show where a sibling comes around and accepts her gay brother, his partner, and their desire to marry would have seemed like a dream come true.

Not only that, but the episode portrays Clayton and Doug so sympathetically that, according to writer Jamie Wooten, while this episode got some hate mail, the show actually received more angry letters about how Bea Arthur's hair was styled.[14]

The episode ends with Blanche finally doing the work she promised she would do two years ago when Clayton came out. She knows that accepting her gay brother will be hard, but it's worth working on because she loves him. That's an accurate reflection of where America was at that point on LGBTQ+ issues at the time: unsure, awkward, with a lot of progress to make—but moving in the right direction.

*

The Golden Girls took its final bow on May 9, 1992, but that wasn't the end of the ladies' involvement with queer matters. All four members of the cast lent their considerable fame to supporting LGBTQ+ causes for the rest of their lives.

Rue McClanahan used her celebrity status to help raise money for LGBTQ+ causes, marching in Pride parades and headlining Broadway benefits for equal rights.

Betty White was an outspoken advocate for equality, appearing in anti-bullying messages and advocating for marriage equality. At a GLAAD awards show in 2013, she told the crowd:

> I'm ninety-one years old ... I've been around the block. I've
> seen a lot of things, and I've done one or two. And I know
> a few things. Not much, but some ... I just want to say to
> all the judgmental people out there, if two people in love
> want to get married, let 'em get married. Just mind your
> own business and don't worry about it.

And of course, always the "Pride of the Lesbians," she remained a loving stepmom to Sarah.

Though Estelle Getty's health was in decline around the end of the series, she continued to work tirelessly on behalf of people with HIV. In 1996, seeing how much help her gay friends and family needed throughout the epidemic, she opened a hospice for people with HIV in Greensboro, North Carolina—the hometown of her nephew Steven, who passed away in 1991. There, she helped ensure that people with HIV could live out their days with dignity and support, rather than suffering alone.

"I am tremendously grateful to the gay community," she told one interviewer. "They put me where I am today. They discovered me, and they stuck by me, and they've been very loyal."[15]

The facility that Getty opened, Beacon Place, remains in operation to this day.

But the biggest impact of all may have come from Bea Arthur, who embraced her status as a gay icon. "The gay community finds me almost a successor to Judy Garland," she told one reporter, before demanding that the gay man interviewing her take her on a tour of SoHo.

In 2005, Arthur got a call from her friend Ray Klausen, a set designer who'd art-directed her 1980s variety show.* Klausen told Arthur about a new nonprofit in New York that supported unhoused queer youths, the Ali Forney Center. Then, as now, queer youths were disproportionately likely to be thrown out of their homes; at the time, the center was struggling to keep up with the need. They had only twelve shelter beds, with more than a hundred youths out on the streets needing a place to sleep every night.

As soon as she got Klausen's call, Arthur leapt into action, volunteering to fly across the country and host a fundraiser for the center. She raised $40,000 in one night and led a media campaign to recruit more donors.

"There's people in this country that kick their kids out of the house

---

* Guest stars: Rock Hudson and Wayland Flowers.

because they're gay," recalled Matthew Saks, Arthur's oldest son. "I think the thought of that really upset her."[16]

Thanks to her fundraising, the center was able to expand their services, but they ran into a new problem three years later. When the 2008 recession hit, donations started slowing down; the center was soon on the cusp of eviction. And in early 2009, Arthur, one of their greatest supporters, passed away.

The staff were heartbroken. But then they found out that Arthur had left $300,000 to the center in her will, allowing them to make it through the recession and then the loss of a building during 2012's Hurricane Sandy. In the years that followed, Arthur's gift allowed the center to establish a dozen new housing sites and a twenty-four-hour drop-in service, helping a thousand youths every year.

In 2017, the Ali Forney Center opened a new building with eighteen long-term beds, The Bea Arthur Residence for LGBT Youth. It's an enduring tribute to the actress who once said, "I would do anything in my power to protect children who are discarded by their parents for being LGBT."

*

At a panel event in 2006, a member of the audience asked Rue McClanahan why *The Golden Girls* was so important for gay viewers. She replied that she used to wonder the same thing, until one night she ran into a fan in Greenwich Village and asked him.

"I said, 'Tell me something,'" she recalled. "'What is it that you gay guys like so much about Blanche?' And he said, 'Are you kidding? We all want to *be* her.'"[17]

That's certainly true—and not just the part about being irresistible to men, though that doesn't hurt.

The Golden Girls was blessed—and blessed viewers—with a constellation of qualities to which any social group might aspire, particularly queer people in the 1980s. It was about a warm, welcoming household where everyone looked after each other; about friends who enjoyed good lives and great sex, even when mainstream society counted them out; and about characters who were loved so deeply that when they died of old age, everyone agreed that they were gone too soon.

DINOSAURS

DAVE: *A lot of dinosaurs eat veggies from time to time. Including . . . me.*

ROBBIE: *You're . . . you're one of THEM? Are you sure? How long have you known?*

DAVE: *Well, I always kind of suspected. Ever since I was twelve, whenever I'd see vegetables, I'd feel kind of . . . hungry.*

On an October evening in 1991, wedged between the domestic contentment of *The Cosby Show* and the gauzy seventies nostalgia of *The Wonder Years*, into America's living rooms stomped a sulky teenage reptile.

When it first aired in the early nineties, there had never been a show quite like the ABC sitcom *Dinosaurs*, and there hasn't been anything like it since. It was a fever-dreamy television stew, composed of equal parts *The Honeymooners* and *The Simpsons*, with a hint of *WandaVision*'s future parodying of sitcom tropes, plus a dash of melancholy fathering reminiscent of *Fiddler on the Roof*. The show's twist is that it takes place 60 million years ago, its main characters all giant talking dinosaur puppets created by The Jim Henson Company.

The premise of the show, which ABC allowed to run for the bare minimum number of episodes required for syndication, is that the lumbering beasts of the Cretaceous lived like modern humans, and in so doing drove themselves to extinction. Like us, the dinosaurs were greedy, thoughtless, hypocritical idiots.

But at least, as audiences were to learn, they weren't all bigots.

*

Dinosaurs originated with puppeteer Jim Henson, cocreator of *Sesame Street*, *The Muppet Show*, *Fraggle Rock*, and many other classic movies, specials, and shows. The show's concept consisted of a single phrase: "the last days of the dinosaurs." Henson, who first developed the Muppets in the 1950s, envisioned a traditional multi-cam sitcom. But here, puppets rather than humans would tell the story of a messy, flawed family in a society that, by giving in to the worst impulses, is ultimately responsible for its own destruction.

It was a fascinating, unique idea, and it went absolutely nowhere for years because nobody believed it could possibly work.

But renewed interest came in the early nineties, thanks to another show about a messy, flawed family. *The Simpsons* was a huge hit for Fox, the struggling fourth network launched to compete with ABC, CBS, and NBC in 1986, and spawned a slate of imitators across primetime—shows that used genres traditionally associated with kids' programs to tell stories that would (hopefully) appeal to grown-ups too. On CBS, there was *Family Dog*, a Tim Burton–designed cartoon about a dysfunctional family as seen by their pet, and a bizarre piscine-noir series called *Fish Police*. On ABC, *Capitol Critters* focused on politically minded rodents living in the walls of the US Capitol. Fox also tinkered with but never aired a Claymation series created by Marlon Wayans.

Though there were a handful of successes, such as MTV's *Beavis and Butt-Head*, nearly all of these *Simpsons* imitators failed. *Dinosaurs* was the rare success in that it lasted more than a single season, perhaps because it hewed so closely to the basic blueprint of *The Simpsons*: structured around a nuclear family, it featured Earl, a dumb dad devoted to life's simple pleasures; his indomitable wife Fran (voiced by future *Arrested Development* matriarch

Jessica Walter); a wisecracking son named Robbie; a proud daughter named Charlene (voiced by *All in the Family*'s Sally Struthers); and Baby, a quippy, catchphrase-generating machine performed by Elmo innovator Kevin Clash.

"We were envious of *The Simpsons*," recalled show writer Tim Doyle in an interview about the creation of *Dinosaurs* many years later. "Not that *The Simpsons* was inherently political, but for some reason we were a remarkably political group of guys who had strong opinions. And there was a lot to react to. This was the end of the Reagan era, and Clinton was on his way in."[1]

It was a fine time to try something new—the weirder the better.

*

In its first season, the show employed dinosaur metaphors to slip contemporary issues into the comedy. Earl learns a mating dance to help Fran overcome postpartum depression; Robbie questions the conventional practice of casting the elderly aside—literally, into tar pits; the family is shunned when they eschew traditional moon-howling rites of passage.

The show also (obliquely) tackles homosexuality, in the episode "I Never Ate for My Father" at the start of season two.[2]

It begins with Earl gleefully celebrating his teenage son's membership in the Young Male Carnivores Association. "I remember the day when I was initiated down at the Y," he says. "Made quite a meat-eater out of me."

Earl is under the impression that Robbie is down at the YMCA eating a smaller dinosaur, as is expected of meat-eaters. Little does he know that Robbie couldn't go through with it, which he confesses to his friend Dave in a scene laden with barely veiled subtext:

ROBBIE: Some carnivore I turned out to be.
DAVE: Did you ever think you're a . . . uh . . . herbivore?
ROBBIE: [Aghast] No way!

No one could accuse the show of subtlety. Standing amid the trees and ferns, Dave nudges Robbie to consider an alternative lifestyle:

DAVE: A lot of dinosaurs eat veggies from time to time. Including . . . me.
ROBBIE: You're . . . you're one of THEM? Are you sure? How long
have you known?
DAVE: Well, I always kind of suspected. Ever since I was twelve,
whenever I'd see vegetables, I'd feel kind of . . . hungry.

Dave even goes so far as to invite Robbie to a local salad bar, leaving
Robbie feeling conflicted over his curiosity about greens and the expectations of his family. When he returns home, gossip about his distaste for
eating smaller dinosaurs has already reached his family. Earl is furious:

ROBBIE: Why should I rip apart some poor mastodon? I mean,
what did it ever do to me?
EARL: It was smaller, that's what it did to you. Bigger eats smaller
in the carnivore kingdom, that's the way it is. That's the way it's
always been.*

That sets up the central conflict of the episode: Earl is uncompromising
when it comes to what he considers to be immutable laws of nature. As a
traditionalist, his response is identical to that of many other sitcom parents
who suspect their kid might harbor radical impulses.

But this is where the show's metaphor starts to get a little blurry:

ROBBIE: You know, it's possible to get nutrition from vegetables.
[The family glares furiously.] . . . Uh-oh.
EARL: Well, it's happened, Frannie. The green menace has crept
into our very home.

---

* Not to split hairs, but in real life an elephant-sized mastodon would almost certainly
have been bigger than the human-sized Sinclair family. *Dinosaurs* had a relationship with
paleontology that was, at best, casual.

That line about the green menace seems to be less a reference to homosexuality than a reference to the Red Scare, a 1950s moral panic around communism, stoked by conservative Senator Joseph McCarthy.

"Are you now or have you ever been an herbivore?" Earl demands, repeating almost verbatim the demand that McCarthy made of witnesses during hearings by the House Un-American Activities Committee: "Are you now or have you ever been a member of the Communist Party of the United States?"

The Red Scare is typically remembered as a witch-hunt for communists—and a pretext for McCarthy to bask in momentary fame. But it was connected to a lesser-remembered hunt for homosexuals, now known as the Lavender Scare. State Department efforts to purge homosexual government workers dated back to the 1940s, with psychiatric screenings meant to detect queers. Those efforts escalated in the 1950s.

Republicans declared that "sexual perverts who have infiltrated our Government in recent years" were "perhaps as dangerous as the actual Communists," and spearheaded investigations to destroy the lives of closeted queer people working in government.[3] McCarthy also wielded homophobia as a defense against criticism: "If you want to be against McCarthy, boys, you've got to be either a Communist or a cocksucker," he said.[4]

"I would like to strip the fetid, stinking flesh off of this skeleton of homosexuality and tell my colleagues of the House some of the facts of nature," bellowed Nebraska Republican Representative Arthur Miller in 1950s on the floor of Congress. Miller was responsible for the 1948 "Sexual Psychopath Law," which criminalized sodomy in Washington, DC—making it punishable by up to twenty years in prison. His speech comes off today as utterly deranged. Imagine delivering these words to your coworkers with a straight face:

> You will find odd words in the vocabulary of the homosexual. There are many types such as the necrophilia, fettichism [sic], pygmalionism, fellatios, cunnilinguist, sodomatic [sic], pederasty, saphism [sic], sadism, and masochist. Indeed, there are many methods of practices among the

homosexuals. You will find those people using the words
as, "He is a fish. He is a bull-dicker. He is mamma and he
is papa, and punk, and pimp." Yes; in one of our prominent
restaurants rug parties and sex orgies go on.[5]

So did *Dinosaurs* mean to reference homosexuality with this episode, or
communism? Probably both, and more—because in the next scene, a third
innuendo is introduced. Fran and Earl search Robbie's room, and discover
a plastic bag full of broccoli.

"Someone at school must have given it to him," Fran says.

Now it's a metaphor for drugs, or perhaps counterculture in general, as
we see when Robbie slips away to the salad bar with Dave. The patrons of
the bar are all sixties-styled hippies with feather earrings and love beads,
listening to a Bob Dylan–like crooner singing "This Lamb Is Your Lamb."

The hippie vibe seems goofy to a contemporary audience, but in 1991,
the sixties were only twenty-five years ago. Adults watching the show would
likely have associated the imagery with a time when *they* were young and
rebelled against *their* parents. Whether the core of the issue is homosexuality or communism or drugs or long hair, parental conflict with kids is at the
heart of this episode.

Earl finds Robbie at the bar and drags him out to a swamp to show him
how to kill and eat smaller creatures. Earl is intent on teaching his son what
he considers an ineffable law of nature: bigger eats smaller. Alas, he hadn't
counted on encountering a swamp monster even bigger than them, and
Robbie is immediately eaten.

Chagrined at the devouring of his son, Earl trudges home and sheepishly delivers the news to his wife. His attitude is that there's nothing they
can do about it—you know, natural selection and all that:

EARL: What do you want me to do, Frannie? The laws of nature
clearly state that bigger eats smaller.

FRAN: The laws of nature also state that we protect our young. No
matter what.

Uh-oh. Earl hadn't counted on this—that there might be *other* laws of
nature, and that they could potentially conflict. As messy as this episode's
metaphors might get, it never strays far from the relationship between parents and their children, and Earl's ironclad bigger-eat-smaller stance has
now taken a heavy toll on his family.

As a statement about the terrible price of parental homophobia, it's a
strong moment for the show: here we see a parent who is clinging so fer-
vently to his fundamentalist, conservative beliefs that he's willing to lose his
child forever, compared to another parent who prioritizes the well-being of
her kid over outdated traditions.

It may seem absurd that a parent would place tradition above their
child's life. But Earl's stubbornness reflects a real and all-too-common parental dynamic faced by queer people of all ages. The same year this episode
aired, an article in the *Journal of Adolescent Health* documented elevated risk
of homelessness and self-harm among gay and bisexual male youth, due in
part to parents who force them out of their homes.[6] It was also the same year
as a landmark court ruling in a case that pitted parents against lovers, rallied
queer activists from coast to coast, and impacted the legal security of every
same-sex couple in the country.

*

The case, known as *In re Guardianship of Kowalski*, began in 1976 when two
women fell in love in a physical education class at St. Cloud State University
in Minnesota. Sharon Kowalski had enrolled in a class taught by Karen
Thompson, and the two women formed a close friendship over the course
of the semester. Neither had identified as a lesbian prior to meeting, and in
fact attended Bible study together at first. But as the months progressed,
they both felt an unfamiliar attraction bloom. Thompson was reluctant to

acknowledge what was happening, but Kowalski insisted they talk, and both women realized they were falling in love.[7]

Three years after that first gym class, Thompson and Kowalski went for a drive together in the country, and surprised each other by both bringing rings to exchange.

A commitment ceremony followed. They bought a house in St. Cloud and moved in together. Four years passed.

On November 3, 1983, a drunk driver named Greg Yeager slammed into a car that Kowalski was driving, killing her niece and leaving Kowalski herself in a coma. When Thompson rushed to the hospital, she was barred from her partner's room—only immediate family were allowed in, she was told. Hospital records listed Kowalski as single.

Thompson was acquainted with Kowalski's parents, Donald and Della, but the two women had endeavored to keep the true nature of their relationship hidden from family members. Now, with Thompson keeping a vigil by Kowalski's hospital bed, the truth couldn't be avoided. Nervous about a confrontation, Thompson wrote a long letter to Kowalski's parents to explain why their daughter's recovery was so personally important to her.

Upon reading Thompson's words, Donald and Della were furious. They began legal proceedings to prevent Thompson from visiting Kowalski ever again. By this point, Kowalski had regained consciousness, but the seriousness of her brain injury left her with a limited ability to understand her surroundings, to communicate, and to move. Her cognitive function was at about the level of a six- or seven-year-old, doctors said. She would need round-the-clock care for the rest of her life—care that Thompson wanted to provide. Donald and Della were determined to stop her.

For two years, Thompson visited Kowalski in her rehab facility, worked with her alongside physical therapists, and adjusted her entire life to aid Kowalski's recovery. With Thompson's help, Kowalski showed remarkable improvement, learning to speak in short sentences, typing messages on a keyboard, and regaining the ability to smile. But all the while, the possibility loomed that her parents might cut off contact. At one session, Thompson recalled Kowalski typing, "Help me, Karen, get me out of here."

After a series of court hearings, Donald Kowalski was awarded unconditional guardianship of his daughter in 1985, and barred Thompson from having any further contact. He moved Kowalski to a nursing home a five-hour drive away. Had the two women been married, there would have been no question about Thompson's right to care for her partner. But the lack of legal recognition rendered the two women legal strangers, and allowed Donald and Della to take control of their daughter's life.

Thompson wouldn't be allowed to see Kowalski again for three years, but in that time she filed appeals, gathered evidence of their relationship, and even built a wheelchair-accessible house so that the two could someday, hopefully, live together again.

Finally in late 1991, on the twelfth anniversary of their commitment ceremony, the Minnesota Court of Appeals issued a ruling:

> We believe Sharon Kowalski has shown areas of potential and ability to make rational choices in many areas of her life and she has consistently indicated a desire to return home. And by that, she means to St. Cloud to live with Karen Thompson again. Whether that is possible is still uncertain as her care will be difficult and burdensome. We think she deserves the opportunity to try.[8]

This was a major victory, and not just for this couple at the center of the case. Thompson's attorney, M. Sue Wilson, told reporters:

> This seems to be the first guardianship case in the nation in which an appeals court recognized a homosexual partner's rights as tantamount to those of a spouse ... Sharon doesn't have the short-term memory to remember what happened

an hour ago, but she does remember Karen and the past, and that she is a lesbian.[9]

Thompson and Kowalski stepped out of their limelight after their victory, content to return together to the home that Thompson had built for them.

Donald, on the other hand, was livid, and continued to refuse to believe that his daughter loved a woman. "I've never seen anything that would make me believe it," he told a reporter over the phone while the case was still proceeding through the courts. "I will not change my mind until Sharon is capable of telling me in her own words."

But it seemed unlikely he would ever hear those words from his daughter—or, for that matter, any others. Kowalski's sister Debra testified in court that her parents had vowed never to visit again if Thompson was named guardian. By refusing to accept their daughter's relationship, they effectively ended their relationship with her forever.

"This case exemplifies the difficulties lesbians and gay men have in safeguarding our relationships," said William Rubenstein, director of the American Civil Liberties Union's Lesbian and Gay Rights Project, after the ruling. "The remarkable thing about this case is not that Karen Thompson finally won guardianship, but that it took her seven years to do so, when guardianship rights for a heterosexual married couple would be taken for granted."

The ruling had implications reaching far beyond just this couple. It came at a time when countless same-sex couples faced the loss of their homes and all their possessions when their partners died from HIV-related causes and hostile families swooped in with legal claims. The lack of relationship recognition left every same-sex couple in the same position as Kowalski and Thompson: legal strangers. It was the nightmare scenario predicted by the 1977 "Cousin Liz" episode of *All in the Family*, occurring at a massive scale.

Same-sex couples could approximate a few legal protections though limited "domestic partnerships," if they were lucky enough to live in a place that offered them, or through novel approaches like adult adoption. But there was only one legal institution that could afford them the protections they needed, particularly in times of crisis. Marriage equality would soon become a top legal priority for queer activists.

"This case, and AIDS, have been the defining events of the 1980s in this area," Rubenstein told the *New York Times*. "It's underscored why we need legal protection, and created a terrific incentive to fight for these kinds of marital rights and recognition of domestic partnership."

This fight, which raged throughout the next three decades, came down to a fundamental conflict between those who prioritize the well-being of family versus those who prized tradition above all else.

*

That is the bind presented to the parents of the recently swallowed Robbie: What is to be done when one is confronted with conflicting values—Earl's "bigger eats smaller" versus Fran's "parents protect their young"? There's no doubt in Fran's mind which should be obeyed and which should be ignored. Some principles, Fran tells Earl, are more important than others.

So back he trudges to the swamp to rescue his son. Step one of Earl's rescue plan is to get eaten by the same monster. (He doesn't seem to have a step two.) Once devoured, Earl finds Robbie hanging out in a surprisingly roomy and well-lit stomach, and the two have an awkward reunion. Neither can figure out how to escape, and soon they start to bicker, which leads to one of the most vividly off-color lines ever broadcast on television:

EARL: Just tell me what it is that you have against me and I will happily jump down this guy's intestines.

As we've clearly entered a traditional sitcom third-act zone of catharsis, Robbie declares that he's exasperated by Earl's attempts to control him; Earl counters that he's frustrated by Robbie's refusal to listen. Robbie counter-counters by asking if Earl ever fought with his father—and Earl realizes that yes, in fact, they used to have arguments just like this one, because Earl didn't care for his father's old-fashioned traditions:

ROBBIE: Well, maybe it's okay if sons have different ideas from
    their fathers, Dad. Maybe that's how we evolve as dinosaurs.
EARL: Yeah. Maybe *that's* the law of nature.

Aha, they've discovered a new law! As much as Earl may have been invested in "bigger eats smaller," he's even more invested in a law of nature that validates his own conflict with his dad. Like Fran, he's making a choice about which values he wants to obey above others. The conflict has been solved, if not their predicament.

"I'm just sorry we're going to be digested now and you're not going to have a son who irritates you as much as you irritate me," Earl says.

There in the slimy pink stomach of a swamp monster, they embrace. And please bear with this next part, because it requires a bit of goofy fantasy logic: the swamp monster, sensing that male bonding is occurring in his stomach, lets out a nauseated roar. Apparently, displays of male affection are so disgusting that their hugging induces him to vomit them back out, which is not exactly a great place for the episode to land. But at least they survive!

While the metaphor of "I Never Ate for My Father" swerves between drugs, communism, homosexuality, and hippies, at its heart it's about how parents deal with the conflict of loving their kid while also disapproving of whatever the kid's into. It's also about the choices that parents make when their values are in conflict. In this episode, the Sinclair parents both decide that when outdated traditions threaten your family, you can choose to part ways with those traditions.

It's a fairly optimistic ending, especially when you consider that three years later, the show ended with the entire cast causing their own deaths.

In the series finale of *Dinosaurs*, the characters' misuse of natural resources causes catastrophic climate change, culminating in an ice age that results in a mass extinction. The final scene shows them huddled together, preparing to die. Earl tries to explain their predicament to the baby:

EARL: Daddy was put in charge of the world, and he didn't take
real good care of it. And now it looks like there won't be much
of a world left for you and your brother and sister to live in.

Sometimes we see the dinosaurs (and by extension, the humans for whom they are a stand-in) at their best, like when they choose to prioritize their children; and sometimes we see them at their worst, like when they cause a mass extinction.

If there's any lesson to learn from those big foam suits, it's that if humanity wants to survive—either as a species, or just as a family—we might try to be a little more like the dinosaurs at their best, and a little less like the dinosaurs at their worst.

FRIENDS

CHANDLER: *I just have to know, okay? Is it my hair?*
RACHEL: *Yes, Chandler, that's exactly what it is. It's your hair.*
PHOEBE: *Yeah, you have homosexual hair.*

As all living organisms on the planet are aware, *Friends* was the apex of NBC's sitcom kingdom for a decade, running from 1994 to 2004 and spawning countless imitators, cafes, and hairstyles. It was a top-ten show for every season it was on the air; it's estimated to generate around $1 billion per year in syndication fees for Warner Bros.;[1] and a University of Toronto study found that it may have contributed to a shift in American slang patterns.[2]

The show came along as NBC was on a triumphant upswing in the early nineties, having shaken off near-bankruptcy over a decade earlier, and went through a variety of changes before it landed in front of viewers—starting with the title, which morphed from *Insomnia Cafe* to *Six of One* to *Friends Like Us*.[3] (That last title was scrapped because executives felt it was too similar to ABC's show *These Friends of Mine*, eventually retitled to *Ellen*.)

As envisioned by its creators, *Friends* was a story of Gen X comings and goings in implausibly roomy Manhattan apartments. At its heart, it's a family show, but the family is more chosen than biological. In the pilot, we meet mopey, lovelorn Ross (David Schwimmer), recently dumped by his lesbian wife; fashionable Rachel (Jennifer Aniston), who's just fled from her own almost-wedding; Monica (Courteney Cox), Ross's perfectionist sister; himbo Joey (Matt LeBlanc); free-spirited Phoebe (Lisa Kudrow); and Chandler (Matthew Perry), the gay one.

Well, not really the gay one, at least not by the time the show made it to air. Chandler is straight, but he's also witty, sarcastic, unlucky in love, and well-dressed, all of which led many to assume at first that he was gay—both on the show and in real life—before everyone was disabused of that notion in the season one episode "The One Where Nana Dies Twice." First aired in November of 1994, it opens with Chandler's coworker Shelly trying to set him up on a date:

SHELLY: Do you want a date Saturday?
CHANDLER: Yes, please.
SHELLY: Okay, he's cute. He's funny . . .
CHANDLER: He's a he?
SHELLY: Well, yeah.

Detecting Chandler's indignation at her assumption that he's gay, Shelly is mortified, and resolves to flush herself down the toilet. But the interaction weighs on Chandler, and the next time he's sitting around with his friends he asks if they ever thought he was . . . well, you know. Throughout the entire scene, nobody even utters the word *gay*, opting instead for "that" and "it":

CHANDLER: Can you believe she actually thought that?
RACHEL: Um . . . yeah.

And a few moments later:

CHANDLER: So, uh, what is it about me?
PHOEBE: I dunno, 'cause you're smart, you're funny . . .

CHANDLER: Ross is smart and funny. Did you ever think that
  about him?
ALL: Yeah, *right*!
CHANDLER: What is it?!
MONICA: Okay, I . . . I dunno, you . . . you just . . . you have a
  quality.
ALL: Yeah, absolutely, a quality.

Now he's even more upset. To misquote Oscar Wilde, to be mistaken as gay by Shelly in Data Entry may be regarded as a misfortune, but to be thought of as "that" by your trendy Manhattan friends feels like a crisis. Chandler has a mystery on his hands: Why do so many people think he's "that"?

*

The answer lies behind the scenes of Chandler's creation.

Friends was spawned by Marta Kauffman and David Crane. Early in the development of the show, Crane (a gay man) entertained the possibility of making Chandler gay, and there are little hints of that original plan scattered throughout the pilot. In the very first scene, the friends are discussing Ross's ex-wife:

JOEY: You never knew she was a lesbian?
ROSS: No, okay. Why does everyone keep fixating on that? She
  didn't know. How should I know?
CHANDLER: Sometimes I wish I was a lesbian. [A beat.] Did I
  say that out loud?

Later, a scene fades out as Chandler describes a recent dream: "Okay, so, I'm in Las Vegas. I'm Liza Minnelli . . ."

Crane later said in interviews that Chandler's sexuality hinged on whether they cast a gay or straight actor in the role—a strategy not dissimilar from the mostly-forgotten 1994 sitcom *Daddy's Girls*, which premiered one day before *Friends* and featured Harvey Fierstein as the first openly gay actor to play a gay lead character on a primetime sitcom.

But Matthew Perry's casting wasn't the end of Chandler's gay aura. Instead of having the character be gay, they decided instead to intentionally make everyone *think* he's gay. According to writer Adam Chase, Kauffman and Crane told everyone to lose the gay storylines but to keep the gay jokes. Their instructions: "Write it gay and play it straight."[4]

That strategy did not escape the audience's notice. There was a flood of articles through the mid-nineties about how gay Chandler seemed, and profiles in which writers very patiently explained that no, Chandler's not gay, really, we promise. *Entertainment Weekly* examined the suspiciously close relationship between Chandler and Joey alongside an article on Ellen's emergence from the closet, with a headline that read simply, "Out?"

Even other members of the cast thought Chandler was gay at first. "When I read the script I thought, 'Chandler, he's the gay character,'" said costar Lisa Kudrow in an interview. "That's the gay character. And then Matthew—oh, he's not gay at all. He's doing it, but the character's not gay—how is he doing that?"[5]

One of the most bizarre acknowledgments of Chandler's gay vibe is a *Saturday Night Live* skit from 1997 that's almost too bizarre to follow. The skit is a parody of *Friends*, and the first disorienting detail is that Matthew Perry appears—but he's playing Joey instead of Chandler. Chandler is played by *SNL* cast member Colin Quinn, and the entire joke of the skit is that Quinn plays Chandler with an exaggerated femme affectation.

"Oh my stars," he swoons in a Snagglepussian voice as Chandler, "it's a wonder I didn't simply faint dead away. Heavens to Betsy!"

As the skit goes on, Perry pretends to break character and get annoyed about Quinn's impression, which he feels is too gay. "I don't play Chandler like some fffff—big gay foppish guy," he fumes, nearly flubbing the line.

From there, the skit gets even more inscrutable. Quinn explains that he wasn't trying to act gay at all; he was simply basing his impression on character actors like Edward Everett Horton. This odd reference seems like it was crafted specifically as bait for a mention in this book, because it's hard to imagine an *SNL* audience nodding, "Ah, yes, Edward Everett Horton, the celebrated character actor whose work, primarily in the 1930s and '40s, hinged on playing coded gay characters."

Horton, born in 1886, was one of those "oh that guy" actors of the black-and-white era, almost always playing fussbudgets. At one point, he calculated, he'd played "thirty-five best friends, twenty-seven timid clerks, and thirty-seven 'frustrated' men."[6]

The *SNL* sketch is oddly endearing (if not explicably funny), in part because it's such a lunatic misunderstanding of gay affectations. But it's just one of many occasions in which Chandler's queerness is regarded as self-evident.

*

As it happened, viewers in 1994 were particularly primed to pick up on queer subtext. *Friends* followed a period that saw relatively few LGBTQ+ characters on American sitcoms, aside from the occasional guest or "very special episode" (code for episodes that dealt with controversial, serious, or taboo topics). Following *Soap*, there was Coco's brief appearance on *The Golden Girls*, a lesbian friend on *Roseanne* played by Sandra Bernhard, and is-he-isn't-he Steven Carrington on *Dynasty*; but aside from them, gays virtually vanished from the main cast of shows around 1990. When they did appear, it tended to be brief, as with a gay man dying of AIDS on an episode of *Designing Women*, or obscured, as with a scene on *Picket Fences* that was reshot with darker lighting so that a same-sex kiss was harder to see.

But there was one place on television that queer people appeared with great regularity in the early nineties, and that was the news. The early nineties saw a surge in activism around issues like marriage, military service, and of course the HIV epidemic. The 1992 presidential election addressed numerous queer issues, and was followed by a march on Washington in 1993.

One month before "The One Where Nana Dies Twice" aired, the Colorado Supreme Court issued a landmark ruling that set the stage for the next several decades of legal advances for queer Americans. The case, *Romer v. Evans*, concerned a ballot measure that Colorado voters had passed in 1992, amending the state constitution to prevent any town from passing nondiscrimination protections for LGBTQ+ citizens. The amendment had drawn widespread condemnation from the ACLU, the League of Women Voters, and numerous Democrats; it also prompted a massive boycott of the state, and a planned spinoff of *Cheers*, still in development at that point, switched its setting from Denver to Seattle.

The Colorado Supreme Court ruled against the measure in October of 1994, determining that it was an unconstitutional burden on queer citizens—a repudiation of the legal tactics that until then had been successfully wielded by the likes of Anita Bryant. The discriminatory Colorado law still wasn't overturned—that would have to wait for a ruling from the Supreme Court of the United States in 1996. But for the time being, it was simply one more reminder, along with all the elections and marches and activism, that gay people were everywhere: they could be your coworkers; they could be your family; they could be your friends. They could even be on *Friends*.

*

Chandler fits particularly neatly into the way that queer characters were depicted on television in the mid-nineties, especially when shows wanted some plausible deniability about a character's sexuality. Don't want to make them gay? That's fine, you can just code them as gay with a few simple flourishes. As Jerry Seinfeld put it in *Seinfeld*'s "not that there's anything wrong with that" episode one year earlier:

JERRY: People think I'm gay.
ELAINE: Yeah, you know, people ask me that about you, too.
JERRY: Yeah, because I'm single, I'm thin, and I'm neat.

ELAINE: And you get along well with women.

GEORGE: Guess that leaves me in the clear.*

Chandler's singleness, thinness, neatness, and friendship with women were all that it took to draw attention to the character, but there are a few other hints. Later in the episode, he finds his coworker Shelly so he can make it abundantly clear to her that he's straight. But then she happens to mention that she was going to set him up with a nerdy guy named Lowell, and Chandler can't help feeling insulted that she wasn't planning to set him up with the office hottie, Brian:

SHELLY: Well, I think Brian's a *little* out of your league.

CHANDLER: Excuse me? You don't think I could get a Brian?
Because I could get a Brian.

Write it gay, play it straight.

By this point in the episode, Chandler's running out of people to tell that he's heterosexual. He winds up at a funeral, for wacky sitcom reasons, and tries to hit on a woman named Andrea. But he's interrupted by Ross, who for other wacky sitcom reasons has taken painkillers that loosen his tongue:

ROSS: [Draping an arm over CHANDLER] I love you, man. And
listen, man, if you wanna be gay, be gay. Doesn't matter to me.

ANDREA: [To a friend] You were right!

The joke there is that Chandler's been hit with some particularly bad luck, romantically; but it's also the start of what would be a recurring joke

---

* Notably, the *Seinfeld* episode features only one actual queer character: an unnamed Marine who thanks Jerry for bringing much-needed visibility to queer issues. He appears on screen for approximately five seconds.

across the run of the series—that someone being mistaken for gay is, on its own, fundamentally funny. It's the punch line in the scenes with Shelly, it's the punch line in the scene where he's "that," and it would become a reliable punch line in future episodes. A few seasons later, when Ross and Rachel are interviewing nannies and one of them is a particularly sensitive man, Ross gets a big laugh when he suspiciously asks, "Are you gay?" In another episode, Chandler accidentally accepts a job transfer to Oklahoma and tries to talk Monica into moving there with him:

> MONICA: Chandler, I don't even wanna see the musical *Oklahoma!*
> CHANDLER: Really? "Oh, What a Beautiful Mornin'"? "Surrey with the Fringe on Top"?
> MONICA: Are you trying to tell me that we're moving to Oklahoma, or that you're gay?

Friends dips its toe in this well quite often, echoing the joke from that early *SNL* skit: Wouldn't it be funny if someone was gay?

To be fair, the show is also responsible for one of the first depictions of a same-sex commitment ceremony on television,* between Ross's ex-wife, Carol Willick, and her partner, Susan Bunch. But the two women were not allowed to kiss. "We were disappointed by that," said Carol's actress, Jane Sibbett, at a *Friends* fan event in 2017. "It just wasn't filmed, that segment of the wedding . . . We wanted to go a little further."[7]

There's also a storyline that certainly wouldn't fly today involving one of Chandler's parents, played by Kathleen Turner. Though the character is generally referred to as a drag queen, the show seems ambiguous about what pronouns and gender identity apply (confusion that is comparable to the at-times nebulous portrayal of Beverly LaSalle on *All in the Family* two decades earlier). More recently, Turner has said that if she was offered the role today,

---

* Officiated by LGBTQ+ rights activist Candace Gingrich, half-sibling of former Speaker of the House Newt Gingrich, in a well-cast cameo.

she would turn it down, and cocreator Marta Kauffman acknowledged that "we didn't have the knowledge about transgender people back then, so I'm not sure if we used the appropriate terms."[8]

What's puzzling about *Friends*'s reliance on the "what if someone was gay" joke is that there is, of course, plenty of fresh comedy to be mined from homosexuality, as *Will & Grace* would prove a few years later. In fact, there were queer comedians already doing great work when *Friends* was on; stand-up comic Bob Smith, for example, had a bit about coming out to his family:

> My mother says, "Bob, you're gay? Are you seeing a psychiatrist?"
> I said, "No, I'm seeing a lieutenant in the Navy."

And of course, there was Scott Thompson on *The Kids in the Hall*, whose Buddy Cole character stared down heterosexuality with the unflinching disdain that straights normally reserved for gays.

It's impossible to know how different *Friends* would have been if they'd cast an out gay actor in the role and allowed Chandler to be gay. Gay actors were in plentiful supply, and *Daddy's Girls* did just that with Harvey Fierstein in a starring role—but *Daddy's Girls* was a flop, *Friends* was a hit, and Chandler's coming out was never to be. For an out gay actor to lead a major network sitcom, America would have to wait a few more years.

It would have been a colossal milestone if *Friends*, one of the most successful television shows ever to exist, had featured a gay lead—particularly at a time when current events had primed audiences to take a particular interest in queer issues. If the show could compel millions of Americans to change their hairstyles, just imagine what it might have done to public attitudes about including queer people in one's friend group.

But if the limit of the show's imagination when it came to gay jokes was, "Are you gay?" maybe it's for the best that that responsibility fell to the shows that came next.

ELLEN

Actor Patrick Bristow was relaxing on a soundstage sofa during a break in shooting one of his many sitcom guest appearances when the star of the show sat down next to him, leaned in, and whispered something shocking.

"I'm thinking of doing what you did," said Ellen DeGeneres.[1]

It was the spring of 1996. Ellen the comedian had recently started therapy, and *Ellen* the ABC sitcom was in desperate need of similar analysis.

Over the last three years, *Ellen* had slipped ever downward in ratings, dropping from fifth place to thirty-ninth. The chief problem seemed to be that nobody seemed sure what the show was about—not viewers, not ABC executives, not even the show's writers. Sometimes it was a comedian-and-friends *Seinfeld* clone about nothing, sometimes a single-gal workplace comedy à la *The Mary Tyler Moore Show*, sometimes a place for slapstick showpieces like *I Love Lucy*. Over its first three seasons, the show had avoided committing to a premise or an identity that would set it apart—including the one that, to insiders, had seemed obvious from the beginning: making Ellen's character a lesbian.

The closest it had come was with Bristow's character, a chipper sing-songy best friend named Peter with the gayest affect on television. The Peter character was originally written straight, but Bristow—who had been openly gay for his entire career—brought such winning verve to the role that showrunners recognized a great thing when they had it, and made him a frequent guest with a partner named Barrett, played by Jack Plotnick.* Now, DeGeneres was considering a similarly queer note for her own character.

With only a few people clued in to what she was contemplating, DeGeneres gathered the cast and crew at her house in June of 1996. Everyone suspected something big was happening—the comedian was typically so private that most of them had never been entrusted with her home address. There, she swore them all to secrecy, and unveiled her vision for season four: they'd tease a coming-out storyline over the first few episodes, then air a big "Ellen's a lesbian" special just in time for November sweeps week.

As it turned out, virtually none of that would go according to plan.

*

In a strange fluke of timing, the same week that DeGeneres held her house party, the Southern Baptist Convention met to discuss a boycott of ABC's parent company, Disney. They didn't know what DeGeneres was planning, of course—their primary objection was to Disney's recent decision to offer health benefits to the same-sex partners of employees. In the absence of marriage equality, such arrangements had grown increasingly common among leading employers. At their meeting, Baptist leaders voted overwhelmingly to boycott.

---

* By pairing these two, *Ellen* created quite the character actor power couple. Among his numerous other roles, Bristow is also often recognized as the "Thrust it! Thrust it!" guy in the movie *Showgirls* and as the Wig Master on *Seinfeld*; Plotnick's vast credits include Paul on *Grace and Frankie*, the voice of elfin Xandir on *Drawn Together*, and the deputy mayor on *Buffy the Vampire Slayer*.

This was music to the ears to professional moral-panicker Donald Wildmon, last seen fuming about *Soap*. His American Family Association seized on the Baptist boycott as a publicity opportunity and broadcast radio ads declaring, "We must show Disney that families are tired of a place where molesters and lesbians are hired to make films and movies that say it's okay to go against morals and grow up gay."[2]

In 1996, America was creeping up to a tipping point on LGBTQ+ issues. Political organizing of activist groups had steadily intensified throughout the HIV epidemic, and demands for equality on issues like marriage, health care, and military service had grown steadily louder, particularly after the 1993 March on Washington. But for all that advocacy, progress had been unsteady: activists suffered a major defeat in 1994, when President Bill Clinton signed a bill banning queer people from serving openly in the military; a major victory in 1995 when he signed a bill banning discrimination by federal contractors; a major defeat in 1996 when he signed a bill barring recognition of same-sex marriages. Were we winning? Losing? It was hard to say.

Against this backdrop, it was impossible to predict how viewers would respond to the star of a floundering sitcom coming out as a lesbian—which *Ellen*'s producers had considered from the start.

"We speculated about it for years," one staffer told *Entertainment Weekly*. "We recognized it would really make the show stand out from all the other six-friends-in-an-apartment shows."[3]

But: "We thought it would be an impossible row to hoe," they went on. DeGeneres was nervous about whether viewers would accept a lesbian lead, insiders said—a not-uncommon feeling in the entertainment industry. Amanda Bearse, who played an uptight neighbor (and her identical lesbian cousin) on *Married . . . With Children*, told *People Weekly* that after she came out in 1993, one agent told her, "If you're under twelve and a tomboy, you're cute. After that you're nothing but a dyke."[4]

Despite the occasional on-screen advances for queer characters and themes over the years, in Hollywood "the homophobia was off the charts," recalled Richard Day, a producer on *Ellen* for its first three seasons. A gay man who'd grown up just outside San Francisco, Day worked on *It's Garry Shandling's Show*, *Mad About You*, *Spin City*, and many more, and found the industry to be universally hostile to queer people behind the scenes. At his first job interview, Day recalled a showrunner telling a gay joke and then asking him directly if he was gay. "I just lied and said no," Day said, years later. "I'm not defending it . . . In 1987, that what's 24-year-old me did."[5]

Day was hired as a writer on the show. Closeted, he overheard many more jokes at the expense of queer people; at one point, one of his colleagues mused that it would be impossible to have a gay comedy writer in the room because it would make it harder to tell gay jokes. Day remembered thinking, *Making a stupid gay joke is more important to them than allowing a whole sector of the population into their profession.*

That straightening—or at least, closeting—of the profession was evident in the on-screen product, Day said. "Hollywood is the only place where the product erases you from the landscape, because you are so repulsive to people, they can't show it."

In that context, it's at least consistent that *Ellen*'s showrunners would be skittish about having a queer lead character. The show even went so far as to downplay chemistry between female characters on the show, such as a guest appearance by Janeane Garofalo during which sparks seemed to momentarily fly. For many writers, the lack of romance where there was obvious potential was a major source of frustration. "Can you imagine *Seinfeld* without sex?" one writer told *Entertainment Weekly*. "There just aren't that many driver's license stories."

*

The decision to have the Ellen character come out started with DeGeneres. She had been open with friends and coworkers for years, but maintained a protective shield around her personal life when it came to the public. The Hollywood closet was a time-honored tradition, but as mainstream attitudes shifted, it became more and more painful to maintain those secrets simply for the sake of a career.

"It's such a disreputable thing, fame and money," said Day. "I mean, they're nice, but only on their own terms. What's the point of those things if you have to give up who you are to get them? Because they're not *that* good . . . The alternative [to being out] is participating in your own oppression."

Word started to leak over the summer of 1996 about a big bold shift in the direction of the show. There had been a smattering of queer characters on primetime before, even a few recurring ones—there was Jodie on *Soap*, Martin Mull's diner-boss character Leon on *Roseanne*, and (if you squinted, at that point) Waylon Smithers on *The Simpsons*. But none of those characters were so prominent as to have an entire show named for them.

The gossip bubbled first around tight-knit TV-industry circles, then out to wider Los Angeles, and by the fall rumors about Ellen—both the actress and the show—were circulating around the county at large. Nothing had been confirmed, but that didn't matter. Innuendo was everywhere: on *NewsRadio*'s Halloween episode, a character sees a woman kissing a man in drag and protests, "What is this, the Ellen DeGeneres show?"

DeGeneres happened to have a comedy album coming out around this time, and found herself in the uncomfortable position of doing a publicity tour on which the album was the *last* thing anyone wanted to talk about. When questions about the next season's rumored twist came up, she would deflect, joking that it was all a misunderstanding—they were going to be adding a character named Les Beán, she told David Letterman, that's all.

On Rosie O'Donnell's talk show, the two women can't help laughing at how evasive they both have to be about what everyone watching already at least suspected about them: "We do find out that the character is Lebanese," DeGeneres deadpans, "there've been clues. You've seen her eating baba ghanoush if you've watched the show at all. And hummus. And [she's a] big big fan of Casey Kasem and Kathy Najimy."

"Hey wait a minute," O'Donnell responds, "I'm a big fan of Casey Kasem . . . maybe I'm Lebanese!"

DeGeneres struggles to keep a straight face. "You could be Lebanese!" she says. "You know, that's odd, because I pick up sometimes that you might be Lebanese!"

This coy teasing was mirrored as season four of *Ellen* began its run in September of 1996. In one episode, Ellen goes house-hunting and a realtor loses track of her:

REALTOR: Ellen? Ellen, where are you?

ELLEN: [Popping out from a doorway] I was in the closet!

Later, the realtor tries to get Ellen excited about home ownership by waving dolls in front of a picture of a house:

REALTOR: Ellen, this could be you. Walking up to your new home.

PETER: Oh, I love this part. It's like a puppet show of your life!

REALTOR: And here's your husband coming home from work.

ELLEN: Oh, I think that puppet's in the wrong show.

"Finally, the world will see me for what I am," she declares at another point, pronouncing her next line very deliberately: "A homeowner."

This teasing was fun at the start of the season, but it lasted far beyond the nine-episode span that DeGeneres had originally envisioned. Behind the scenes, executives at ABC and Disney were waffling over the timing of the coming-out episode (now titled "The Puppy Episode" after one network executive suggested that the show instead shake things up by having the Ellen character adopt a puppy).

As the season progressed, there never seemed to be the right time for "The Puppy Episode" to air. One week there was an investor meeting that executives were wary about overshadowing; another week there were big-ticket events on other networks that presented too much competition. There was also, of course, constant concern about riling the already volatile hornet's nest of conservative boycotters.

As a result, the show's innuendo stretched through the fall season into 1997, with neither DeGeneres nor the network able to confirm anything. Gay fans, frustrated by the will-she-won't-she waffling, took to sending boxes of waffle mix to ABC in protest.

*

Meanwhile, the national mood on LGBTQ+ issues remained as volatile as ever—but courts provided a few slivers of hope by ruling on cases that had been winding their way through the legal system for years.

The first cause for optimism came from the Supreme Court of the United States in the *Romer v. Evans* case. Two years earlier, the Colorado Supreme Court had ruled against a law that blocked towns from implementing civil rights protections that covered sexual orientation. Now, the highest court in the land had affirmed that decision, ruling that the law could not stand because it served no purpose other than to harm certain vulnerable citizens: "Inexplicable by anything but animus towards the class that affects," wrote Justice Anthony Kennedy in *Romer v. Evans*. "It lacks a rational relationship to legitimate state interests."

This was the first time that the country's highest court had ruled on LGBTQ+ issues since 1986, when it upheld state bans on sodomy. This new ruling was essentially a signal from Kennedy that the court's temperature had changed—and an invitation for queer activists to challenge a whole host of prejudicial laws, which they set about doing immediately. The precedent established by *Romer* would, in the years to come, pave the way for US Supreme Court rulings that overturned anti-sodomy laws and bans on marriage equality.

"It has not given us equality," Chai Feldblum, general counsel to the Human Rights Campaign, told reporters in 1996. "All it has done is open the door."[6]

The second piece of good news came at the end of 1996 and caught just about everyone off-guard, including the two women at its heart.

In June of 1990, thirty-year-old Ninia Baehr was living in Hawaii near her mother, Clara Jane "C.J." Baehr, who worked at a local public television station. Meeting her mom after work one day, Baehr's eye was caught by a pretty woman walking past a car in the parking lot—a coworker of her mother's, as it turned out.

"Oh, that's my wonderful friend Genora," C.J. said. "And I'd be happy if she was your friend too."[7]

C.J.'s matchmaking was a bit bumpy at first. Baehr had been comfortably out of the closet for her entire adult life, but Genora Dancel was far more private. When Baehr first dropped by the station and introduced herself to her mother's friend, Dancel was so nervous she kept backing up until she was pressed against the wall.

But opposites attracted, and before the end of the year the two women were making plans for a commitment ceremony—nothing legally recognized, of course, just a little party.

Then Baehr came down with an ear infection. She had no health insurance, but Dancel did, so she called the local gay community center to see if there was any way to use her partner's benefits. The answer, she was told, was no—or more accurately, not yet. As it happened, a group of organizers at the community center were planning to apply for marriage licenses, fully expecting to be denied, and then sue the state for the right to marry. Would she like to join them?

That was how a simple ear infection grew into a constitutional lawsuit.

"Honey, this is a good thing for somebody to do," C.J. told her daughter after Baehr joined the group. "But why don't you let a long-term, established couple, somebody who's been together for thirty years, do it?"

Reflecting on her decision years later, Baehr could only laugh. "You know," she said, "I was really, really in love."

The group formed an organization called the Hawaii Equal Rights Marriage Project in 1990 and got to work, splitting their time between filing legal documents and giving interviews to the media for what turned out to be years of exhausting slogging from one court to another—first a trial court that dismissed the case; then the State Supreme Court, which issued a partial ruling; then a split decision; then a remanding back to trial court; then an appeal; and so on, and so on. The legal system ground slowly by, until finally, on December 3, 1996, Judge Kevin S.C. Chang handed down the news that Baehr and Dancel had been waiting for.

"Defendant presented little or no evidence which addressed how same-sex marriage would adversely affect the public," Chang wrote, and ordered the state to begin issuing licenses.[8]

"Plaintiffs hope to marry soon," read the headline of the *Honolulu Advertiser*—though, as it turned out, "soon" would have to wait, as Chang immediately paused his ruling so that opponents could appeal.

Still, between the rulings in the *Romer* and *Baehr* cases, it seemed like the tide might be turning for equality—if not in public opinion, at least in the legal landscape.

*

It was with that spirit of optimism that the cast of *Ellen* assembled in March of 1997 to film "The Puppy Episode"—as *Time* magazine described it, "amid an atmosphere that seemed half party, half support group."[9]

The regular cast and crew had spent nearly a year waiting for the two-week shoot and had been through the wringer between the vacillations of Disney and ABC, the incessant rumor mill, and security measures like having to pass through metal detectors to enter the soundstage.

For those two weeks, the mood shifted between screaming elation (studio audience cheers throughout were deafening) and fear (production was briefly halted by a bomb threat).

To the public, ABC executives did their best to manage expectations somewhere between those two extremes. "Obviously this is an experiment," said ABC entertainment president Jamie Tarses. "We're not sociologists. We don't know how this is going to be received."[10]

But they had a few clues. JCPenney and Chrysler quietly paused their sponsorship for the impending coming-out broadcast, and Wendy's stepped away as a sponsor on *Ellen* altogether.

"*Ellen* is going to take a hit on this," predicted *Law & Order* creator Dick Wolf to *Time* magazine. "If it was my show, I probably wouldn't have done it. This is one specific area that a large percentage of the population is still very uncomfortable with."

A survey conducted by *Entertainment Weekly* and International Communications Research found that nearly a quarter of Americans would be "personally offended" if a character on a TV program were gay, that a little over 40 percent would prevent their children from watching such a show, and that 44 percent felt that "the trend of more gay characters on TV" was a bad thing, compared to 31 percent who felt that it was good.

With data points like those, the anxiety about audience reaction was hard to shake—though it rankled DeGeneres that ABC was being so cautious.

"When Disney or ABC were worried about boycotts or this or that, I kept saying to everybody, 'I'm the one who's going to get the biggest boycott,'" she later told *Time*. "You can cancel the show, you can go and make another one. It's not going to hurt you. I'm the product here."[11]

Meanwhile, as viewers waited for "The Puppy Episode" to air, they could look forward to other primetime programs dipping their toes in the wake generated by *Ellen*'s publicity. *Roseanne* gave the character Bev a girlfriend; *NYPD Blue* picked up a lesbian cop; on *Dr. Quinn, Medicine Woman*, Walt Whitman was scheduled to stop by town.

Anticipation for the coming-out episode reached an even higher pitch thanks to LGBTQ+ organizers who seized on the opportunity. GLAAD encouraged members to host "Come Out with Ellen" house parties, and the Human Rights Campaign distributed watch-party kits that included invitations, posters, and a trivia game. They'd initially planned to send out three hundred; they wound up shipping three thousand.

Finally, the air date approached: April 30, 1997. Split into two half hours, it features Laura Dern as a new friend named Susan who assumes that DeGeneres's character is gay, sending her into an immediate panic:

ELLEN: [Intensely nervous] I think I know what's going on, it's
    not enough for *you* to be gay, you gotta recruit others, you know.
SUSAN: Yeah, I'll have to call national headquarters and tell them
    I lost you. Damn, just one more and I would have gotten that
    toaster oven.
ELLEN: What is that? Gay humor? 'Cause I don't get it.

After that, Ellen spirals for a bit, fleeing to the arms of a male acquaintance named Richard for a hookup before realizing she can't bring herself to sleep with him. Later, speaking with a therapist (played by Oprah Winfrey), Ellen agonizes over her romantic anxiety—with dialogue that seems like a diagnosis of the show's multiseason search for an identity:

ELLEN: It's not like I'm looking for perfection, you know, I just
    want someone special, someone I click with.
THERAPIST: And obviously you didn't click with Richard?
[ELLEN shakes her head.]
THERAPIST: Has there ever been anyone you felt you clicked
    with?
[ELLEN nods.]
THERAPIST: And what was his name?
ELLEN: Susan.

It's a strain, but Ellen finally brings herself to say the words out loud to Susan: "I'm gay." (She happens to lean toward a PA system just as she says them, broadcasting her coming out to an entire airport.)* The studio

---

* When watching this scene, keep an eye out for a white-haired woman in the crowd of airport bystanders; that's Betty, Ellen's real-life mother.

audience goes wild, but this is just the midpoint of the hour-long story; later that night, Ellen dreams she's in a lesbian grocery store, which she describes to her therapist the next day:

THERAPIST: Have you had this dream before?

ELLEN: Oh, no. Usually I'm at the hardware store having lesbian keys made up.

THERAPIST: Ellen, if you keep this to yourself, you're just going to continue to have these dreams. And then it's going to show up in your waking life as these little clues that get more and more obvious. And eventually . . . tiresome.

This is a clear dig at the unexpected dragging-out that had been forced by Disney and ABC. Now that she's finally free to proclaim herself, the first friend she tells is Patrick Bristow's Peter character, who gave the show its first openly gay energy starting two seasons earlier. They're hanging out at Ellen's house assembling a snack tray:

PETER: You know what you need? A melon baller.

ELLEN: I'm gay.

[PETER is visibly startled.]

ELLEN: So, where would I find one of those melon ballers?

PETER: [Elated] Oh, Ellen, at the grocery store, at the grocery store! I'm so proud of you!

The episode ends with her friends all welcoming her out of the closet, accompanying her to a lesbian coffee house, and in a jokey final scene, filling out "official" lesbian paperwork so Susan, as a gay recruiter, can win a toaster oven.

In the context of modern television events, it's difficult to imagine just how massive a media commotion the airing of "The Puppy Episode" was. It was the water-cooler moment of the year; watch parties at queer bars spilled out into streets; it handily trounced every other show in the ratings that week. It was a night of unbridled jubilation.

There were detractors, of course. One ABC affiliate in Birmingham refused to air the episode. But even there, the party couldn't be stopped: A local gay comedian named Kevin Snow worked with Pride Birmingham and GLAAD to rent an auditorium with a satellite feed of "The Puppy Episode" with thousands in attendance. When a news crew from the censoring affiliate station arrived to report on the scene, they were booed.[12]

It had taken so long for ABC to approve the broadcast that there were only two episodes left in the season—one in which Ellen tells her parents, and another in which she comes out at work—and then work got underway on season five. But that wasn't how it was originally supposed to go.

A year earlier, when the plan was to hint at the coming out episode and then air it in November, DeGeneres had hoped to spend the rest of the season showing her character adjusting to her new life and growing comfortable with herself—essentially, finding the identity that the show had lacked for so long—and then to end the series with season four.

But the ratings success of "The Puppy Episode" prompted ABC to keep it going, and DeGeneres lacked the authority to stop them.

"People made a bad deal for me when it started," she later told *Entertainment Weekly*.[13] But knowing she'd be back in the fall—like it or not—she started formulating some new plans for the next phase of her show. It wasn't going to be anything like it had been.

As the summer break approached, DeGeneres started getting letters from viewers, letting her know how important her show had become for them—including those who wrote that they'd considered suicide until her show made them feel less alone. "I got a sense of pride for the first time in my life," DeGeneres said, and with each letter she received the more determined she was to stop dancing delicately around her character's sexuality.

The show's incoming producer for season five, Tim Doyle, agreed. "Everyplace I went, I said, 'Well, here's what I'm gonna do: I'm gonna tell this story about a gay woman looking for love. That's gonna be the show this season,'" he said in a later interview. "I just kept saying it. I said, 'I'm only gonna take this job if I can do a show about this gay woman looking for love. That's the only thing I'm interested in. That's the only thing that makes a difference for television.'"[14]

When *Ellen* returned in the fall, viewers were going to see an entirely new side to the character. As her then-partner, Anne Heche, observed about DeGeneres at the time: "She's become an activist."[15]

*

The summer of 1997 was a good time to feel hopeful about what activism could achieve.

On April 29—one day before "The Puppy Episode" aired—Hawaii's legislature approved a measure to extend a few limited marriage-like benefits to same-sex partners. It was lawmakers' way of reacting to Baehr and Dancel's lawsuit, still meandering through the courts but headed toward what looked increasingly like a victory. The legislature's long-shot hope was that a few legal breadcrumbs would be enough for the court to say "close enough" and dismiss the case without granting full marriage equality.

It was progress of a sort—a few useful new rights, like survivorship benefits and health coverage—with the possibility remaining that the marriage lawsuit could prompt even more down the line.

"I think it's great that we'll get something," said Pat Lagon, one of the other plaintiffs in the case. "It's better than nothing."[16]

Meanwhile, there were signs of similar progress in Alaska. Jay Brause and Gene Dugan, a couple who ran a theater in Anchorage, had filed a suit similar to Hawaii's, and after bouncing through courts for years, a victory was looking increasingly likely. Momentum for marriage equality was clearly building in the two states most recently admitted to the Union.

But there was also cause for concern. At the time, polling showed that 70 percent of Hawaii voters disapproved of marriage equality, and along with the "marriage-lite" bill in Hawaii, lawmakers there also approved a possible constitutional amendment banning same-sex marriage. It would go before voters in the fall, and if approved it would instantly cut off the legal avenue being used by the gay couples' lawsuit. Alaska's legislature approved a similar measure.

When it came to queer liberation, both in politics and pop culture, the future remained murky.

*

By October 29, 1997, *Ellen* was a few episodes into season five. DeGeneres was at home, about to watch the broadcast of the fifth episode of the season. This had been a particularly contentious episode to shoot, as it featured Ellen's first kiss with another woman. Initially approved by the network, at the last moment ABC's Standards & Practices department insisted that it be shot from an angle that obscured the characters' faces.

Though she knew that the kiss had prompted heavy debate before broadcasting, DeGeneres was unprepared for what aired at the start of the episode.

"This program contains adult content," said a somber male voice over a black screen with white warning text. "Parental discretion is advised."

It was as if nothing had changed at ABC since the warning at the start of *Soap* twenty years earlier.

Furious, DeGeneres immediately called the network and demanded to speak with then-president Bob Iger. The warning was personally offensive to her, she told him, and described the heartbreaking letters she'd received from teen viewers over the summer. Iger was resolute that the warning would stay.

In a later interview with Diane Sawyer for ABC's *Primetime*, he explained his position: "Depicting characters who are gay on television and physical acts . . . I believe is adult content," he said.

Iger wasn't the only one feeling uncomfortable about the new season. Just as Tim Doyle had promised, season five focused heavily on storylines about a woman adjusting to life as a newly-out lesbian. Ellen goes dating;

Ellen learns gay slang; Ellen hires a gay plumber; Ellen meets the Indigo Girls.

For many gay viewers, this was thrilling, groundbreaking television—like a little queer film festival beamed into millions of American homes every week. But other viewers found it a bit inaccessible, especially heterosexuals who began to feel like the show simply wasn't meant for them anymore.

"It's excluding a large part of our society," Chaz Bono, entertainment media director at GLAAD, told *Variety*. "A lot of the stuff on it is somewhat of an inside joke. It's one thing to have a gay lead character, but it's another when every episode deals with pretty specific gay issues."[17,*]

That "inside joke" feeling was borne out by ratings. When the episode with the warning aired, *Ellen* was averaging around 15 million viewers—losing over 2 million from its lead-in, *The Drew Carey Show*. That drop grew over the next few months, resulting in a drop-off of around 5 million viewers.

"After a while people get tired of being educated," the show's former co-executive producer, Jonathan Stark, told *Entertainment Weekly*. "I love watching Ellen as a comic, not a spokesperson."

The emerging consensus was that the show had become too gay too fast—that straight viewers just couldn't relate.

"What alternative did we have?" Doyle asked the *Los Angeles Times*, defending the show's newfound queer focus. "Are we going to write stories about her getting locked in a meat locker?"[18]

That spring, ABC replaced *Ellen* on the schedule with the decidedly more heterosexual *Two Guys, a Girl and a Pizza Place*. Though no decision had yet been made about giving *Ellen* a sixth season, nobody was under any illusions about what was coming.

---

* Bono was frequently misquoted as calling the show "too gay," words he never used. Later he walked back his criticism, explaining, "Ellen saw everything that was wrong for gays in this country and wanted to change all that . . . to really effect change, you have to go at a pace people can follow."

After shooting the final scene of the final episode of season five in the spring of 1998, DeGeneres stood before the cast and crew and delivered a tearful speech of gratitude. "I can't thank you all enough," she told the crowd, stopping frequently to collect herself and hold back tears. "You've been part of this very controversial show, and I'm sure you get a lot of shit from people . . . The fact that you've supported me through all of this means a whole lot to me. It's been a wonderful run."[19]

Her heartfelt words were slightly undercut by her appearance: having just filmed a spoof of classic sitcom moments, she stood in a vat of coffee beans, wearing a peasant dress that evoked Lucille Ball in a vat of grapes.

As the cast and crew applauded, DeGeneres somberly stepped off the set, changed out of her costume, and drove off the lot.

*

Ellen's cancellation wasn't the only queer bombshell to drop in 1998. In November, voters in Hawaii and Alaska voted to amend their state constitutions to specifically ban marriage equality, effectively cutting off any hope of prevailing in the lawsuits filed by same-sex couples.

For Ninia Baehr and Genora Dancel, the loss carried a particularly harsh sting, as their relationship had reached an end after seven years together. "The pressure to look like a perfect couple, or to try to embody what people thought a couple who deserved to get married should look like . . . it was a lot," Baehr said.[20]

And that was just the start of what would turn out to be a string of bad news for LGBTQ+ organizers. Using Alaska and Hawaii as test cases, conservative forces had identified a new strategy to block civil rights advances—amending state constitutions—and in the decade to come, they would replicate those campaigns again and again in dozens of states.

For a few brief, optimistic years in the middle of the nineties, it looked as though queer Americans had reached the point where they could realistically expect equality—equal rights, equal treatment, equal prominence in the media. With public attitudes improving, nondiscrimination measures passing, and queer characters appearing in ever-larger numbers in mass media, the country appeared to have finally found a tipping point. At the very least, it couldn't hurt to ask for an equal piece of the pie.

But that optimism had proven premature. Those small advances were met with an even bigger backlash, one that seemed to wipe away whatever progress had been made in the last decade.

Clearly, it wasn't enough to advance toward equality; whatever gains LGBTQ+ Americans made, they'd also have to come up with a strategy to protect their advances as well.

That's exactly what was about to happen.

WILL
&
GRACE

NBC EXECUTIVE: *You will never see two gay men kissing on network television.*
JACK: *Wha—It's a gay network, for God's sake! The symbol is a peacock!*

On September 21, 1998, *Will & Grace* debuted on NBC at what seemed like the worst possible moment.

Ellen's coming-out in the spring of 1997 and near-immediate cancellation a year later had left audiences and critics convinced that primetime sitcoms with gay leads were cursed to fail. Now here came *Will & Grace*, premiering just months after *Ellen*'s last episode aired. It was met with equal parts skepticism and bewilderment that the network—riding high on the success of *Seinfeld*, *Friends*, and the soon-to-shutter *Mad About You*—was about to repeat ABC's mistake.

But not only did *Will & Grace* prove the critics wrong, it went on to become a colossal hit, putting popular gay characters in front of millions of Americans every week for eight years—plus three more with an eventual revival. By the time the cast took their final bow, the show had accumulated eighteen Emmy wins, spent several years as one of the highest rated shows on television, and helped kick-start the Smithsonian Institution's LGBTQ+ history collection.[1]

Not everyone was a fan, though. Its first few years on the air were marked by angry disapproval from viewers who felt that it would have a negative impact on public attitudes toward gay men.

But nobody could have anticipated the impact it wound up having—an impact that would, in time, help sway the president of the United States.

*

The story of *Will & Grace* started in the late 1970s, when two thirteen-year-old kids met through their temple's drama program in Beverly Hills, became best friends, and started dating in their teens.[2] Jason "Max" Mutchnick was the outgoing drama club extrovert; Janet Eisenberg was the fun partner in crime, glad to have a boyfriend who loved shopping as much as she did. The two were inseparable throughout high school, dated through college, and then moved to New York's Greenwich Village, where the relationship continued to blossom. Perhaps you can see where this is going: before long, Mutchnick told Eisenberg he needed some time apart, and after a move to Los Angeles, he worked up the nerve to tell her that he was gay.

Furious, Eisenberg broke off contact for a year—until finally their mutual friend David Kohan, who they'd known since drama club days, sat them both down to talk through their feelings. With Kohan's help, Mutchnick and Eisenberg rebuilt their relationship as best platonic friends, a relationship that would eventually prove an invaluable source of support and inspiration.

Years passed, and all three found their way into the entertainment industry, Eisenberg as a commercial casting director and Mutchnick and Kohan as writers on shows like *The Wonder Years* and *Dream On*. In 1996, they created the mid-season replacement *Boston Common*, a sitcom that could be reliably found near the bottom of the ratings each week and departed the airwaves after about a year. But in a stroke of luck, one of the few people who had noticed the show's existence was NBC entertainment president

Warren Littlefield, who invited the two to pitch a show to fill the slot that had been occupied by *Mad About You*.[3]

Scrambling, Mutchnick and Kohan concocted a somewhat convoluted premise about a San Francisco couple and their neighbors, which included a pair based loosely on Mutchnick and Eisenberg. But the concept wasn't quite recognizable as *Will & Grace* yet—the focus was squarely on two straight couples, with the gay guy and his straight friend popping in as minor next-door neighbor characters.

Reactions to this early version of the show were less than enthusiastic. According to Mutchnick, one executive asked, "What do you think of having the character of Will not be gay?"[4]

In the aftermath of *Ellen's* demise, the entire television industry was experiencing tremendous jitters about any show with queer characters.

It wouldn't be the first time that queer representation suffered a setback on primetime. After gay and lesbian characters tiptoed their way to some prominence in the early 1970s, the Family Viewing Hour wiped them away. After the Family Viewing Hour was overturned, a late-seventies resurgence in queer characters was undone by a conservative course-change after the election of Ronald Reagan in 1980. Queer characters gradually returned to television over the 1980s, but shows—particularly comedies—tended to avoid depictions of gay men due to associations with the growing HIV epidemic. Now, following *Ellen's* cancellation, television was primed for another step backwards, closing the door that DeGeneres had opened.

But Littlefield wasn't ready to dismiss the pitch from Kohan and Mutchnick just yet. When they presented the show to him, he responded with interest, particularly when they got to the characters based on Mutchnick and Eisenberg. Littlefield asked them to make a few changes to their proposal, and a few cuts—but to their surprise, he didn't want them to eliminate the gay character and his straight best friend. He wanted them to cut everyone else.

"I said, 'That's the center of the show,'" Littlefield recalled in a later interview. "'That's the relationship I want to examine.'"[5]

Littlefield was willing to buck the conventional wisdom of the time in part because he'd proposed a similar show a decade earlier to NBC's then-president Brandon Tartikoff. At the time, Littlefield recalled, Tartikoff told him, "Get the fuck out of here."

The mid-1980s wasn't an optimal time for NBC to green-light a show with a gay lead. But now, Littlefield thought, the network might finally be ready, particularly thanks to the verisimilitude that Mutchnick and Eisenberg's real-life friendship lent to the concept. While most TV executives were shying away from gay characters, Littlefield decided to give Mutchnick and Kohan a chance to buck the trend and prove everyone else wrong with a show now titled *Will & Grace*.

But other NBC executives weren't on board. Don Ohlmeyer, president of NBC's West Coast division, hated the concept and derisively called the show "Grace & Gay."

Instead of fighting him, Littlefield decided to, in his words, "string him along." At first Littlefield told Ohlmeyer, "It's just an idea. Nothing usually comes of them." As Mutchnick and Kohan drafted up a pilot, Littlefield told Ohlmeyer, "It's just a script. Most of them don't go anywhere."

But in reality, it was full steam ahead on the *Will & Grace* project. Its big break came when the already-legendary TV director Jim Burrows expressed interest. Burrows had cut his teeth in theater, working on Broadway comedies and following in the footsteps of his father, famed playwright Abe Burrows. Jim Burrows escaped to television in the mid-1970s, directing episodes of *The Mary Tyler Moore Show*, *The Bob Newhart Show*, and *Taxi* under the tutelage of Jay Sandrich (director of, among many other classics, the episode of *The Mary Tyler Moore Show* with Phyllis's gay brother, *Cheers*'s "The Boys in the Bar," and the pilot of *The Golden Girls*).

With Burrows interested in directing the pilot of *Will & Grace*, Ohlmeyer's objections suddenly held a lot less water—and it also didn't hurt that while television was timidly avoiding queer characters, the hottest trend in films was gay men and their female best friends. The year before, in the summer of 1997, *My Best Friend's Wedding* was a huge hit, followed by *As*

Good as It Gets in December; then came *The Object of My Affection* and *The Opposite of Sex* in the spring of 1998.

"The gay-man/hetero-gal duo has become the pop-culture relationship du jour," declared *Entertainment Weekly*. "Gay men and straight women are to the '90s what Oscar and Felix were to the '70s."[6]

As they waited for the network wheels to turn and their show to co-alesce, Mutchnick and Kohan spent four tense months feverishly faxing Littlefield the grosses from those hit films—and then the go-ahead finally came and it was time to start casting.

Early in the process, it seemed as though they'd struck gold when actor Eric McCormack read for the part of Will and Debra Messing for Grace. Though neither was an established, household name, they had years of television acting experience—mostly in bit parts—and immediately grasped the characters. In his audition, McCormack imbued Will with a breezy blend of confidence and vulnerability; Messing allowed Grace to laugh at Will's quips, a friendly character note that harkened back to the real-life friendship of Mutchnick and Eisenberg. Rounding out the growing cast were Megan Mullally—not yet speaking in what would become her trademark squeak—and Sean Hayes, a hardworking, mostly commercial actor with an impulsive, frantic energy. Of Hayes, Jim Burrows noted, "He could be our Kramer or our Urkel."[7]

Even before they were locked in, it was hard to imagine anyone else in the parts, but there was just one problem: all four actors turned them down.

For his part, McCormack was nervous about signing a contract for the long-term commitment that a sitcom required. Messing was exhausted from her role on a recently canceled ABC show. Hayes, busy making a splash at Sundance in the film *Billy's Hollywood Screen Kiss*, threw the *Will & Grace* script in the trash, assuming he'd soon be awash in TV offers. And Mullally was more interested in playing lead roles, going so far as to blow off an audition so she could stay home and make breakfast.

In later interviews, none of the actors said that their reluctance had anything to do with the show's queer content—but it's impossible that the *Ellen* factor wasn't on everyone's mind. "The Puppy Episode" and DeGeneres's tearful departure a year later was the biggest industry shake-up since *Bewitched* switched Darrins, and signing onto a primetime sitcom with a gay lead was as risky a move as a low-profile actor could make.

But Mutchnick, Kohan, and Burrows weren't willing to lose their perfect cast without a fight. They all leapt into action to try to persuade them with phone calls, meetings, and hasty deal-making. Mutchnick and Kohan reached one particularly persuasive turning point when they showed up at Messing's house one evening with a bottle of vodka, leading to a heart-to-heart long into the night.

One by one, all four actors came around and agreed to sign on.*

Finally, they were ready to see if this crazy idea could work.

*

The pilot was filmed in the spring of 1998. It begins with Will Truman sprawled on the couch, ogling George Clooney on *ER*, while on the phone with his pal Grace Adler, who's lounging in bed next to her boyfriend:[8]

WILL: Was that Danny?
GRACE: Mm hmm. Jealous?
WILL: Honey, I don't need your man. I got George Clooney.
GRACE: Sorry, babe. He doesn't bat for your team.
WILL: Well . . . He hasn't seen me pitch.

In the episode, Grace is about to marry Danny, but Will disapproves, telling her she deserves someone better. After a bit of a tiff over his lack of support, Grace comes to realize that he's right and the two trudge down to a bar to drown their sorrows at their perpetual singlehood.

The night of taping, everything went perfectly. The studio audience was

---

* When heterosexual Eric McCormack called his mother to tell him he'd be playing a gay lawyer, she reportedly sighed, "Oh, Jesus, Eric. Not a lawyer."

crazy for the show, and Jim Burrows kept having to pause the scenes to let the laughs die down. After they were done and everyone headed home, McCormack and Messing found themselves sitting, exhausted, on the sofa at the back of the set. Messing was hoping that the pilot would at least get picked up, but McCormack was feeling more confident: he took her hand and said, "I think we're going to be sitting here for a long time."

Will & Grace was scheduled to premiere in the fall of 1998, and over the summer, NBC sent the cast and creatives out to do previews for entertainment reporters. The reaction, they found, was alarming, particularly at the Television Critics Association summer meeting. With *Ellen*'s audience advisories still fresh in everyone's memories, Mutchnick, Kohan, Burrows, and the lead actors sat before an audience of critics who peppered them with questions about how they could possibly expect this show to succeed, with particular focus on their plans for physical displays of affection.

"We will do a show that makes us laugh and is entertaining and if we find an entertaining way to do a kiss," Burrows said after the eighth question about whether they'd show gay romance, "we will do that."[9]

Later, when one of the critics mistook Burrows for *Cheers* cocreator James Brooks, Burrows managed to calm the tension somewhat by telling the sheepish reporter, "The only way to make it up is to come up and kiss me."

The reporter obliged, climbing onto the stage to kiss Burrows on each cheek. "Look what I had to do!" the director declared. "I had to kiss a guy to break the ice!"

Though Burrows was able to ease the tension that day, it clearly wasn't enough to assuage skepticism about *Will & Grace*. Following the critics' gathering, newspaper reports made frequent comparisons between the upcoming show and the recently canceled *Ellen*—not exactly the association NBC wanted to establish in viewers' minds.

So the team came up with a novel solution: they'd let viewers think, at least at first, that *Will & Grace* might not be a show with a gay lead at all. As the premiere approached, NBC's marketing team went out of its way to suggest that it would be a will-they-won't-they romcom with two straight leads, like *Friends* or *Cheers.*

"They're not a couple," declared an early promo for the show. "They're a couple of friends." The ads made no mention of Will's sexuality, and could easily be interpreted as a show about a straight man and woman who just haven't realized yet what a perfect couple they are.

Burrows recommended that they go even further. In the pilot, he had Will and Grace share a brief kiss so that audiences might think he could eventually go straight.

"I knew how difficult homosexuality would be to middle America," Burrows recalled in an interview with the Archive of American Television. "I told Max and David, 'I think we should try the first year to make America believe that Will's going to recant and marry Grace.' . . . To make sure that when people would tune into the show, they would think this is going to happen. Once you got 'em in there, then they could see how funny it is."[10]

The initial de-gaying of Will worked so well, in fact, that when NBC showed the scene to a test audience, many missed that he was meant to be gay at all. "They said, 'He's not gay. They just don't have any chemistry,'" recalled NBC vice president Kate Juergens.

In interviews, Littlefield emphasized that Will Truman was no Ellen Morgan. "*Ellen* was about one woman's odyssey," he said. "We have a different concept, a unique relationship between these two people."[11] A path was paved for viewers who wanted to believe that romance might blossom between the show's leads, a tease reminiscent of the "other values" line that ABC had trotted out to describe Jodie on *Soap.*

Finally on September 21, 1998, *Will & Grace* had its premiere. Ratings-wise, it did fine—not great, just good, landing in forty-first place for the week, sandwiched by *Suddenly Susan* and *Boy Meets World.*

"The most important thing for us is to plant a couple of seeds," Littlefield said in an interview that week.[12]

Those seeds certainly took their time to sprout. Though the show's initial following was devoted, it wasn't particularly large. Critics described it as having "breakout potential" rather than having broken out; though it was NBC's only new sitcom to show "any spark," another critic wrote, "it's not enough to set the network on fire again."[13] Within a month, Littlefield had been fired from his long-held position at NBC.

Even more worryingly, as the series progressed, it came in for criticism from an unexpected source: gay viewers complained that it leaned too heavily on stereotypes, with the Will character pushed to the far edge of masculinity and Jack absurdly femme. "A Greenwich Village clone if ever we saw one," wrote *The Bay Area Reporter*,[14] and *The Advocate* printed angry letters calling the characters "neutered,"[15] and the show just "more of the same."[16]

In an interview, lesbian comedian Michele Balan echoed a frequent complaint about the show—that it seemed to avoid any acknowledgment of same-sex romance. "The guy isn't even gay," she said.[17]

Responding to the mounting criticism, McCormack could only shrug. "We're damned if we do, damned if we don't," he told *Entertainment Weekly*. "If we don't have a date in the first three episodes, we're hypocritical . . . If we do, that will be the show, the show will be about, 'Did you watch the kiss last night?'"

Dissatisfaction from gay viewers reached a crescendo near the end of the first season, just as *Will & Grace* ran its most controversial episode—one that made repeated use of the f-slur. In the episode, first aired in April of 1999 and titled "Will Works Out," Jack starts attending Will's gym, embarrassing his friend with over-the-top flamboyance. "Hello, press this," Jack sings across the room as he enters the gym.[18]

Will is aghast. Worried about what people will think of him, he confides in Grace that he can't stand to be seen in public with Jack:

> GRACE: Jack was just being Jack. You're overreacting. Who cares if Jack's at the gym?
> WILL: Well, sometimes he's just . . . I don't know, sometimes he's just such a . . . fag.
> GRACE: Wow.

Wow indeed! It's one thing to hear a slur from Archie Bunker in the 1970s, but its deployment by *Will & Grace* is effectively shocking.

As it happened, that word was approaching a turning point in 1999. The same year, Merriam-Webster removed it from their thesaurus as a synonym for "homosexual," along with "fruit" and "pederast."[19] Meanwhile, World Championship Wrestling discontinued the gay-baiting characters known as the West Hollywood Blondes, due in part to the crowd's tendency to roar slurs at them whenever they appeared. "How many gay bashings and gay murders have to be committed in this country for you to remove such hurtful portrayals from your broadcasts?" wrote GLAAD entertainment media director Scott Seomin to WCW's parent company, Turner Network Television.[20]

Seomin's words were no hyperbole. That year, the use of such slurs was a crucial piece of evidence in the conviction of a soldier who bludgeoned Private Barry Winchell to death for dating a transgender woman.[21] The year before, one of Matthew Shepard's killers used the slur to refer to his victim while being interviewed by police.[22]

Once a casually tossed-off epithet, a new cultural understanding was emerging around the f-slur—that it wasn't just a funny-sounding word, but was often the last thing a queer person might hear before getting bashed.

Unbeknownst to Will, Jack overhears the exchange with Grace and decides to confront him in a scene where he angrily mocks the ease with which the slur falls from Will's mouth. He also throws a critique of his own back at Will, accusing him of being a coward for hiding his homosexuality when around heterosexuals:

WILL: Whatever. I tell people when I'm ready, on my timetable.
JACK: Oh, I know what this is—the fifteen faces of Will. Well, listen, Will, I am what I am.
WILL: And that makes you what, the gay Popeye?
JACK: [After a beat] I'd rather be a fag than afraid.

Not only does Jack's dialogue reference Harvey Fierstein's lyrics from *La Cage aux Folles*, but it serves as a rebuke to critics who'd accused the characters of being simple, shallow stereotypes. This episode shows a new side to Jack, his wounded pride hinting at a painful past that he overcame to become comfortable with himself.

After some reflection, Will realizes that he was wrong, and resolves to stop distancing himself from his friend. The next day, he introduces one of his heterosexual gym buddies to Jack, hiding nothing about his own homosexuality or his friendship with the most flamboyant man in the room. Afterwards, Jack begrudgingly recognizes Will's growth:

JACK: Well, that was almost a nice thing you did there, Will Truman.
WILL: It's a start. What more do you want?
JACK: I'd like you to realize that this is not about me, this is about you.
WILL: I do realize that.
JACK: And I'd like an apology.
WILL: I'm sorry.
JACK: And a little respect.
WILL: You have that.
JACK: And a full-time membership to this gym.
WILL: I respect you too much to pay for . . .
JACK: Okay, forget the respect, just full-time membership.
WILL: Fine.

This episode was one of the best of the season, and it hinted at how the show could set itself apart by tackling topics that other sitcoms couldn't touch. But the bold language came at a cost.

"I guess we lost a sponsor," director Jim Burrows recalled. "The network, they were scared."[23]

Spooked, NBC cracked down on anything that might cause more

advertisers to flee. The show's position was particularly precarious as the season ended, since the ratings were still just middling—not bad enough to cancel, but far from a hit. At this point *Will & Grace* was getting beat by reruns of *Everybody Loves Raymond*.

But despite the struggle to find its audience, NBC renewed the show for a second year. Behind the scenes, cocreator Max Mutchnick wanted to get much more political—and just in the nick of time.

*

Around the same time that *Will & Grace* first hit the airwaves, conservative leaders were quietly rallying their forces for an unprecedented nationwide campaign to oppose equal rights for queer Americans.

The collapse of the marriage equality lawsuit in Hawaii was a key motivating factor. When Ninia Baehr and Genora Dancel filed their lawsuit in 1991, one of their chief arguments was that Hawaii's ban on marriage equality violated a right to privacy enshrined in the state constitution. They had a good chance of succeeding—or at least, they did until November of 1998, when voters amended the constitution to carve out an exemption for laws that blocked same-sex couples from marrying.

Encouraged, conservative groups from around the country convened a meeting in October of 1998 to plan similar measures. Their strategy was to place as many marriage bans on ballots across the country as possible, knowing that voters' anti-gay animus virtually guaranteed victory. One of their top targets: California.

"A California initiative would divert and dry up the sizable national resources of the opposition," wrote one anti-gay activist in a memo. "Gay activists would mount a formidable campaign in the expensive California media markets, thereby drying up much of their national funding."[24]

California Senator Pete Knight introduced an anti–marriage equality ballot measure in 1999. Bearing the official title "Proposition 22," it quickly became known as the "Knight Initiative." Though California already barred same-sex couples from marrying, the Knight Initiative sought to amend state law to prevent the recognition of same-sex licenses obtained in other states. With polls showing that voters supported it by a wide margin, the initiative seemed sure to pass.

That was when Mutchnick got involved.

Prompted by a friend to donate to the "No on Knight" campaign, Mutchnick reached out to campaign leaders and offered to have the cast of *Will & Grace* record a TV ad asking Californians to vote no. The campaign, headed by veteran organizer Mike Marshall, was desperate for any help that they could get, and immediately accepted the offer.

But privately, Marshall was concerned. Putting an ad on television in California was a massive expense, and fundraising had been weak. The campaign, expecting to lose, planned to use what money they had to build infrastructure for future campaigns that (they hoped) had a better chance of succeeding. Mutchnick's well-meaning offer had the potential to be a massive drain on their very limited resources.

Nevertheless, in late 1999, the cast assembled and shot a short message:

DEBRA MESSING: Proposition 22, known as the Knight Ini-
    tiative, would legalize discrimination against gay and lesbian
    Americans and their families.
MEGAN MULLALLY: You can make a difference. We urge you
    to say no to discrimination by voting no on Knight.
SEAN HAYES: One more time, please.
ALL: No on Knight.

Marshall flew from San Francisco to Los Angeles to watch the taping. "You're going to use this, right?" Mutchnick asked him.

"Yeah, yeah," Marshall told him, while thinking to himself, "What the fuck?"[25] The script, which Mutchnick had insisted on writing, was completely off-message (discrimination was *already* legal, so Messing's line made no sense) and the cast's delivery was low energy and depressing.

Upon returning to campaign headquarters, Marshall started cooking up a plan to make the best possible use of the footage. Rather than air it as is, he decided, they'd hold a press conference, dressed up like a news report with a satellite feed that local stations could access and air as if it was a news package they'd produced. A story about a sitcom cast recording a political ad carried a fun, newsworthy hook, and sure enough, numerous local affiliates wound up taking the bait. That meant that viewers saw soundbites carefully crafted by the campaign *around* the ad, rather than the content of the ad itself.

The day after the press conference, Mutchnick called Marshall with good news for the campaign and terrible news for *Will & Grace*. At this point, it was December of 1999, and ratings for *Will & Grace*'s second season were so low that NBC was seriously considering cancellation. Airing a political ad could attract exactly the kind of controversy *Will & Grace* had been trying to avoid, and Mutchnick begged Marshall not to air the ad. It was a huge relief for Marshall that he was off the hook for airing the expensive commercial, but the outlook for *Will & Grace* was worse than ever.

Mutchnick took a red-eye to New York to plead his case, and managed to buy his show a little more time to find its audience. And as season two progressed, the show started to take a new approach.

While season one tended to feature the kind of wacky premises you could find on a lot of other sitcoms (Jack gets sentenced to pick up trash; the gang eavesdrops on a bickering couple through a heating vent; Grace brings home a puppy), in season two the show started incorporating more storylines about issues that were specifically gay.

In the episode "Acting Out," Will, Grace, and Jack gather excitedly to watch one of their favorite shows broadcast a groundbreaking gay kiss. But when it airs, they're dismayed to see the camera pan away to the fireplace.

"Get off the flames and follow the flamers!" Jack howls, slapping the TV.[26]

This was something that happened on real TV shows all the time. A romance on *Dynasty* was handled almost identically, in an episode where—instead of kissing—a same-sex couple is shown reciting poetry at each other from across a room. A decade later, Fox executives made *Melrose Place* insert an awkward cutaway at the moment two men's lips touch.[27] And on CBS, *Picket Fences* filmed a scene in which two young women kissed, but the network made the producers reshoot the scene so that it's too dark to see what's going on.[28]

Furious that their favorite show censored a same-sex kiss, Will and Jack storm into the NBC offices to complain. They get brushed off by a network official named Craig, with language that is probably similar to what Max and David heard from real-life NBC executives:

> WILL: Look, we are loyal viewers and consumers. And we find your policies unfair and discriminatory. What you need to understand . . .
>
> CRAIG: No, sir, what *you* need to understand is that this network has a responsibility to its audience. Now, I understand your disappointment. Believe me . . . I understand. [Leaning toward JACK] Hi.
>
> JACK: Hi.
>
> CRAIG: But you will never see two gay men kissing on network television.
>
> JACK: Wha—It's a gay network, for God's sake! The symbol is a peacock!

On their way out of the building, they wind up in a crowd outside a taping of the *Today Show*. Will, angry that they weren't being listened to, waits until a camera is close, then grabs Jack in an exaggerated kiss just as Al Roker pauses near them, thereby getting the gay-kiss broadcast they'd sought.

This moment was based on a real-life incident: about a year earlier, two men lured Al Roker's camera close on the real *Today Show* by holding a sign indicating that one of them wanted to propose to his girlfriend. When given the opportunity, one of the men declares, "I'm so happy! I love . . . Rich!" And he turns his head to kiss his companion.

A little startled, Roker steps away, laughing, "Oh, lovely! . . . See, they wouldn't do that on *Will & Grace*."

So naturally, when the *Will & Grace* writers saw that, they took it as a challenge and wrote it into their show.

This was the show's first same-sex kiss, something that critics had predicted would be an epicenter of controversy. It's a clever, subversive mood for the show to use it as a comment on how timid the networks had been about such mundane displays of affection. It was a point that only a show with gay characters could make, and it showed off what made *Will & Grace* unique.

The writers' increased focus on gay issues is also evident on a season two Thanksgiving episode titled "Homo for the Holidays,"[29] which includes a big coming-out scene for Jack. Though this is precisely the move that many people believed had doomed *Ellen*, NBC not only aired the episode but believed in it enough that they gave it a one-time tryout on Thursday instead of its usual Tuesday.

At the time, Thursday was NBC's Must See TV night, a destination for the network's biggest blockbusters: *Frasier, Seinfeld, Friends, ER*—some of the top rated shows not just on NBC, but on all of television. To put a coming-out episode on that night was a big roll of the dice.

In the episode, Jack's mother, Judith, comes over for Thanksgiving. Jack is nervous because she—somehow—doesn't know that he's gay. His friends encourage him to come out to her, but he's worried about what she'll say. During dinner he keeps tiptoeing up to a coming out and then backing away with one distraction or another.

Finally, Will takes Jack aside and gives him some advice about being honest and authentic—advice that's not so different from what Jack suggested in season one's gym episode—and a reminder of how Jack helped him come out years earlier:

> WILL: You pulled me aside, and you said, 'Aren't you tired yet?'
> And I was tired . . . So you . . . took me to clubs and introduced
> me to people, made me realize what I'd been missing by not be-

ing myself. And I'm thankful for that ... Now here's my secret: I admire you, Jack. Because you are more yourself than anyone else I have ever known.

JACK: Will, look, I appreciate what you're trying to do, but ... This is different. My mother will fall apart. She's ...

WILL: Jack, Jack, Jack, Jack, Jack. Aren't you tired yet?

And Jack's coming out winds up going pretty well. Far from falling apart, she's supportive:

JUDITH: You could never disappoint me. I just want you to be happy. Looking back on it ... There have been clues ... you do have a lot of flamboyantly gay friends. I mean, look at Will.

Both the kiss and the Thanksgiving episodes were warmly received. *The Baltimore Sun* called the coming-out episode "twice as smart and funny" as *Friends*, and "one of the comedy high points of the fall season." It wound up being the highest-rated episode for the show's entire second season, validating the Thursday night spotlight.[30]

Beyond that, *Will & Grace* was finally finding its voice by incorporating real-life gay experiences that no other sitcom of the time could touch. And after struggling with so-so ratings, it was finally starting to get attention. In season one, awards shows had barely recognized *Will & Grace*—it received just one Emmy nomination, a fact that *Frasier*'s David Hyde Pierce criticized on live TV that year. Recognizing all of the other nominees in the supporting actor category by name, he slipped in "Sean Hayes," then quips, "Oh, he wasn't? Well, he should have been."[31]

After season two, *Will & Grace* was nominated for eleven Emmys, and Hayes won Outstanding Supporting Actor in a Comedy Series specifically for the kiss and coming-out episodes. "David Hyde Pierce," Hayes said in his acceptance speech, "thank you for singlehandedly nominating me last year."[32]

This prestige was great, but it didn't help with their main problem—ratings. Stuck on Tuesday nights, *Will & Grace* still hadn't attracted a sizable audience by the end of season two, and once again the show was in danger.

But for its third season, NBC moved the show to a permanent slot on Thursday, hoping to replicate the success of the one-time Thanksgiving tryout. This was a huge vote of confidence from the network executives, many of whom had rejected the show when it was still in the development stage. They were clearly thinking of it very differently now, and believed in *Will & Grace* so much that they bumped *Frasier* to make room.

Thanks to that move, the show's ratings soared. Now situated between *Friends* and *ER*, *Will & Grace* went from drawing around 11 million viewers to nearly 20 million. It went from the forty-fourth rated show to being in the top twenty, and in the next season, the top ten.

Thursday was clearly where *Will & Grace* belonged, in the middle of the American institution that was Must See TV. Formerly feared to be devastatingly niche, written off by critics before it even aired, *Will & Grace* was now wildly popular and reaching more people than nearly any other show on television. After season three it was smooth sailing for *Will & Grace* for five more years.

During that time, other networks attempted a handful of gay-focused clone sitcoms, but none lasted long. In 2000, Fox commissioned *Don't Ask*, a pilot starring John Goodman as a single dad in West Hollywood—it never aired, and was eventually retooled into a show called *Normal, Ohio*. In 2001, CBS's *Some of My Best Friends* was a loose adaptation of the 1997 film *Kiss Me, Guido*.[33] Also that year, Ellen briefly returned in a sitcom titled *The Ellen Show*.* None made it past the end of their first season, and that series of failures only served to reinforce the feeling that audiences still weren't ready for network sitcoms with queer leads.

*

* Created by *Arrested Development*'s Mitch Hurwitz and *Seinfeld*'s Carol Leifer.

The *Will & Grace* audience began to drift around season eight, and in 2006 the time came for the show to wrap things up. That year, there was a noticeable vacuum when it came to gay leads in primetime—just 1.3 percent of scripted network shows featured LGBTQ+ characters in 2006, GLAAD found; and of the three major networks, NBC now had the least queer-inclusive content.[34]

But before long, new shows with prominent gay leads started to appear, like *Ugly Betty* in 2006, *Gossip Girl* in 2007, *True Blood* in 2008, and *Glee* and *Modern Family* in 2009.

These shows tended to feature more diverse queer characters than *Will & Grace*, with a wider range of backgrounds and relationships. They were hits and among the top-rated shows on television, resonating especially with younger viewers. At last, it seemed, the post-Ellen curse on shows with gay leads had finally started to lift.

And if that alone was *Will & Grace*'s biggest impact on American culture, that would be enough to qualify it as one of the most significant shows of its time. But its legacy didn't end there.

*

In May of 2012, then–vice president Joe Biden appeared on *Meet the Press* and was asked—unexpectedly—if he supported gay marriage.[35]

This was six months before Barack Obama and Biden were up for reelection. No presidential administration had ever supported marriage equality, which was still seen as a deeply controversial topic. In 1996, Obama indicated his support for marriage equality when he ran for the Illinois Senate,[36] then endorsed civil unions but not marriage when he ran for US Senate in 2004, and again stopped short of endorsing marriage in 2007 during his presidential campaign. In 2010, he acknowledged that "attitudes evolve, including mine," without going so far as to offer a change of heart.[37] It seemed deeply unlikely that Biden would deviate from Obama's position.

But as the journalist Richard Ben Cramer wrote in *What It Takes*, a

1992 tell-all about presidential politics: "Joe Biden had balls. Lots of times, more balls than sense."

"The president sets the policy," Biden began, and then went on, "I am absolutely comfortable with the fact that men marrying men, women marrying women, and heterosexual men and women marrying another are entitled to the same exact rights, all the civil rights, all the civil liberties. And quite frankly, I don't see much of a distinction beyond that."

As the *Meet the Press* interview continued, Biden laid out the factors that brought him around on marriage equality. Among them, he said, "I think *Will & Grace* probably did more to educate the American public than almost anything anybody has done so far. People fear that which is different. Now they're beginning to understand."

Vice presidential comments generally don't make headlines, but these certainly did.

The cast of *Will & Grace* was flabbergasted. "I'm thrilled Biden has come out in support of gay marriage and am beyond proud of what he said," Debra Messing tweeted.

"Three cheers for VP Joe Biden!" Eric McCormack tweeted. "Now who ELSE is gonna step up?"

The answer, it turned out, was Barack Obama, who arranged an interview several days later to declare that he, too, supported the freedom to marry—the first sitting president to do so.[38]

The year that Biden credited *Will & Grace* with educating the public was also the first year that polls showed a majority of Americans supported marriage equality—up from just a quarter of Americans when *Will & Grace* premiered in the late nineties.

Was Biden right, that a sitcom could really be a factor in changing American minds? Fortunately, while the show was on the air, media researchers Edward Schiappa, Peter B. Gregg, and Dean E. Hewes conducted a study to answer that question.

Past research had already shown that having frequent, sustained contact with queer people in real life can lead a person to be more likely to support equal rights; now, the researchers wanted to see if that held true for people whose contact was with queer characters on TV. The team examined viewers of various piece of queer media—*Will & Grace*, *Six Feet Under*, *Queer Eye for the Straight Guy*, and a stand-up special by the comedian Eddie Izzard—and compared the attitudes of viewers before watching and after.

The results suggested that under the right conditions, prejudicial attitudes can indeed lessen after someone is exposed to fictional queer characters. Viewers who already knew gay people showed little change—their real-life social contacts had already had an impact. But for those with few queer people in the lives, under the right conditions shows like *Will & Grace* seemed to nudge them in the direction of adopting more tolerant attitudes toward queer strangers.

Will & Grace happened to come at a pivotal moment for television, when many of its gatekeepers were swept up in a fear of gay characters that could have wiped away the representation that *Ellen*'s coming-out episode had achieved. But instead, *Will & Grace* was able to pick up the work started by shows that came before it, and then broaden its reach across millions of people for years and years.

"I was just happy to get a job," said Sean Hayes in an interview when *Will & Grace* was nearing its finale. "Little did I know that the byproduct of the show would be so much bigger than any of us . . . What the characters go through on *Will & Grace* is what the country is going through. They live in the same world as the audience, so it's a reflection of that."

He concluded, "The baton was passed to us. We twirled it a little bit. And now we're going to pass it to those other people."[39]

But nobody could anticipate just how enthusiastically that baton was about to get picked up.

MODERN FAMILY

MITCH: You know who had straight parents? Adolf Hitler.

By the turn of the millennium, the American sitcom was dead—or at least that's what the experts believed.

After a golden age in the nineties, network sitcoms seemed to drop off a cliff in the 2000s, with audiences abandoning the traditional multi-cam studio-audience format. In 1991, nine of the top ten shows on television were sitcoms; by 2006, none were.

"We're constantly trying to convince some of our friends at the networks that the [studio sitcom] isn't dead," Eric Tannenbaum, producer of *Two and a Half Men,* told a reporter.[1] By the middle of the decade, that seemed to be a losing argument: by 2006, the number of traditional studio sitcoms on ABC, for example, had dropped from eighteen in the network's heyday to zero. Fox had just six, and three of them were animated. Sitcoms, industry watchers agreed, had reached their expiration date.

Among the viewers who'd abandoned the genre was Norman Lear, who admitted in 2007 that he no longer had any interest in the format. "We're in a golden age of television drama," he told one interviewer. "I don't know why there's no topical humor in sitcoms now."[2]

Dramas were where all the attention was. "They've been able to put old wine in a new bottle," said CBS head Les Moonves, referring to the success of shows like *The Sopranos*, *CSI*, and *24*—old stories in new packaging. "That was harder to do in sitcoms."[3]

But was there, somewhere, a "new bottle" for sitcoms? Could they be repackaged in a way that audiences would be willing to taste?

As it turns out, yes, there was; and it arrived on September 23, 2009—coincidentally, just after America embraced a presidential candidate who had arrived under the slogan, "Change."

*

Modern Family was a departure from the decades-old sitcom formula of two parents with wacky kids and nosy neighbors. Though it was a half-hour family comedy helmed by sitcom veterans, the show was a great big ensemble that smashed together a variety of diverse family structures. There were couples that divorced, kids born out of wedlock, second marriages, age gaps—and most unusual of all for broadcast TV, a gay couple raising an adopted baby.

On their own, none of these types of families was entirely new to television, but dropping them all into one show was a novel move. Same-sex parents were particularly rare. Though gay characters had become somewhat more common, couples were still often relegated to side characters (Lee and Bob on *Desperate Housewives*; James and Tom on *How I Met Your Mother*); cable (Keith and David on *Six Feet Under*); or tragedy (Willow and Tara on *Buffy the Vampire Slayer*). For *Modern Family* to launch with a prominently featured gay couple—one that is happy, well-adjusted, and not destined for heartbreak—was a risky move for a new show in a genre that everyone assumed was in the process of expiring.

So how did it happen?

It began with a disaster. In 2007, Fox launched a new sitcom called *Back to You* that seemed like the surest of sure bets: it was about two bickering newscasters at a local television station, reluctantly reunited by the revelation that they share a daughter, and starred Kelsey Grammer from *Frasier* and Patricia Heaton from *Everybody Loves Raymond*. It was directed by sitcom royalty Jim Burrows. It was created by a team with a track record of success going back to the 1980s.

It didn't even last a season.

Back to You was symptomatic of everything that was causing audiences to flee network sitcoms. It was a retread of decades-old tropes, worsened by overly meddlesome network executives who pushed for flavor-of-the-week guest stars and disorienting cast changes. The show's cancellation in May of 2008 was seen as yet another sign that the end of sitcoms was nigh.

It also looked like time might be running out for the producers who created the show, Steven Levitan and Christopher Lloyd (not to be confused with Christopher Lloyd the actor). Levitan and Lloyd had spent their entire careers working on classic sitcoms. Levitan's prior credits included *The Larry Sanders Show*, *Wings*, and *Just Shoot Me!* Lloyd's included *The Golden Girls* and *Frasier*. Now, it appeared as though the medium in which they'd honed their talent no longer had a use for them. As *Back to You* flopped, they both started frantically trying to figure out plan B.

"Basically, we were just looking not to get kicked off the lot," Levitan said at a Paley Center forum in 2010.

In between brainstorming half-baked ideas, they both noticed that the funniest stories they told each other were true ones about their families. A lightbulb lit up over both of their heads: maybe that's the sort of show they should develop.

Over the course of 2008, the show began to take shape: a humongous family ensemble shot in mockumentary style, something few American shows had attempted at that point.

But as they tossed around ideas and locked the good ones in place, one aspect of their proposal became a point of concern.

At first, they intended to have one of the show's households led by a single mom, but they found it difficult to cook up single-mom storylines that fit with the other characters. In a moment of inspiration, they spun that one character out into two gay dads, and potential storylines started falling into place. But they soon realized that a gay couple could be a turn-off for some viewers.

"We said from the beginning, 'This probably means we probably won't be a giant hit,'" Levitan said in an interview with the Television Academy Foundation. In another interview, he recalled his thinking at the time: "Well, there goes the middle of the country."[4]

This concern wasn't unfounded, considering the hostility that gay couples had recently attracted in real life. Though public attitudes toward queer individuals had warmed somewhat since *Ellen*'s coming-out episode, attitudes toward couples were another matter. Starting around 2000, voters in over thirty states had chosen to prevent same-sex couples from getting married. That marriage had appeared so frequently on ballots was no accident: according to George Bush campaign lackey Ken Mehlman, fellow Bush advisor Karl Rove engineered nationwide gay-marriage referendums to drive conservative voter turnout for presidential elections.

Those ballot measures included a particularly intense showdown in California, the state where *Modern Family* would be set, in 2008—just as Lloyd and Levitan were developing their new show.

It was a ballot battle that had been percolating since the days of *Will & Grace*—or, if you want to connect even more historical dots, since the days of *Bewitched*. Back in 1971, California eliminated gendered pronouns from state law in an effort to make laws more equitable, but lawmakers realized too late just *how* equitable they had become when rumors began circulating that homosexuals might attempt to obtain marriage licenses. Officials quickly moved to pass a revision, limiting marriage to "a man and a woman."

That wording remained intact until 2000, when voters passed the Knight Initiative, clarifying that same-sex marriages from out of state would not be recognized either. The failure of the No on Knight campaign was a setback, but was also an opportunity for California's queer activists to marshal resources for future campaigns.

That was followed by several years of legal wrangling. Then, in 2008, the California Supreme Court ruled that the Knight Initiative was unconstitutional and allowed same-sex couples to get married. But that was followed a few months later by yet another ballot measure, this one called Proposition 8, that ended marriage equality in California just months after it had begun.

It was a wild back-and-forth for marriage in California, but voters had spoken. Americans—including those in the supposedly liberal state in which *Modern Family* was to be set—had made it clear that they felt discomfort with same-sex couples being considered equal to heterosexuals. That left Levitan and Lloyd in a precarious position: either risk alienating viewers by making their gay couple prominent members of the core cast, or play it safe by making them background characters as sitcoms had tended to do in the past.

Their concern deepened when they ran the idea for the show past a friend (whom they declined in interviews to identify). The friend, a prominent gay writer, absolutely hated the plan to include gay dads. He told Levitan and Lloyd to scale back the gay content, and that "no one's going to watch" unless Mitch and Cam were reduced to minor supporting roles.

But the more they mulled it over, the worse they felt about making the "safe" choice. If they were going to make a show called *Modern Family*, it seemed strange to remove the kind of family that had only just begun to appear on modern TV shows.

"We both said you can't do a show about this without this," Levitan told the Television Academy Foundation in an interview. "Yes, it'll turn off a large portion of America, but it has to be."

In the end, they decided to keep the gay dads as central characters. ABC green-lit the show in late 2008, and the show debuted in September of 2009 with everyone's fingers crossed that the choice wouldn't backfire.

*

From its very first episode, it was clear that *Modern Family* was a different kind of sitcom. Shot in an *Office*-ish mockumentary style, the pilot introduces three households: curmudgeonly Jay (Ed O'Neill, best known for his role on *Married . . . With Children*) and assertive Gloria (Sofía Vergara) are recently married and deeply in love but have a significant age and culture gap; busybody Claire (Julie Bowen) and doofus Phil (Ty Burrell) married young and are raising three kids, each exhausting in a different way; fussbudget Mitch (played by Broadway veteran Jesse Tyler Ferguson) and sentimental Cam (character actor Eric Stonestreet) are a gay couple who just adopted a baby and are still a bit shell-shocked by how much fatherhood is about to change their lives. The pilot's end-of-episode twist is that all three households are different branches of the same family tree—Jay is the father of Claire and Mitch from his previous marriage—and the pilot lays out its weekly template of goofy extended family–comedy hijinks, inevitably capped by a few lines of heartfelt insight.

As one of the most prominent gay couples ever to appear on television, Mitch and Cam drew particular interest. They're a well-matched pair: Mitch is an uptight lawyer, while Cam is a former music teacher who's a bit more outgoing and—as Barbara Walters described him in one special—"swishy."

When we first meet the couple, they're on an airplane, bringing home their newly adopted daughter, Lily. They're prepared for people to disapprove: when a passerby comments on "the baby with those cream puffs," Mitch takes offense and stands up to lecture the entire airplane about referring to gay couples with such a demeaning term . . . until Cam points out that Lily is, in fact, eating cream puffs.

Despite their fears, the show almost never shows Cam and Mitch encountering homophobia, and instances of bigotry turn out to be misunderstandings. But behind the scenes, the showrunners were still concerned about how viewers would react. So in the first few episodes, the writers carefully gave Mitch and Cam storylines that are less about gay issues and more about parenting. We see them freak out about accidentally locking their daughter in the car for a few minutes, arrange her building blocks in an attempt to impress other parents with her stacking skills, and get lost at Costco while trying to buy diapers:

MITCH: Look how cheap they are! Oh, you know what we should
    do? We should get enough for like the next year or two, right?
CAM: Where would we keep them?
MITCH: [Looking around the store] They sell sheds.

As Ferguson put it in an interview with New Mexico Public Television, the topics of their stories were "all these things that every parent can relate to . . . realizing they're not too different from us . . ."[5]

In fact, with Mitch positioned as the breadwinner of the household and Cam as a stay-at-home parent, the gay couple comes off as one of the more traditional on the show. If you disregard their gender, you could easily exchange their storylines with an episode of *Leave It to Beaver*.

This tactic of depicting the gay couple as relatable parents was highly effective. The show was an instant hit, landing in the top five sitcoms that year with around ten million viewers per week.

Coverage of the show was glowing: "Something funny is happening on television," wrote one critic with a mixture of surprise and relief. "The obvious choice for best new fall comedy—and possibly best series," wrote the *Hollywood Reporter* in a review of the pilot, adding, "Is the sitcom staging a comeback? If previous ones were this clever, the genre never would have fallen off."[6]

Far from being the liability that the showrunners feared, Mitch and Cam were called out as a particular highlight. "The sparkling centerpiece of the family," the *Los Angeles Times* called them, adding, "*Modern Family* has single-handedly brought the family comedy back from the dead."[7] Barbara Walters placed the couple on her list of the "Ten Most Fascinating People" that year.

And beyond cultural critics, the show had a meaningful impact on viewers. At a Paley Center forum, Eric Stonestreet recalled meeting a young man who told him that the show helped him work up the courage to come out to his mother. Her response, he said, was, "Well, are you a Mitch or a Cam?"

But there was also some criticism awaiting the show. Of course, there was a conservative backlash, as expected. The group One Million Moms—which despite their name has never been able to muster more than a few thousand social media followers—urged members to boycott ABC, writing that "the homosexual content . . . is highly offensive and not family-friendly programming." Jack Hanick, a one-time producer at Fox News, accused the show's depiction of homosexuality of causing the "destruction of the traditional family." Bryan Fischer, successor to Donald Wildmon at the American Family Association, called Mitch and Cam "corrosive," "twisted," and "a little bit of poison."[8]

None of that was a surprise, though it seemed to have little impact on the show's impressive ratings.

Other criticism came from unexpected quarters: gay viewers who noticed that all though season one, *Modern Family* didn't exactly treat Mitch and Cam the same as the straight couples. The show depicted frequent physical affection between Jay and Gloria or between Claire and Phil, but Mitch and Cam seldom touched, rarely hugged, and never kissed.

Fans started an online petition on Facebook, urging the show to let the gay couple kiss, which quickly picked up steam. Jesse Tyler Ferguson tweeted that he'd sign the petition himself (then later deleted the tweet).

Behind the scenes, not everyone was so eager to see a kiss happen. *Will & Grace* had deftly maneuvered this gauntlet about a decade before. But same-sex kisses still carried a frisson of controversy: In 2008, the characters Luke and Noah kissed on *As the World Turns*, drawing condemnation from conservatives. In 2009, CBS's *Early Show* blurred a same-sex kiss between *American Idol* star Adam Lambert and his keyboardist. ("The Adam Lambert image is a subject of great current controversy," a CBS rep explained in a statement, bizarrely adding that the footage "for all we know, may still lead to legal consequences."[9])

Because many viewers still regarded gay kisses on TV as controversial—even inappropriate to air—*Modern Family* was once again in a tricky position. On one hand, they'd just managed to get audiences comfortable with a gay couple in the core cast, and showing a kiss could alienate that middle part of the country they'd been so worried about. But on the other hand, if the show kept treating Mitch and Cam differently, it made them seem, as a family, less legitimate than the straights.

As the season wore on, the lack of physical contact became more and more obvious, and backlash from queer fans became harder to ignore. At a Q&A with the cast and crew in 2010, one fan took the mic and called the showrunners out to their faces: "As a lesbian, I would like to know when we're going to see Cam and Mitch get some on-screen action, kissing or something," she said, drawing applause from the audience. In response, Eric Stonestreet deflected with a joke, but it was clear that many fans wouldn't stand for the icy barrier between the two gay dads for much longer.

Modern Family finally gave the fans what they wanted early in season two, with an episode titled "The Kiss." In the opening scene, Cam expresses annoyance at Mitch for not being affectionate enough for the entirety of their relationship—just as fans had been saying all along:

> CAM: I remember once at a New Year's Eve party, stroke of midnight, he high-fived me . . . Gays don't high-five.*

In response to Cam's dismay, Mitchell tries to dodge the issue, just like the show had been doing:

> MITCH: I'm the one who makes speeches on airplanes every time someone looks at us weird. I'm the one who gives my dad hell when he refers to you as my "friend."
> CAM: That's different. That's confrontation. But you know what takes real strength?
> MITCH: Whining?

---

* While maybe not appropriate for New Year's Eve, a high five is not entirely heterosexual; remember from the chapter about *Cheers* that the gesture was likely invented by a gay man.

CAM: Affection.

MITCH: Oh, this is insane.

But then things get awkward at a big family gathering, when Cam leans in for a kiss and Mitch dodges away, causing Cam to crash over the back of a couch. Finally, in one of *Modern Family*'s trademark act-three soul-bearings, the entire family hashes out their issues over public displays of affection: Claire points out that their father, Jay, raised them to be affection-avoidant, and that may have contributed to Mitch developing a shyness around showing love that is, in fact, always present. Mitch, in turn, recognizes that public affection is important to Cam (and, one might say, to the fans of the show), so he promises to try a little harder. With that, we finally get to see Mitch and Cam enjoy their first on-screen kiss. It's brief, but the shot is cleverly framed to include both their kiss as well as Jay giving Claire a peck on the cheek—emphasizing that familial affection comes in various forms and is entirely unremarkable.

And for any worries about public reaction, there was no backlash at all. The episode won a Humanitas Prize for its writing, it was one of the highest-rated episodes of the season, and it beat every other scripted show that week except for *Glee* (which happened to be the Britney Spears episode, so good luck beating that).

The cleverest aspect of this solution to the kissing conundrum is that Mitch's discomfort provides a reason for the show to gradually work up to showing more affection over time. Over season two, and in the seasons that followed, there's a noticeable increase in kisses between Mitch and Cam woven into the jokes, and their affection soon feels so natural that it's hard to imagine it was ever a source of controversy.

"For a lot of people, they might be the first gay couple that they know," Ferguson told the *Wall Street Journal*. "We call our show the Trojan horse— we sneak into peoples' rooms and before they know they love us we're already in."[10]

Mitch and Cam were now one step closer to truly being equal to the straight couples on the show—with one exception. They still couldn't get legally married. At least, not yet.

*

For the first few years of *Modern Family*'s run, marriage remained banned in California thanks to the Prop 8 vote, and relationship recognition of any kind was prohibited at the federal level.

Behind the scenes, many members of the *Modern Family* cast had become involved in the fight for marriage equality, particularly Jesse Tyler Ferguson, who played Mitch. He appeared at fundraisers, in TV commercials, and as a celebrity spokesperson on behalf of the freedom to marry; he and his then-boyfriend (now-husband), Justin Mikita, formed a foundation called Tie the Knot to raise money for equality-focused organizations.

Mikita was a convenient bridge between the activism opportunities of Ferguson's celebrity profile and the complex legal wrangling over Proposition 8. While Ferguson played a lawyer on TV, Mikita was an attorney in real life and oversaw fundraising efforts at the American Foundation for Equal Rights (AFER), the nonprofit leading the multimillion-dollar effort to challenge Prop 8 before the US Supreme Court.*

At this point, queer organizers were up against a formidable foe in the form of a massive conservative legal machine that had been laying the groundwork to block marriage equality ever since the rumblings of a lawsuit in Hawaii in the early nineties. Groups like the National Organization for Marriage, the Alliance Defense Fund, and Liberty Counsel had created an entire industry that pumped conservative donors for cash, and then used armies of well-funded lawyers, lobbyists, and marketers to push back on LGBTQ+ equality at every opportunity. They also had powerful politicians backing them up—among them California governor Arnold Schwarzenegger, who was responsible for, among other tasks, defending Proposition 8 against AFER's lawsuit.

---

* Full disclosure: I was AFER's communications manager.

And although public opinion on the freedom to marry was gradually improving through *Modern Family*'s first few seasons, polling still indicated that a majority of Americans remained opposed to allowing same-sex couples to wed. As the show matured through its second, third, and fourth seasons, it was looking like marriage equality might never come—either for fictional couples or those in real life.

And then, one day in June, everything changed.

*

The day began with a bizarre ritual in Washington, DC, that over the years has come to be known as the "Running of the Interns." Because no recording is allowed inside the US Supreme Court, news networks developed a system years ago to be the first to report on new rulings: they assign interns to loiter in the court's lobby when rulings are expected, grab the photocopied pages the moment they're released, and then race down the steps of the court to hand-deliver the documents to on-air journalists stationed on the sidewalk in front of cameras.

When interns started pouring down the steps on the morning of June 26, 2013, they carried in their hands the Supreme Court's ruling in the case against Proposition 8. It was short—just thirty-five pages—and by a five-to-four margin, it was revealed, Proposition 8 was no more.

Modern Family was just heading into a summer break on the day that the ruling came down, but the writers leapt into action to figure out how to respond. They'd already been planning some form of ceremony for Mitch and Cam—"There was no backup plan," writer Jeffrey Richman told the *Hollywood Reporter*, confessing that when the ruling arrived, he felt relief as a writer before he felt it as a gay man.[11]

But once again, there was a risk of alienating conservative viewers. Television had depicted a handful of same-sex ceremonies starting with *Roc* in the early nineties and continuing through *Friends*, *Roseanne*, *Northern Exposure*, and more recently shows like *The L Word* and *All My Children*. But just as with same-sex kisses, these ceremonies tended to be a source of controversy. Two stations in the South refused to air *Northern Exposure's* wedding-themed episode; meanwhile, Focus on the Family, an evangelical group with a particular focus on anti-gay rhetoric, declared outrage over *All My Children's* ceremony.

Once again, *Modern Family* found itself in a delicate position. By 2013, public opinion was split roughly 50/50 on the issue of marriage equality, and the show stood to lose the middle-American audience they'd worked so hard to attract and retain.

So the writers took what they'd learned with the kiss episode three years earlier, and crafted a season-long arc that focused on wedding-related hijinks. It starts with the season five premiere, in which the overturning of a marriage ban (which is not identified by name) prompts all of the couples on the show to reflect on the moments that made them fall in love. Mitch and Cam, meanwhile, are ecstatic that they can now marry, but soon find themselves in an unofficial contest with each other to engineer the ideal romantic proposal. Each one wants to be the first to ask the question, and to do it in the most perfect setting possible.

As one amorous scheme after another goes haywire, they eventually wind up with a broken-down car on the side of the road in the middle of nowhere at night. Attempting to replace a flat tire, they both kneel down next to the car, then raise their eyes up to each other, their thoughts perfectly in sync, and both say in unison . . .

"Yes."

"I remember sitting at my computer writing the ending," writer Jeffrey Richman told entertainment journalist Marc Freeman, who wrote an oral history of the making of the series. "Suddenly I had tears in my eyes."[12]

"A lot of the writers, and specifically the gay writers, were so emotional about this movement toward marriage equality," said Jesse Tyler Ferguson in that same oral history. "They were funneling it into their art, and I was funneling it into Mitch and Cam. It was very easy to ride those emotions from your real life into your artistic life."

"I think you don't realize how invested in these characters you are,"

Richman told the *Hollywood Reporter*, "until this huge thing that had been denied to them suddenly is not an obstacle for them."

But not every obstacle was out of the way. Over the course of season five, Mitch and Cam plan their wedding and, of course, endure more comedic mishaps. Just as with the kiss, the show focuses on storylines relatable to a wide audience, gay or straight—like squabbling over invitations and debating their balloon budget.

And while most of the mayhem is comedic, other issues are more serious. Mitch's dad, Jay, has never been totally comfortable with his gay son, and now he can't keep his discomfort hidden:

> JAY: This whole wedding thing is weird to me ... Why do you need
>   to make it into a spectacle?

As the wedding approaches, Mitch learns that Jay had been taking pains to keep it a secret from his macho golf buddies:

> JAY: I mean, I'm just saying, I don't know how this stuff plays out
>   with my guys from the club.

In the two-part season finale, disasters escalate on the day of the wedding. There's a fire near the venue; Cam's parents are on the verge of divorce; a swarm of butterflies attacks the grooms; and in a harebrained scheme to retrieve a tuxedo from an unexpectedly closed dry cleaner, their daughter, Lily, crawls into a drop-off chute and is then snagged and carried away by the garment conveyor.

After the entire wedding party is forced to spend the day traipsing from one unsuitable venue to another, the meals lost and the guests drenched by lawn sprinklers, the entire affair is starting to look like an unredeemable fiasco. "Is this really how you want to get married?" Cam asks Mitch. "Let's just call time of death on this."

They're about to cancel the entire thing when someone speaks up: Jay has been watching his son persevere through one setback after another all day long, after waiting years for the opportunity to declare his commitment to the man he loves. The importance of the day now clear to him, Jay makes a few calls and secures the perfect backup venue: his macho golf club. (In real life, a hillside overlooking a Trump property.)

At the tail end of season five, after years of fighting for equality in real life and having persevered through one setback after another on the show, Mitch and Cam finally get to walk down the aisle, glowing in a dusty orange California sunset.

This season finale was the culmination of years of work to balance concerns about middle America's willingness to accept a gay couple against the desire to have Mitch and Cam be truly equal—in their prominence, physical affection, and finally legal recognition, just as thousands of real-life couples got married all across California.

Among those couples was Jesse Tyler Ferguson and his partner, Justin Mikita, just before filming his TV wedding (with *Angels in America* playwright Tony Kushner officiating).

"I have two husbands, you guys," Ferguson laughed at an awards show in 2019. "Remember when we could have zero husbands? Now we can have *two*."[13]

*

The triumph at the Supreme Court and at *Modern Family*'s wedding altar coincided with a surge in public support for the freedom to marry in 2012. For the first time, surveys showed that a majority of Americans favored marriage equality, and voters in multiple states approved ballot measures legalizing marriage—breaking a thirty-one ballot-measure losing streak.

There were numerous reasons for the public's change of heart, from Obama's endorsement that year to political advertising to the expansion of legal protections to individual conversations. But if we extrapolate from research conducted around other shows with queer leads, Mitch and Cam likely played a meaningful role as well.

Remember the hypothesis put forth by the researchers who studied *Will & Grace* (among other shows)? Viewers who don't regularly interact with queer people can experience a decline in prejudicial attitudes when they see fictional queer characters in significant roles over a long period of time—say, as a committed gay couple who get significant screen time in every episode of a show over the course of multiple seasons.

Changing public opinion certainly was not Steven Levitan and Christopher Lloyd's goal when they came up with *Modern Family*. But by including Mitch and Cam, and crafting storylines that made them appealing to a wide audience, *Modern Family* managed to create the perfect conditions for viewers to accept gay dads as just another part of the family.

Instead of being the risk that doomed the show, it "turns out Mitch and Cam are two of the most popular characters on the show," Levitan said in an interview with the Television Academy. "Two of the reasons why America loves 'em so much."[14]

Modern Family ran for another six years, and then took a bow in 2020. In the series finale, Cam gets a job offer in Missouri, close to the family that he left behind when he moved to California to be with Mitch. The series ends with Mitch, Cam, Lily, and a new baby named Rexford heading out on a new adventure . . . to the middle part of America, exactly the place that, when the show was being developed, they feared would never accept them.

But it makes sense that they'd feel comfortable finding a new home in the Midwest. Around the time that *Modern Family* debuted, public support for marriage equality in Missouri was running 32 percent to 59 percent opposed; close to when the show ended, that had flipped to 58 percent support to 35 percent opposed. That shift was mirrored in television demographics: when *Modern Family* began, GLAAD noted that "LGBTQ characters accounted for just 3 percent—18 total—of all primetime scripted broadcast series regulars." When the show ended, that had quintupled to ninety LGBTQ+ characters.

"As an actor you just want to work," Ferguson said at a Paley Center event where he received an award for LGBTQ+ Achievements in Television. "If you get to work on a show that people actually like and has good enough ratings to stay on TV, even better," he went on. "And if you get to be on a show that contributes in a social way . . . that's the cherry on top of the sundae."[15]

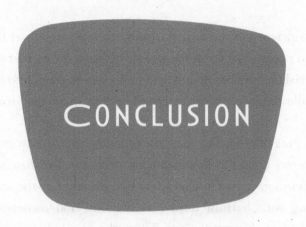

CONCLUSION

In the late 1930s, radio broadcasters discovered something troubling in the lyrics of the popular Cole Porter song "My Heart Belongs to Daddy."

The number, ostensibly sung by a young ingenue describing her devotion to a man, has lyrics laden with both innuendo and plausible deniability. For example, the singer describes herself preparing a dinner for two, then notes, "I just adore / his asking for more," a seemingly innocent phrase until singer Mary Martin recorded the song in 1939 and added a sly pause, transforming the lyric into "I just adore / his ass ... king for more."

Radio stations were already on the lookout for naughtiness in Porter's work. Censors had previously sounded the alarm over what they perceived as a troubling trend in his other hits: "Let's do it / let's fall in love," went the lyrics of one, and "I've got such a yen / so do it again," went another, sung with euphoric sighs by Bernice Parks. "You do something to me," croons Ella Fitzgerald in yet another Porter song. In each of these numbers, radio officials decided, the verb "to do" was getting up to some funny business. The songs were banned from airwaves for their suggestiveness.

"My Heart Belongs to Daddy" seemed headed for a similar fate, and was scrutinized by radio networks' song-clearance departments. Finally, a decision was reached: censors declared that the song was suitable for broadcast, but only if sung by women. Radio, it would seem, could tolerate a mild heterosexual entendre, but not daddies staking claims on the hearts of men.[1]

This debate was just one early skirmish in a tug-of-war over the nation's airwaves that's continued for nearly a century. From the earliest years of radio and television, queer content would find a way to creep into broadcasts, inevitably followed by a pearl-clutching backlash that wiped it away—but not for long.

After a period of virtual invisibility in television's first few decades, coded characters hinted at homosexuality on shows like *Bewitched*; vocal real-life activism gave rise to characters like Beverly LaSalle on *All in the Family*, along with harmful misrepresentations; and conservatives who clamored for censorship got their wish with the Family Viewing Hour.

This led to a particularly decisive showdown in the mid-1970s, roughly fifty years after the country's first television broadcast in 1928 and fifty years before the publishing of this book in 2023. With depictions of homosexuality lumped alongside explicit sex and violence as unfit for broadcast, the Family Viewing Hour threatened to undo the hard-won visibility of the preceding few years. Fortunately, it was vulnerable to challenge—a challenge unveiled at 10 AM on October 30, 1975, when a group of television luminaries gathered at the headquarters of the Writers Guild of America to declare war on ABC, CBS, NBC, and the US government.[2]

Assembled there on a stage before reporters were some of the nation's top television talents, both in front of and behind the camera: actors like Mary Tyler Moore, Alan Alda, and Carroll O'Connor, and creators like Danny Arnold, Larry Gelbart, Norman Lear, Susan Harris, and more.[3]

They had come to announced a lawsuit over the Family Viewing Hour, which they deemed an illegal government intrusion on free speech. This move was a gamble—should they lose, it could establish a dangerous precedent, opening the doors to further government crackdowns. But courts proved receptive to their claims, and within a year the Family Viewing Hour vanished as quickly as it had come. Almost immediately, viewers could enjoy a surge in queer characters like Jodie on *Soap*, Mr. Plager on *The Bob Newhart Show*, and George's transgender friend Edie Stokes on *The Jeffersons*.

The tug-of-war continued.

The inclusivity of the late seventies soon cooled with the election of Ronald Reagan, after which broadcast television tended to shy away from provocative topics, but this trend reversed itself only a few years later as viewers defected to more daring shows on cable television and networks scrambled to lure them back. The presidential election of 1992 prompted a handful of programs tackling queer military service and relationship recognition. That was followed by a backlash to *Tales of the City*'s queer romance that was so intense, there were Congressional hearings about defunding PBS for having dared broadcast it. A few years later, *Ellen*'s coming-out episode was a major step forward, but the show's swift cancellation seemed to indicate a further backslide, thankfully held at bay by the success of *Will & Grace*.

And then, starting around 2000, TV gays entered an extended renaissance. Politically, America enjoyed a string of civil rights successes with the decriminalization of sodomy, the repeal of the military's ban on openly queer servicemembers, and the gradual recognition of marriage equality. Culturally, television offered unprecedented levels of gay characters and even queer-led series like *Glee*, *Modern Family*, and *Schitt's Creek*.

Looking back over the last twenty years of television, it might seem as though the tug-of-war might've finally ended, that conservative activists were sufficiently exhausted by their failures, that the moral arc of the universe had finished bending, and that television was finally, safely, gay for good.

Or maybe not.

As I write these words at the end of 2022, there are signs of a long-delayed backlash coming that could dwarf those of the previous century.

In schools across the country, we're seeing queer-inclusive books banned. Teachers and librarians fired. Curricula scrubbed of affirming role models. A moral panic that began by scapegoating trans students is now expanding to brand all queer people as a threat to kids. If history is any guide, the current moral backlash to inclusive material in schools could easily expand into campaigns to wipe queer characters from media intended for all audiences.

If that happens, we would lose one of the most powerful forces behind the expansion of civil rights for queer people over the last few decades. Positive media depictions of minority groups in fiction have a demonstrable real-life impact on public attitudes fostering tolerance and empathy. Over the last twenty years, America has experienced a steady reduction in discriminatory attitudes toward queer people; if those positive depictions were to disappear, the widespread institutionalized bigotry of the past could more easily return once again.

So what can be done?

In the past, a variety of techniques have proved useful in pushing back against conservative attempts to purge queer people from media. There were lawsuits like the one that overturned the Family Viewing Hour. There was political activism, such as the Stonewall uprising and vociferous campaigns for marriage equality, military service, and access to HIV care. There were diversifying sources for entertainment, such as the rise of cable TV and independently produced online media. And there was pushback from professionals within the media industry, who insisted on including queer stories in their work.

All of these tactics helped pull broadcast television's tug-of-war in the direction of featuring more queer characters and more positive depictions. And if a backlash is, indeed, headed our way, all of these tactics will be needed to prevent the last twenty years of progress from being reversed.

If that sounds like a lot of work, that's because it will be. But it's work that was worth it in the past to bring us to this point, and it's work that will matter to future generations, because media and culture teach us about the world and ourselves, shape our values, and inform our dreams of what could be. Television isn't just a piece of furniture to watch; it's a conversation, a tool, a weapon, a war, a party, an instrument, and an opportunity. It's a project to participate in rather than passively watching in the dark.

Fifty years after radio censors forbade male voices from declaring that their hearts belonged to daddy, an activist named Vito Russo started work on *The Celluloid Closet*, a celebration of queer images in cinema that he screened at fundraisers for the newly formed Gay Activists Alliance. Those screenings eventually became a book, which led to Russo's cofounding of the Gay and Lesbian Alliance Against Defamation to combat negative media depictions at local levels. The book became a documentary, released in 1996 just as GLAAD established itself nationally. The screenings, the book, and the film were all urgent calls to action—calls that, today, remain as vital to make as they are to answer.

"We have cooperated for a very long time in the maintenance of our own invisibility," Russo concludes in *The Celluloid Closet*. "And now the party is over."[4]

ACKNOWLEDGMENTS

Boundless thanks are due to all my teachers who saw a weird little nerd enter their classrooms and knew, somehow, that with their help he might walk out a writer: David Kolakoski, Stephen Carpenter, Joseph Cipollini, Deborah Fager, Patricia Picchioni, Catherine McKinstry, and most of all Peter Moore, whose response to my impenetrably discursive physics class lab reports was, "I can't wait to read your first book."

Thanks as well to my parents, who ensured that our house was filled with a constant supply of books to read and who, I suspect, always knew I'd do something like this.

I'm particularly grateful to everyone who spoke to me about television history, particularly Norman Lear, Marsha Posner Williams, and Richard Day, who were so generous with their time and insight. Thanks as well to Stan Zimmerman and Jeffrey Duteil, who spoke to me for my YouTube series.

I'm also indebted to Alonso Duralde, Dave White, Anthony Oliveira, Drew Mackie, Dashiell Silva, Chase Burns, and James Jorden for helping me workshop titles for this book. Thank you for not letting me call it *Tube of Pansies*.

This book would not be possible without the amazing writing, research, and storytelling of my fellow media and pop culture writers: Steven Capsuto, whose invaluable book *Alternate Channels* is the most dog-eared on my shelf; Brett White, whose knowledge of television history puts mine to shame; Drew Mackie and Glen Lakin, whose podcast *Gayest Episode Ever* is required listening; and Professor Bryan Wuest, whose scholarship, craft, and friendship is an inspiration (and whose name I am so sorry for misspelling in the acknowledgments of my last book). Above all, I am indebted to the work of Vito Russo, whose work is the North Star by which I hope to navigate.

Thanks to the entire crew at Seattle's Overcast Coffee Company, who maintained the optimal level of caffeination required for me to clatter away at a keyboard for hours.

I'm particularly thankful to everyone who helped me navigate the world of grown-up publishing, particularly my agent Lauren Abramo and everyone at Dystel, Goderich, and Bourret. Thanks to photographer Nate Gowdy for ensuring that I looked presentable, and to everyone at Ben-Bella Books and Smart Pop: Robb Pearlman, whose vision established the structure of this book; Leah Wilson, who helped to nudge it all into place; Glenn Yeffeth, who kept the momentum going; Vy Tran and Leah Baxter, who are masters of fine details; Jessika Rieck, who finessed each page; Ariel Fagiola and Alicia Kania, who got the manuscript into the right hands; and Heather Butterfield, who ensured that once the words were written, they would be read.

In my career, I've been tremendously fortunate to work with some of the greatest editors in the world, whose feedback and encouragement made me proud to be a writer: Eve Batey, Jackson West, Brock Keeling, Chase Burns, and Tyler Trykowski. Thanks for joining me in a fandom of the written word.

And thanks most of all to James, my best friend.

NOTES

INTRODUCTION

1. Waters, Harry F. "99 and 44/100% Impure." *Newsweek*, 1977.
2. Baume, Matt. Conversation with Marsha Posner Williams. Personal, March 26, 2022.
3. Baume, Matt. Conversation with Marsha Posner Williams. Personal, March 26, 2022.
4. Capsuto, Steven. *Alternate Channels: Queer Images on 20th-Century TV*. New York: Steven Capsuto, Books and Translation Services, 2020.
5. US Bureau of the Census. *Statistical Abstract of the United States, 1982–83*. 103rd ed. Washington, DC, 1982.
6. "What Is the American Family Association?" American Family Association, August 22, 2017. Video, 1:37. https://youtu.be/LFjbIOkjcJI.
7. "What Is the American Family Association?" American Family Association, August 22, 2017. Video, 1:37. https://youtu.be/LFjbIOkjcJI.
8. "Norman Lear with Emerson College." *The Interviews*. Television Academy Foundation. June 2, 2021. https://interviews.televisionacademy.com/interviews/norman-lear-with-emerson-college.

BEWITCHED

1. Regier, John W., and Gary Markowitz, writ. *M*A*S*H*. Season 2, episode 22, "George." Aired February 16, 1974, CBS.
2. Adelman, Jerry, Daniel Gregory Browne, and Ann Marcus, writ. *Mary Hartman, Mary Hartman*. Season 1, episode 103, "Episode #1.103." Aired May 26, 1976, in syndication.
3. Metz, Walter. *Bewitched*. Detroit, MI: Wayne State University Press, 2007.
4. Mann, William J. *Behind the Screen: How Gays and Lesbians Shaped Hollywood, 1910–1969*. New York: Penguin, 2002.

5. Avedon, Barbara, and Sol Saks, writ. *Bewitched.* Season 1, episode 2, "Be It Ever So Mortgaged." Aired September 24, 1964, ABC.

6. Saks, Sol, and Danny Arnold, writ. *Bewitched.* Season 1, episode 4, "Mother, Meet What's His Name." Aired October 8, 1964, ABC.

7. Mitchell, Stewart. Essay. "In the Founding of Massachusetts: A Selection from the Sources of the History of the Settlement 1628–1631, 23." Boston: Massachusetts Historical Society, 1930.

8. Shurtleff, Nathaniel B., and David Pulsifer. *Records of the Colony of New Plymouth, in New England, Vols. 1 & 2.* New York: AMS Press, 1855.

9. Morgan, Edmund S. "The Puritans and Sex." *New England Quarterly* 15, no. 4 (1942): 591. https://doi.org/10.2307/361501.

10. S.G. "Now Is the Time." *Los Angeles Evening Citizen News,* January 23, 1962.

11. "Officer Spells Out Sex Deviate Data." *Los Angeles Evening Citizen News,* February 13, 1962.

12. "From the Desk of Dave Heyler." *Los Angeles Evening Citizen News,* March 11, 1963.

13. "Prey-on-Boys Sex Ring Is Smashed." *Los Angeles Evening Citizen News,* May 1, 1962.

14. Steele, Robert C., and Jim Foshee. *Banned from California: Jim Foshee, Persecution, Redemption, Liberation . . . and the Gay Civil Rights Movement.* Yuma, AZ: Wentworth-Schwartz Publishing Company, LRCS, 2020.

15. "LA Chief Ires Assemblyman." *San Francisco Examiner,* May 25, 1963.

16. Arvidson, Marilyn. "Morals Squad Takes Homo Issue to Parents." *Miami Herald,* April 12, 1966.

17. "Jail for SD's." *Los Angeles Evening Citizen News,* February 6, 1963.

18. "Homosexuals Mistreated, Washington Pickets Say." *Dayton Daily News,* May 30, 1965.

19. Slade, Bernard, and Sol Saks, writ. *Bewitched.* Season 1, episode 7, "The Witches Are Out." Aired October 29, 1964, ABC.

20. Shockley, Jay. "Picket in Front of U.S. Army Building, First-Ever U.S. Gay Rights Protest." NYC LGBT Historic Sites Project. Partner Program of the Fund for the City of New York, July 2018. https://www.nyclgbtsites.org/site/picket-in-front-of-u-s-army-building-first-ever-u-s-gay-rights-protest/.

21. Pela, Robert L. "The Legend of Lizzie." *Advocate,* July 30, 1992.

22. Tibbles, Doug, writ. *Bewitched.* Season 3, episode 1, "Nobody's Perfect." Aired September 15, 1966, ABC.

23. Greene, John L., writ. *Bewitched.* Season 7, episode 25, "Samantha's Psychic Pslip." Aired April 1, 1971, ABC.

24. Evans, Maurice. *All This . . . and Evans Too!: A Memoir.* Columbia: University of South Carolina Press, 1987.

25. Ennis, Thomas W. "NEWS OF REALTY: SALE IN 'VILLAGE'; Albee, Playwright, Buys the Home of Maurice Evans." *New York Times*, May 25, 1965.

26. Ennis, Thomas W. "NEWS OF REALTY: ALBEE HOUSE SOLD; Jerry Herman, Composer, Buys 'Village' Dwelling." *New York Times*, April 19, 1968, C34.

27. *The Tonight Show Starring Johnny Carson*. "Paul Lynde/McLean Stevenson/Bob Uecker/Carol Wayne." Aired April 30, 1976, NBC.

28. Hadleigh, Boze. *Hollywood Lesbians: Conversations with Sandy Dennis and Others*. New York: Barricade, 1994.

29. See, Carolyn. "Think Plastics!" *TV Guide*, February 7, 1970.

30. Starr, Seth Michael. *Hiding in Plain Sight: The Secret Life of Raymond Burr*. New York: Applause Theatre & Cinema, 2009.

31. Hy, Gardner. "Hudson, Nabors 'Marriage' a Hoax." *Post-Crescent (Appleton, WI)*, August 15, 1971.

32. "Sheila Kuehl Discusses Helping Dick Sargent Come out on Television—EMMY TVLEGENDS.ORG." Television Academy Foundation Interviews, August 7, 2015. Video, 5:44. https://youtu.be/PJZzwEbYmSg.

33. "Just for the Record: Episode #125 Christopher Street West Association Gay Pride Parade 1992, Part 2." Amistad Research Center, October 6, 2022. Video, 59:39. https://vimeo.com/363584193.

34. Terracuso, John, writ. *In the Life*. Season 1, episode 2, "Coming Out (Laughing)." Aired November 1992, PBS.

ALL IN THE FAMILY

1. Lear, Norman, writ. *All in the Family*. Season 1, episode 1, "Meet the Bunkers." Aired January 12, 1971, CBS.

2. Baume, Matt. Conversation with Norman Lear. Personal, July 12, 2022.

3. Styler, Burt, and Norman Lear, writ. *All in the Family*. Season 1, episode 5, "Judging Books by Covers." Aired February 9, 1971, CBS.

4. Baume, Matt. Conversation with Norman Lear. Personal, July 12, 2022.

5. Martin, Douglas. "Arthur Evans, Leader in Gay Rights Fight, Dies at 68." *New York Times*, September 14, 2014.

6. Gross, Larry P. *Up from Invisibility: Lesbians, Gay Men, and the Media in America*. New York: Columbia University Press, 2002.

7. "Homosexuals Hold Protest in 'Village' After Raid Nets 167." *New York Times*, March 9, 1970.

8. Miller, Johnny. "Drag Queen Don McLean Dies." *SFGATE*, February 9, 2012. https://www.sfgate.com/entertainment/article/Drag-queen-Don-McLean-dies-3173277.php.

9. Baume, Matt. Conversation with Norman Lear. Personal, July 12, 2022.

10. Day, Gerry, and Bethel Leslie, writ. *Family*. Season 2, episode 10, "Rites of Friendship." Aired December 28, 1976, CBS.

11. Shilts, Randy. *The Mayor of Castro Street: The Life and Times of Harvey Milk*. New York: St. Martin's Griffin, 1988.

12. Neubacher, Jim. "Radical Councilmen Happy to Quit; Establishment Glad to See Them Go." *Detroit Free Press*, March 24, 1974.

13. Carelli, Richard. "High Court Upholds 'Gay' Case Ruling." *Lansing State Journal*, October 3, 1977.

14. Baume, Matt. Conversation with Norman Lear. Personal, July 12, 2022.

15. Kaiser, Charles. "3 Sentenced in Attack Using Bats Against 6 in Central Park in '78." *New York Times*, October 17, 1979.

16. Shilts, Randy. *The Mayor of Castro Street: The Life and Times of Harvey Milk*. New York: St. Martin's Griffin, 1988.

17. "Reaction to Dan White Verdict." The Fruit Punch Collective, May 23, 1979. Audio, 44:15. https://archive.org/details/pra-AZ0203.

18. Ghaziani, Amin. *The Dividends of Dissent: How Conflict and Culture Work in Lesbian and Gay Marches on Washington*. Chicago: University of Chicago Press, 2008.

ALICE

1. Von Hoffman, Nicholas. "This Is 'Year of the Fag' on TV." *Journal Times*, October 15, 1976.

2. Crowe, Cameron. "Playboy Interview: David Bowie." *Playboy*, September 1976.

3. Jahr, Cliff. "Elton John: It's Lonely at the Top." *Rolling Stone*, October 7, 1976.

4. Day, Gerry, and Bethel Leslie, writ. *Family*. Season 2, episode 10, "Rites of Friendship." Aired December 28, 1976, CBS.

5. Donovan, Martin, writ. *Alice*. Season 1, episode 2, "Alice Gets a Pass." Aired September 29, 1976, CBS.

6. Parker, Rod, writ. *The Nancy Walker Show*. Season 1, episode 1, "The Homecoming." Aired September 30, 1976, ABC.

7. Sheehan, Tony, writ. *Barney Miller*. Season 3, episode 2, "Quarantine: Part 1." Aired September 30, 1976, ABC.

8. "NBC Snips Comedian David Brenner's Show." *Rocky Mount Telegram*, September 1, 1976.

9. Parker, Rod, writ. *Maude*. Season 3, episode 12, "Maude's New Friend." Aired December 2, 1974, CBS.

10. Regier, John W., and Gary Markowitz, writ. *M*A*S*H*. Season 2, episode 22, "George." Aired February 16, 1974, CBS.

11. Rothman, Lily. "How a Closeted Air Force Sergeant Became the Face of Gay Rights." *Time*, September 8, 2015. https://time.com/4019076/40-years-leonard-matlovich/.

12. Clair, Dick, and Jenna McMahon, writ. *The Mary Tyler Moore Show*. Season 3, episode 17, "My Brother's Keeper." Aired January 13, 1973, CBS.

13. Neuwirth, Allan. *They'll Never Put That on the Air: An Oral History of Taboo-Breaking TV Comedy*. New York: Allworth Press, 2006.

14. Charles, Glen, and Les Charles, writ. *Phyllis*. Season 2, episode 7, "Out of the Closet." Aired November 1, 1976, CBS.

15. Shilts, Randy. *The Mayor of Castro Street: The Life and Times of Harvey Milk*. New York: St. Martin's Griffin, 1988.

16. Holston, Noel. "'Born Innocent' Riles Parents." *Orlando Sentinel*, September 12, 1974.

17. Montgomery, Kathryn C. *Target: Prime Time: Advocacy Groups and the Struggle over Entertainment Television*. New York: OUP USA, 1991.

18. "Television: Too Candid Camera?" *Time*, September 30, 1974.

19. Cowan, Geoffrey. *See No Evil: The Backstage Battle over Sex and Violence on Television*. New York: Simon and Schuster, 1980.

20. Schneider, Alfred R., and Kaye Pullen. *The Gatekeeper: My Thirty Years as TV Censor*. Syracuse, NY: Syracuse University Press, 2001.

21. Black, David. "Inside TV's 'Family Hour' Feud." *New York Times*, December 7, 1975.

22. Brown, Les. "TV 'Family Hour' to Be Challenged." *New York Times*, October 22, 1975.

23. "NBC Announced 3 New Sitcoms." *Los Angeles Times*, November 16, 1976.

24. Jones, Patricia, and Donald Reiker, writ. *The Bob Newhart Show*. Season 5, episode 3, "Some of My Best Friends Are . . ." Aired October 9, 1976, CBS.

25. Carter, Bill. "Homosexuality on TV: Just a Passing Fad?" *Baltimore Sun*, October 24, 1976.

26. Jones, Paul. "Homosexuals on Television: Should They Be Included?" *Atlanta Constitution*, October 9, 1976.

27. Shales, Tom. "Widow 'Alice' Is Loud, Bold, and Brassy." *Tampa Times*, October 15, 1976.

28. Von Hoffman, Nicholas. "A Gay Time on TV." *Pocono Record*. October 13, 1976.

29. Rintels, David W. "'Why We Fought the Family Viewing Hour.'" *New York Times*, November 21, 1976.

30. Formicola, Jo Renee, Mary C. Segers, and Paul J. Weber. *Faith-Based Initiatives and the Bush Administration: The Good, the Bad, and the Ugly*. Brantford, ON: W. Ross MacDonald School, Resource Services Library, 2005.

BARNEY MILLER

1. "Danny Arnold, 70, Creator of 'Barney Miller'." *New York Times*, August 22, 1995, sec. D.

2. Tardan, Dennis. "A Reasonably Spontaneous Conversation with Danny Arnold." Tardan Media, May 26, 2020. Video, 29:47. https://youtu.be/0dtYqi8fC7A.

3. Lait, Jack, and Lee Mortimer. *New York: Confidential!* New York: Ziff-Davis Publishing Company, 1948.

4. Franke-Ruta, Garance. "An Amazing 1969 Account of the Stonewall Uprising." *Atlantic*, January 24, 2013.

5. Di Brienza, Ronnie. "Stonewall Incident." *East Village Other* 4, no. 32, July 9, 1969.

6. Gordon, Steve, Danny Arnold, Theodore J. Flicker, writ. *Barney Miller.* Season 1, episode 2, "Experience." Aired January 30, 1975, ABC.

7. US Congress. House. *Equality Act.* HR 15692. 93rd Cong, 1974.

8. Cowan, Geoffrey. *See No Evil: The Backstage Battle over Sex and Violence on Television.* New York: Simon and Schuster, 1980.

9. Capsuto, Steven. *Alternate Channels: Queer Images on 20th-Century TV.* New York: Steven Capsuto, Books and Translation Services, 2020.

10. Schneider, Alfred R., and Kaye Pullen. *The Gatekeeper: My Thirty Years as TV Censor.* Syracuse, NY: Syracuse University Press, 2001.

11. "Hal Linden." *The Interviews.* Television Academy Foundation. January 26, 2016. https://interviews.televisionacademy.com/interviews/hal-linden.

12. Tardan, Dennis. "A Reasonably Spontaneous Conversation with Danny Arnold." Tardan Media, May 26, 2020. Video, 29:47. https://youtu.be/0dtYqi8fC7A.

13. "All in the Family Tops by Nielsen for 1974–1975." *Times Record,* June 2, 1975.

14. Cowan, Geoffrey. *See No Evil: The Backstage Battle over Sex and Violence on Television.* New York: Simon and Schuster, 1980.

15. *Doe v. Commonwealth's Attorney of Richmond.* 435 US 901 (31976).

16. O'Neill, Tim. "Doe v. Commonwealth's Attorney: A Set-back for the Right of Privacy." *Kentucky Law Journal* 65, no. 3 (1977): 748–63. https://uknowledge.uky.edu /cgi/viewcontent.cgi?article=2385&context=klj.

17. Kibbee, Roland, Danny Arnold, and Reinhold Weege, writ. *Barney Miller.* Season 3, episode 19, "Asylum." Aired February 24, 1977, ABC.

18. Healy, Dan. "A History of Homophobia." *St. Petersburg Times,* March 28, 2014.

19. Regula, Michael. "Why the End of Communism Didn't End Antigay Hate in Russia." *Advocate,* November 17, 2015. https://www.advocate.com/world/2014/02/07/why-end -communism-didnt-end-antigay-hate-russia.

20. Rivers, Daniel. "'In the Best Interests of the Child': Lesbian and Gay Parenting Custody Cases, 1967–1985." *Journal of Social History* 43, no. 4 (Summer 2010): 917–43. https://doi.org/10.1353/jsh.0.0355.

SOAP

1. O'Connor, John J. "TV VIEW; Unhappiness Within the Industry." *New York Times*, December 2, 1979.

2. Wieder, Robert. "The Lady Behind the 'Soap' Lather." *Vancouver Sun*, November 19, 1977, sec. Weekend Magazine.

3. Banks, Miranda. *The Writers: A History of American Screenwriters and Their Guild*. New Brunswick, NJ: Rutgers University Press, 2016.

4. Baume, Matt. Conversation with Marsha Posner Williams. Personal, March 26, 2022.

5. Knopf, Terry Ann. "Controversy Has Forced ABC to Clean up 'Soap.'" *Fort Worth Star-Telegram*, September 10, 1977, sec. C.

6. Wildmon, Donald E., and Allen Wildmon. *I Had a Vision: God Had a Plan*. Tupelo, MS: American Family Association, 2013.

7. Warga, Wayne. "Susan Harris' Soap: Is the Bubble Going to Burst?" *Los Angeles Times*, October 23, 1977, sec. Calendar.

8. Conger, John J. "Proceedings of the American Psychological Association, Incorporated, for the Year 1974: Minutes of the Annual Meeting of the Council of Representatives." *American Psychologist* 30, no. 6 (1975): 620–51. https://doi.org/10.1037/h0078455.

9. Brown, Les. "Homosexuals Move to Protect Civil Rights on TV." *New York Times*, August 8, 1977.

10. Hoffman, Ken. "Gays Challenge 'Soap' Portrayal." *Florida Today*, September 11, 1977, sec. D.

11. Deeb, Gary. "ABC Soft-Pedals New Fall Series, 'Soap'." *Macon News*, August 21, 1977, sec. TV Teletime.

12. "The Censor's Memo to 'Soap's' Producers." *San Francisco Examiner*, October 9, 1977.

13. Baume, Matt. Conversation with Marsha Posner Williams. Personal, March 26, 2022.

14. "Gays' Letter Outlines Objections to 'Soap'." *Bangor Daily News*, September 17, 1977.

15. Schwartz, Tony. "Psychic Consulted on TV Programs." *Province (BC)*, March 15, 1981, sec. B.

16. Baume, Matt. Conversation with Marsha Posner Williams. Personal, March 26, 2022.

17. "Billy Crystal Interview." *The Interviews*. Television Academy Foundation. February 27, 2019. https://interviews.televisionacademy.com/interviews/billy-crystal.

18. Murphy, Mary. "'I Felt a Lot of Rage'." *TV Guide*, 1980.

19. Faber, Nancy. *People Magazine* 12, no. 2, July 9, 1979.

20. Harakas, Margo. "In the Courts, Women Face Uphill Battle." *Palm Beach Post*, July 8, 1980.

21. Murphy, Mary. "'I Felt a Lot of Rage'." *TV Guide*, 1980.

22. Montgomery, Kathryn C. *Target: Prime Time: Advocacy Groups and the Struggle over Entertainment Television*. New York: OUP USA, 1991.

23. Selcraig, Bruce. "Reverend Wildmon's War on the Arts." *New York Times Magazine*, September 2, 1990, sec. 6.

CHEERS

1. Littlefield, Warren, and T. R. Pearson. *Top of the Rock: Inside the Rise and Fall of Must See TV*. New York: Anchor Books, 2013.

2. "Ken Levine and David Isaacs Interview." *The Interviews*. Television Academy Foundation. March 30, 2015. https://interviews.televisionacademy.com/interviews/ken-levine?clip=28868#interview-clips.

3. Pomerantz, Earl, writ. *Cheers*. Season 1, episode 2, "Sam's Women." Aired October 7, 1982, NBC.

4. Fierstein, Harvey. *I Was Better Last Night: A Memoir*. New York: Alfred A. Knopf, 2022.

5. David, Larry, Jerry Seinfeld, and Carol Leifer, writ. *Seinfeld*. Season 6, episode 15, "The Beard." Aired February 9, 1995, NBC.

THE GOLDEN GIRLS

1. Colucci, Jim. *Golden Girls Forever: An Unauthorized Look Behind the Lanai*. New York: Harper Design, 2016.

2. Gussow, Mel. "Theater: 'Divorce of Judy and Jane.'" *New York Times*, April 27, 1972.

3. *Matlovich v. Secretary of the Air Force*. 591 F. 2d 852 (D.C. Cir. 1978).

4. Colucci, Jim. *Golden Girls Forever: An Unauthorized Look Behind the Lanai*. New York: Harper Design, 2016.

5. Endler, Michael, and Thad Mumford, writ. *Maude*. Season 6, episode 9, "The Gay Bar." Aired December 3, 1977, CBS.

6. Baume, Matt. Conversation with Stan Zimmerman. Personal, July 5, 2021.

7. Glicksman, Frank, Al C. Ward, and Barry Oringer, writ. *Medical Center*. Season 5, episode 4, "Impasse." Aired October 1, 1973, CBS.

8. Cordes, Sarah, and Rick Egusquiza. "Betty White: Pride of the Lesbians." *National Enquirer*. July 3, 2012.

9. "LaRouche-Backed AIDS Measure on the Ballot Again." *Ukiah Daily Journal*, June 5, 1988.

10. Shannon, Kelley. "Groups Want Judge Out for Remarks about Homosexuals." *Advocate-Messenger.* December 20, 1988.

11. "Robert Eichberg, 50, Gay Rights Leader." *New York Times*, August 15, 1995, sec. B.

12. Speer, Kathy, Terry Grossman, Barry Fanaro, and Mort Nathan, writ. *The Golden Girls.* Season 4, episode 15, "Valentine's Day." Aired February 11, 1989, NBC.

13. Wolfson, Evan, and David Westfall. "Samesex Marriage and Morality: The Human Rights Vision of the Constitution," 1983.

14. Colucci, Jim. *Golden Girls Forever: An Unauthorized Look Behind the Lanai.* New York: Harper Design, 2016.

15. Hadleigh, Boze. "Estelle by Starlight." *Advocate*, October 10, 1989.

16. "Bea Arthur Residence." The Ali Forney Center, November 29, 2016. Video, 2:45. https://youtu.be/820aR6Q8dno.

17. "The Golden Girls at PaleyFest LA 2006: Full Conversation." The Paley Center for Media, May 13, 2020. Video, 1:15:23. https://youtu.be/W5z9zHcgQSg.

DINOSAURS

1. Golembewski, Vanessa. "How a '90s Kids Show Predicted the Downfall of Humanity." Dinosaurs TV Show—Innovative 90s Sitcoms. Refinery29, April 26, 2016. https://www.refinery29.com/en-us/2016/04/109127/dinosaurs-tv-show-anniversary.

2. Ulin, Rob, writ. *Dinosaurs.* Season 2, episode 3, "I Never Ate for My Father." Aired October 2, 1991, ABC.

3. "PERVERTS CALLED GOVERNMENT PERIL; Gabrielson, G.O.P. Chief, Says They Are as Dangerous as Reds—Truman's Trip Hit Gabrielson Warns Industry." *New York Times*, April 19, 1950.

4. Cuordileone, K. A. "'Politics in an Age of Anxiety': Cold War Political Culture and the Crisis in American Masculinity, 1949–1960." *Journal of American History* 87, no. 2 (2000): 515. https://doi.org/10.2307/2568762.

5. U.S. Congress, House. 81st Cong., 2nd sess. *Congressional Record* 96, no. 4, daily ed (March 31, 1950): 4527.

6. Kruks, Gabe. "Gay and Lesbian Homeless/Street Youth: Special Issues and Concerns." *Journal of Adolescent Health* 12, no. 7 (1991): 515–18. https://doi.org/10.1016/0197-0070(91)90080-6.

7. Thompson, Karen, and Julie Andrzejewski. *Why Can't Sharon Kowalski Come Home?* Tallahassee, FL: Spinsters Ink, 1989.

8. *In re Guardianship of Kowalski*, 478 N.W.2d 790 (Court of Appeals of Minn. 1991).

9. Lewin, Tamar. "Disabled Woman's Care Given to Lesbian Partner." *New York Times*, December 18, 1991, sec. A.

FRIENDS

1. Thompson, Arienne. "You'll Never Believe How Much Money the 'Friends' Cast STILL Earns Today." *USA Today*, February 27, 2015.

2. Tagliamonte, Sali, and Chris Roberts. "So Weird; So Cool; So Innovative: The Use of Intensifiers in the Television Series Friends." *American Speech* 80, no. 3 (2005): 280–300. https://doi.org/10.1215/00031283-80-3-280.

3. Lauer, Matt. "'Friends' Creators Share Show's Beginnings." NBCNews.com. NBC-Universal News Group, May 6, 2004. https://www.nbcnews.com/id/wbna4899445.

4. Lee, Veronica. "With Friends like These . . ." *Guardian*, June 13, 1997.

5. "Lisa Kudrow on the First Time the 'Friends' Cast Met—Televisionacademy.com/ Interviews." Television Academy Foundation Interviews, June 20, 2014. Video, 2:18. https://youtu.be/Nh1BiKQPpYs.

6. Mann, William J. *Behind the Screen: How Gays and Lesbians Shaped Hollywood, 1910– 1969*. New York: Penguin, 2002.

7. Kelly, Emma. "Carol and Susan Weren't Allowed to Kiss When They Got Married on Friends." *Metro*. Metro.co.uk, December 12, 2019. https://metro.co.uk/2017/09/15 /carol-and-susan-werent-allowed-kiss-when-they-got-married-on-friends-6931148/.

8. Martinelli, Michelle R. "'Friends' Co-Creator Marta Kauffman Explains Why Fans Love the Show's Sports Episodes." *USA Today*. Gannett Satellite Information Network, May 1, 2019. https://ftw.usatoday.com/2019/04/friends-marta-kauffman -anniversary-finale-sports-moments-thanksgiving.

ELLEN

1. Tracy, Kathleen. *Ellen: The Real Story of Ellen DeGeneres*. New York: Kensington, 2005.

2. Dickerson, Marla. "Religious Conservatives Intensify Boycott Against Disney." *Los Angeles Times*, July 2, 1996.

3. Jacobs, A.J. "Out?" *Entertainment Weekly*, October 4, 1996.

4. Gliatto, Tom. "Outward Bound." *People*, May 5, 1997.

5. Baume, Matt. Conversation with Richard Day. Personal, April 2, 2022.

6. White, Keith. "Anti-Gay Rights Law Rejected." *Press & Sun-Bulletin* (Binghamton, NY), May 21, 1996.

7. Baume, Matt. *Defining Marriage: Voices from a Forty-Year Labor of Love*. Self-published, CreateSpace, 2015.

8. "Excerpts from Judge's Gay-Wedding Ruling." *Honolulu Advertiser*, December 4, 1996, sec. A.

9. Handy, Bruce. "Roll Over, Ward Cleaver." *Time*, April 4, 1997.

10. Zurawik, David. "'Ellen' Breaks with the Past." *Baltimore Sun*, April 27, 1997, sec. E.

11. Handy, Bruce. "Roll Over, Ward Cleaver." *Time*, April 4, 1997.

12. Kemp, Kathy. "Crowd Cheers Ellen." *Birmingham Post-Herald*, May 1, 1997, sec. B.

13. Cagle, Jess, and Joe Flint. "As Gay as It Gets." *Entertainment Weekly*, May 8, 1998.

14. Capsuto, Steven. *Alternate Channels: Queer Images on 20th-Century TV.* New York: Steven Capsuto, Books and Translation Services, 2020.

15. Cagle, Jess, and Joe Flint. "As Gay as It Gets." *Entertainment Weekly*, May 8, 1998.

16. "Hawaii Legislature Expands Rights of Same-Sex Couples." *Ashbury Park Press*, April 30, 1997.

17. Lovell, Glenn. "Bono: 'Ellen' Too Gay." *Variety*, March 8, 1998.

18. Lowry, Brian. "Ratings, Not Sexuality, Steer Future of 'Ellen.'" *Los Angeles Times*, March 11, 1998.

19. Barbato, Randy, and Fenton Bailey, dir. *The Real Ellen Story*. Aired September 30, 1997, Bravo.

20. Baume, Matt. *Defining Marriage: Voices from a Forty-Year Labor of Love*. Self-published, CreateSpace, 2015.

WILL & GRACE

1. Kutner, Max. "A Proud Day at American History Museum as LGBT Artifacts Enter the Collections." Smithsonian.com. Smithsonian Institution, August 19, 2014. https://www.smithsonianmag.com/smithsonian-institution/will-grace-affirms-role-american-history-180952400/.

2. Colucci, Jim. *Will & Grace: Fabulously Uncensored*. New York: NBC Studios, 2004.

3. Littlefield, Warren, and T. R. Pearson. *Top of the Rock: Inside the Rise and Fall of Must See TV*. New York: Anchor Books, 2013.

4. "Creators of *Will & Grace* Max Mutchnick and David Kohan on Will & Grace Revival." CNBC, September 25, 2017. https://youtu.be/NBAnAWpB6j4.

5. "Warren Littlefield Interview Part 3 of 3." *The Interviews*. Television Academy Foundation. July 16, 2012. https://interviews.televisionacademy.com/interviews/warren-littlefield.

6. Jacobs, A. J. "Gay Men & Straight Women: Why Hollywood Just Loves Them." *Entertainment Weekly*, October 23, 1998.

7. Natale, Richard. "Will Power." *Advocate*, September 15, 1998.

8. Kohan, David, and Max Mutchnick, writ. *Will & Grace*. Season 1, episode 1, "Pilot." Aired September 21, 1998, NBC.

9. Endrst, James. "Ellen Heir Sneaks into Town." *Hartford Courant*, August 7, 1998.

10. "James Burrows." *The Interviews*. Television Academy Foundation. September 30, 2009. https://interviews.televisionacademy.com/interviews/james-burrows.

11. Natale, Richard. "Will Power." *Advocate*, September 15, 1998.

12. "CBS Rides Sunday Night to Ratings Victory." *San Francisco Examiner*, September 30, 1998, sec. C.

13. Endrst, James. "Network TV Is Going Down the Tube." *Hartford Courant*, November 13, 1998.

14. Brownworth, Victoria A. "The Fall Season and the Ick Factor." *Bay Area Reporter*, September 3, 1998.

15. "Reader Forum." *Advocate*, July 6, 2004.

16. "Reader Forum." *Advocate*, October 13, 1998.

17. Dodds, Richard. "'Bi-Comical' Jewish Lesbian Comic: Oy Vey!" *Bay Area Reporter*, January 20, 1999.

18. Kohan, David, Max Mutchnick, and Michael Patrick King, writ. *Will & Grace*. Season 1, episode 19, "Will Works Out." Aired April 22, 1999, NBC.

19. Carvajal, Doreen. "Thesaurus Takes Action to Remove Gay Slurs." *New York Times*, January 20, 1999, sec. A.

20. De Moraes, Lisa. "TNT Tosses Gay-Bashing Spectacle Out of the Ring." *Washington Post*, October 12, 1999, sec. C.

21. Clines, Francis X. "For Gay Soldier, a Daily Barrage of Threats and Slurs." *New York Times*, December 12, 1993, sec. 1.

22. Osborne, Duncan. "Trashing Matthew Shepard." *Gay City News*, December 1, 2004.

23. "James Burrows." *The Interviews*. Television Academy Foundation. September 30, 2009. https://interviews.televisionacademy.com/interviews/james-burrows.

24. Baume, Matt. *Defining Marriage: Voices from a Forty-Year Labor of Love*. Self-published, CreateSpace, 2015.

25. Baume, Matt. *Defining Marriage: Voices from a Forty-Year Labor of Love*. Self-published, CreateSpace, 2015.

26. Kohan, David, and Max Mutchnick, writ. *Will & Grace*. Season 2, episode 14, "Acting Out." Aired February 22, 2000, NBC.

27. Pergament, Alan. "'Melrose Place' Season Finale Backs Off on Gay Kiss Scene." *Buffalo News*, May 18, 1994.

28. Tropiano, Stephen. "When a Kiss Is Not Just a Kiss." *PopMatters*, May 28, 2003. https://www.popmatters.com/tropiano030528-2496174507.html.

29. Kohan, David, Max Mutchnick, and Alex Herschlag. *Will & Grace*. Season 2, episode 7, "Homo for the Holidays." Aired November 25, 1999, NBC.

30. Zurawik, David. "Shows as Yummy as Pie TV." *Baltimore Sun*, November 24, 1999.

31. "The 51st Annual Primetime Emmy Awards." Broadcast, September 12, 1999.

32. "The 52nd Annual Primetime Emmy Awards." Broadcast, August 26, 2000.

33. Tropiano, Stephen. *The Prime Time Closet: A History of Gays and Lesbians on TV.* New York: Applause Theatre & Cinema Books, 2002.

34. "Where We Are on TV Report: 2006–2007 Season." GLAAD, September 15, 2018. https://www.glaad.org/publications/tvreport06.

35. Melick, Rob, dir. *Meet the Press.* Aired May 6, 2012, NBC.

36. Smith, Ben. "Obama Backed Same-Sex Marriage in 1996." *Politico*, January 13, 2009. https://www.politico.com/blogs/ben-smith/2009/01/obama-backed-same-sex -marriage-in-1996-015306.

37. Steinmetz, Katy. "See Obama's 20-Year Evolution on LGBT Rights." *Time*, April 10, 2015. https://time.com/3816952/obama-gay-lesbian-transgender-lgbt-rights/.

38. Earnest, Josh. "President Obama Supports Same-Sex Marriage." National Archives and Records Administration, May 10, 2012. https://obamawhitehouse.archives.gov /blog/2012/05/10/obama-supports-same-sex-marriage.

39. Kohan, David, and Max Mutchnick, writ. *Will & Grace.* Season 11, episode 18, "It's Time." Aired April 23, 2020, NBC.

MODERN FAMILY

1. Hughes, Mike. "Are Studio Sitcoms Dying?" *Sheboygan Press*, August 17, 2006.

2. Garvin, Glenn. "'70s Sitcom King Says Form Is Dead." *Miami Herald*, June 3, 2007.

3. Boedeker, Hal. "Death of Sitcoms Is Feared, but Unlikely." *Orlando Sentinel*, August 26, 2005.

4. Freeman, Marc. *Modern Family: The Untold Oral History of One of Television's Ground-breaking Sitcoms.* New York: St. Martin's Press, 2020.

5. Grant, Gene. "Episode 717 | Jesse Tyler Ferguson." NM PBS, October 25, 2013. Video, 18:39. https://youtu.be/vds7kAMMs7Q.

6. Garron, Barry. "'Modern Family' Season 1: TV Review." *Hollywood Reporter*, September 22, 2009.

7. McNamara, Mary. "'Modern Family'." *Los Angeles Times*, September 23, 2009.

8. Isquith, Elias. "Religious Right Leader Says 'Modern Family' Is Like 'Poison.'" Salon. Salon.com, March 28, 2014. https://www.salon.com/2014/03/27/ religious_right_leader_says_modern_family_is_like_poison/.

9. Itzkoff, Dave. "CBS Is Criticized for Blurring of Video." *New York Times*, November 28, 2009.

10. Peeples, Jase. "Watch: Jesse Tyler Ferguson Dishes on Historic 'Modern Family'

Wedding." *Advocate*. Advocate.com, May 15, 2014. https://www.advocate.com /arts-entertainment/television/2014/05/15/watch-jesse-tyler-ferguson-dishes-historic -modern-family.

11. Rose, Lacey. "'Modern Family' Writer Reveals Emotional Backstory of 'Historic' Gay Marriage Proposal (Exclusive)." *Hollywood Reporter*, September 25, 2013.

12. Freeman, Marc. *Modern Family: The Untold Oral History of One of Television's Groundbreaking Sitcoms*. New York: St. Martin's Press, 2020.

13. "Debra Messing and Jesse Tyler Ferguson on LGBTQ+ Achievements in Television." The Paley Center for Media, June 22, 2020. Video, 5:00. https://youtu.be /Czm4YfcKUT4.

14. "Steve Levitan." *The Interviews*. Television Academy Foundation. April 15, 2013. https://interviews.televisionacademy.com/interviews/steve-levitan.

15. "Debra Messing and Jesse Tyler Ferguson on LGBTQ+ Achievements in Television." The Paley Center for Media, June 22, 2020. Video, 5:00. https://youtu.be /Czm4YfcKUT4.

CONCLUSION

1. Capsuto, Steven. *Alternate Channels: Queer Images on 20th-Century TV*. New York: Steven Capsuto, Books and Translation Services, 2020.

2. Cowan, Geoffrey. *See No Evil: The Backstage Battle over Sex and Violence on Television*. New York: Simon and Schuster, 1980.

3. Black, David. "Inside TV's 'Family Hour' Feud." *New York Times*, December 7, 1975.

4. Russo, Vito. *The Celluloid Closet: Homosexuality in the Movies*. New York: Harper & Row, 1987.

INDEX

A

ABC. *see also individual shows*
   censor role at, 74–75
   in competition with Fox, 166
   and Family Viewing Hour,
     58, 61, 248
   struggling shows of, 76–77
   traditional sitcoms on, 229
Abzug, Bella, 71
Albee, Edward, 20
Alda, Alan, 51, 248
Alfred Hitchcock Presents, 29
Alice, 49–66
Alice (*Soap* character), 112
Alice Doesn't Live Here Anymore
   (film), 52
Ali Forney Center, 161–162
Alley, Kirstie, 129
All in the Family, 4, 9, 24,
   27–47, 59, 95, 126, 248
All My Children, 240, 241
American Family Association, 191
American Foundation for Equal
   Rights (AFER), 239
The Andy Griffith Show, 4
Aniston, Jennifer, 180
"The Annual Reminder," 18, 31
Antonowsky, Marvin, 95
Arnold, Danny, 10, 60, 67–70,
   72–74, 76–80, 83–84, 91–92, 248

Arthur, Bea, 50, 95, 139, 140,
   160–162
As Good as It Gets, 132,
   210–211
Asher, William, 10
Ashley, Warren, 145n

B

Back to You, 230–231
Baehr, Ninia, 196, 197, 202,
   205, 218
Bailey, Jim, 35
Baker, Gilbert, 46
Baker, Richard John, 32
Balan, Michele, 215
Barney Miller, 50, 61, 67–92
The Bea Arthur Residence of
   LGBT Youth, 162
Beard, Fred, 57
Bearse, Amanda, 191
Bell, Book and Candle (film), 10
Benevides, Robert, 22
Benson, 117
Berle, Milton, 35
Bernhard, Sandra, 183
Beverly LaSalle (*All in the
   Family* character), 32–38,
   41–43, 47, 126, 248
Bewitched, 5, 9–25, 212, 248
Beyt, Peter, 155–156

Biden, Joe, 225–226
The Birdcage, 131
bisexuality, 50, 110–111, 171.
   see also LGBTQ+ people
Blair, Linda, 52, 56–57
The Bob Newhart Show, 61–62,
   120, 210
Bono, Chaz, 204
Born Innocent (TV movie), 56–58
Bosom Buddies, 35
Boston Common, 208
Bowen, Julie, 234
Bowie, David, 50, 111
Boys Beware, 15, 55
The Brady Bunch, 53n, 76
Brause, Jay, 202
Brenner, David, 50
Bristow, Patrick, 189, 190, 200
Britt, Harry, 44
broadcast licenses, 57–58
Broderick, Matthew, 130
Brothers, 118, 143
Bryant, Anita, 39, 98, 99, 113
Burke, Glenn, 122
Burns, Allan, 60
Burr, Raymond, 22
Burrell, Ty, 234
Burrows, Jim, 120, 210–214,
   217, 231
Burstyn, Ellen, 52

Burton, Tim, 166
Butler, Owen, 116–117

C
Cafiero, Renée, 18
Cagney & Lacey, 118
Carol (*Soap* character), 110–113
Carson, Johnny, 21
CBS, 4. *see also individual shows*
　in competition with Fox, 166
　dramas on, 230
　and Family Viewing Hour,
　　58, 60–61, 79, 248
The Celluloid Closet, 250–251
Chang, Kevin S.C., 197
Chaplin, Charlie, 34
Charles, Glen, 120
Charles, Les, 120
Chase, Adam, 182
Cheers, 5, 119–133, 184, 210
A Chorus Line (show), 59
Citizen News, 13–15
Civil Rights Movement, 11, 15–16
Clash, Kevin, 167
Clift, Montgomery, 151*n*
Clinton, Bill, 191
Coalition for Better Television
　(CBTV), 3
Coco (*The Golden Girls*
　character), 140–141, 143, 183
Colasanto, Nick, 120
Colucci, Jim, 152, 156
comedy, 4–6, 35. *see also* sitcoms
coming out, 9, 187, 190
　on *Bewitched*, 16–17
　on *Ellen*, 194–195, 197–
　　201, 212, 227, 232, 249
　on *The Golden Girls*,
　　145–146, 149–153
　making decisions about,
　　145–146
　on *M*A*S*H*, 9
　National Coming Out Day,
　　151
　on *Will & Grace*, 222–223
The Corner Bar, 73

The Cosby Show, 125, 137
Cox, Courteney, 180
Cramer, Richard Ben, 225–226
Crane, David, 181, 182
Crenna, Richard, 117
Crystal, Billy, 2, 103–105, 109,
　115, 116, 118
Curtis, Tony, 58

D
Daddy's Girls, 129, 187
Dancel, Genora, 196, 197, 202,
　205, 218
Danson, Ted, 120
Darryl Driscoll (*Barney Miller*
　character), 50, 61, 79–86,
　88–91
The David Susskind Show, 2
Davis, Sid, 15
Day, Doris, 82
Day, Richard, 192, 193
Dean, Beverly, 101
Defense of Marriage Act, 157
DeGeneres, Ellen, 182,
　189–195, 198, 201–203, 205,
　209, 212, 224
DeLarverie, Stormé, 69
DeLeon, Jack, 73
Dern, Laura, 52, 199
Diamond, Selma, 136–137
Di Brienza, Ronnie, 70
Dieter, Newt, 72–74, 80, 87,
　99, 105
Dilday, William H., Jr., 57
Dinosaurs, 165–171, 175–177
discrimination, 18, 89, 113, 184,
　219, 250. *see also* legal rights/
　protections
Disney, 190, 191, 194, 198, 200
Divine, 36, 131*n*
Dog Day Afternoon (film), 59
domestic partnerships, 174–175
Don't Ask, 224
Doyle, Tim, 167, 201–204
Dr. Quinn, Medicine Woman, 198
drag, 32–38, 186

Dugan, Gene, 202
Duke Astin, Patty, 117
DuMont Network, 4
Duteil, Jeffrey, 144, 149
Dynasty, 118, 126, 140–141,
　220–221

E
East Coast Homophile
　Organizations, 16
Eichberg, Robert, 151
Eisenberg, Janet, 208–210
Eisner, Michael, 103
Ellen, 189–206, 209, 212–213,
　227, 232, 249
The Ellen Show, 224
Equality Act of 1974, 71
ER, 222
The Ernie Kovacs Show, 2
Evans, Arthur, 31
Evans, Maurice, 20

F
The Facts of Life, 126
"fag," 215–217
Falwell, Jerry, 3, 116
families, 10–11, 142, 230
Family, 37, 50, 61
Family Viewing Hour, 56,
　58–61, 65, 76, 79, 97, 209, 248
Fay, 95
Federal Communications
　Commission (FCC), 57–58, 65
Feinstein, Dianne, 44
Feldblum, Chai, 195
female impersonators, 32–38
Ferguson, Jesse Tyler, 234, 239,
　241, 243–245
Ferguson, Warren J., 64–65
Fierstein, Harvey, 129–133, 138,
　187, 217
Fitzgerald, Ella, 247
Flowers, Wayland, 161*n*
Ford, Gerald, 56
Foshee, Jim, 14
Fox network, 166, 221, 229–231

Foxx, Red, 49, 127
Franken, Al, 119
Franklin, Michael H., 60
Frasier, 127–128, 222–224
Frasier Crane (character), 127–128
Freebie and the Bean, 34
Friends, 4, 128n, 179–187, 222, 240
Fruit Punch Collective, 43–44

G
Gail, Max, 68
Garofalo, Janeane, 192
Gay Activists Alliance (GAA), 31, 32, 251
Gay and Lesbian Alliance Against Defamation, 251
Gay Media Task Force (GMTF), 72, 73
gay people. *see* LGBTQ+ people
Gelbart, Larry, 60, 248
gender
    pronouns referring to, 186–187, 232
    sexual orientation vs., 108
Get Smart, 11
Getty, Estelle, 130, 138–140, 141n, 143–144, 146, 154–155, 161
Gingrich, Candace, 186n
GLAAD, 198, 201, 204, 225, 244, 251
Glass, Ron, 68
Glee, 225, 249
Gold, Ronald, 99
The Golden Girls, 5–6, 125, 135–163, 183, 210
Goodman, John, 224
Gossip Girl, 225
Grammer, Kelsey, 127, 230–231
Grant, Lee, 95
Greenwich Village, 67, 69, 70, 84
Gregg, Peter B., 226–227
guardianship, 171–175
Guillaume, Robert, 104, 117

H
Hail to the Chief, 117
Hairspray, 36, 131n
Harman, Barry, 52
Harris, Sam, 94, 100, 101
Harris, Susan, 2, 94–96, 104, 105, 115–118, 137–142, 248
Hawaii Equal Rights Marriage Project, 196–197
Hayes, Sean, 211, 219, 223, 227
Heaton, Patricia, 231
Heche, Anne, 202
Hello, Larry, 119
Henson, Jim, 166
Herman, Jerry, 20
Hervey, Winifred, 144
Hewes, Dean E., 226–227
Hill Street Blues, 140
Hirschkop, Philip, 84–85
HIV epidemic, 150, 153–156, 161, 183, 209
Holbrook, Hal, 75
Holiday, Billie, 103n
Hollibaugh, Amber, 43–44
Holston, Noel, 57
homophile organizations, 3, 16, 70
homophobia, 43, 167–171, 191–192, 242
homosexuality. *see also* LGBTQ+ people
    censored version of, 75–76
    as a crime, 13, 84–85
    decriminalization of, 56, 59, 249
    media depictions of, 133, 247–249
    as mental illness, 15, 23, 32, 55, 56, 98, 110, 113
    moral panic around, 169
    polls on, 113
    in Soviet Union, 87–88
Horton, Edward Everett, 183
Hot L Baltimore, 32, 73, 76
Hudson, Rock, 22–23, 82, 109, 161n

Hunt, Helen, 117
Hurt, John, 59
Hurwitz, Mitch, 224n

I
Iger, Bob, 203
I Love Lucy, 4, 189
I'm a Big Girl Now, 117
I Married a Witch (film), 10
Inherit the Wind, 139
In re Guardianship of Kowalski, 171–175
Isaacson, Madeleine, 114
It's Garry Shandling's Show, 192
It Takes Two, 117

J
Jack (*Alice* character), 62–63
The Jeffersons, 32, 126, 144
The Jim Henson Company, 165
John, Elton, 50, 111
Johnson, Jay, 104
Jones, Jeffrey, 141
Juergens, Kate, 214

K
Kameny, Frank, 51
Kate & Allie, 126
Kauffman, Marta, 181, 182, 187
Kaye, Danny, 35
Kennedy, Anthony, 195
The Kids in the Hall, 187
Klausen, Ray, 161
Knight, Pete, 218
Knight Initiative, 218–220, 232–233
Koch, Ed, 71
Kohan, David, 208–214, 221
Korman, Harvey, 35
Kowalski, Sharon, 171–175
Kozachenko, Kathy, 39, 84
Kristofferson, Kris, 52
Kudrow, Lisa, 180, 182
Kuehl, Sheila, 24, 25
Kushner, Tony, 243

L

La Cage aux Folles, 131, 217
Lagon, Pat, 202
Lavender Scare, 169
Lear, Norman, 5, 27, 28, 31–32, 34, 47, 50, 60, 73, 95, 229, 248
Leave It to Beaver, 11
LeBlanc, Matt, 180
legal rights/protections, 184, 218, 226, 243
    anti-discrimination laws, 46, 71, 98, 184, 191, 205–206
    decriminalization of homosexuality, 56, 59, 249
    guardianship, 171–175
    health benefits, 190, 196–197
    marriage equality (*see* marriage equality)
    for same-sex couples (*see* same-sex couples)
Leifer, Carol, 224*n*
lesbians. *see also* LGBTQ+ people
    on *All in the Family*, 50
    on *Ellen*, 189–191, 203–205
    Ellen character's coming out, 194–195, 197–201
    on *The Golden Girls*, 144–149
    jokes about, 193–194
    as parents, 89, 112–114
    and *In re Guardianship of Kowalski*, 171–175
    Roseanne kiss, 5
    teaching how to react to, 146–149
Let My People Come (musical), 60
Levin, Charles, 140
Levine, Ken, 120, 141*n*
Levitan, Steven, 231–233, 244
LGBTQ+ characters, 183, 244, 248–249
    controversy over, 1–3, 6–7, 99
    depictions of, 2–7, 29, 56, 72–74, 184–187

    in early 2000s, 249
    during the eighties and into the nineties, 118
    explicitness of, 9
    gay-man/hetero-woman relationship, 132, 210–211
    in mass media, 206
    as plot devices, 125–126
    as primetime leads, 225
    recurring, 73
    setbacks for, 209
    viewers' attitudes toward, 227
LGBTQ+ people, 161–162, 171
    activism by/for, 16–18, 23, 46–47, 98–103, 183, 191, 195, 198, 202, 239
    backlash on issues regarding, 249–251
    civil rights for, 250
    coming-out decisions of, 145–146
    in early nineties' news, 183–184
    gay culture, 56, 70, 82
    gay proposals, 153
    jobs restricted for, 40
    jokes at expense of, 192
    Lavender Scare, 169
    liberation movements, 3, 28, 31–32, 46, 56, 69, 203
    marriage equality for (*see* marriage equality)
    media portrayal of, 248–251 (*see also* LGBTQ+ characters)
    in the military, 51, 84, 191, 249
    national mood on issues, 195–197
    as parents, 89, 111–113, 230–233
    persecution of, 13–15
    police shakedowns of, 80
    in politics, 38–41, 46–47, 84 (*see also individual people in politics*)
    public awareness of, 46, 64

    public perception of/beliefs about, 3, 28, 55–56, 98, 150, 232, 244
    slurs used for, 215–217
    Smithsonian LGBTQ+ history collection, 208
    teaching how to react to, 146–149
    television examples for, 151, 159–160
    violence against, 13, 42–43, 69–70, 216
    visibility of, 3, 31, 130, 248
Lilith Sternin-Crane (character), 127–128
Linden, Hal, 68, 76
Littlefield, Warren, 138, 209–210, 213, 215
Lloyd, Christopher, 231–233, 244
Long, Shelley, 120
Love, American Style, 76, 95
Love, Sidney, 139
The Love Boat, 118, 126, 144
Lubin, Arthur, 11
The L Word, 240
Lynde, Paul, 20–21

M

Mad About You, 192, 207, 209
Mandan, Robert, 50
The Many Loves of Dobie Gillis, 24
March on Washington, 46–47
Marcus Welby, M.D., 2, 32, 55–56, 72
Markham, Monte, 149
marriage equality, 249
    in Alaska, 202, 203, 205
    on *All in the Family*, 39–41
    Biden and Obama on, 225–226
    in California, 218–220, 232–233, 239, 240
    Defense of Marriage Act, 157
    denial of marriage licenses, 32
    on *The Golden Girls*, 153, 156–160

in Hawaii, 197, 202–203, 205, 218
legislation/ballots for, 44–45, 191, 218–220, 230, 232, 239, 240
Loving v. Virginia, 85
on *Modern Family*, 239–243
public support for, 243–245
and *In re Guardianship of Kowalski*, 171–175
Marshall, Mike, 219–220
Martin, Mary, 247
Marty Morrison (*Barney Miller* character), 70–73, 79–83, 85–91
Mary Hartman, Mary Hartman, 9, 32
Mary Kay and Johnny, 4
The Mary Tyler Moore Show, 5, 24, 51–52, 120, 144, 189, 210
M*A*S*H, 51
The Masquerader, 34
Mater, Gene, 4
Matlovich, Leonard, 51, 84, 139
Mattachine Society, 16
Maude, 2, 32, 50–51, 95, 123, 140
McCarthy, Joseph, 169
McClanahan, Rue, 123n, 139–140, 152, 160, 162
McCormack, Eric, 211, 212n, 213, 215, 226
McCoy, 59
McLean, Don Seymour, 34
Medical Center, 144
Mehlman, Ken, 232
Melrose Place, 221
Messing, Debra, 211–213, 219, 226
Miami Vice, 136–137
Mikita, Justin, 239, 243
Milk, Harvey, 16n, 28, 30n, 39, 43, 44, 56, 84, 113
Miller, Arthur, 169–170
Miller, Denny, 53
Mills, Olan, 23
Mister Ed, 11
Mitchell, John, 60
Modern Family, 225, 229–245, 249

Montgomery, Elizabeth, 10, 18–19, 25
Moonves, Les, 230
Moore, Mary Tyler, 248
Moore, Robert, 51n
Moorehead, Agnes, 12, 21
Morgan, Edmund, 13
Mosk, Stanley, 15
Mull, Martin, 193
Mullally, Megan, 211, 219
Mulligan, Richard, 104
The Munsters, 11
Murder, She Wrote, 126
Mutchnick, Jason "Max," 208–214, 218–221
My Best Friend's Wedding, 132, 210
My Favorite Martian, 11
"My Heart Belongs to Daddy" (song), 247–248
My Living Doll, 11
My Mother the Car, 11

N
Nabors, Jim, 22–23
The Naked Civil Servant, 59
Nakia, 77
The Nancy Walker Show, 50, 61
National Coming Out Day, 151
National Federation for Decency (NFD), 3, 97
National Gay Task Force, 72, 84, 99
NBC. *see also individual shows*
in competition with Fox, 166
and Family Viewing Hour, 61, 79, 248
mid-eighties slate of, 135–137
poll on homosexuality by, 113
queer-inclusive content of, 225
"We're Proud" campaign, 119–120
Nettleton, Lois, 144, 149
Neuwirth, Bebe, 127
Night Court, 118, 126
Normal, Ohio, 224
Norman . . . Is That You?, 49, 127

Northern Exposure, 240
NYPD Blue, 198

O
Obama, Barack, 225, 226, 243
The Object of My Affection, 132, 211
Occasional Wife, 11
O'Connor, Carroll, 248
O'Donnell, Rosie, 193–194
Officer Zatelli (*Barney Miller* character), 88, 90
Ohlmeyer, Don, 210
O'Leary, Jean, 151
Olfson, Ken, 61
The Opposite of Sex, 211

P
Pacino, Al, 59
parental homophobia, 167–171, 242
Parks, Bernice, 247
The Partridge Family, 76, 95
PBS, 64, 249
Perlman, Rhea, 120
Perry, Matthew, 180, 182
personal connections, understanding marginalized groups through, 43–46
Phyllis, 53
Picket Fences, 221
Pierce, Charles, 35
Pierce, David Hyde, 223
Plotnick, Jack, 190
Police Woman, 32, 72
Porter, Cole, 247–248
Posner, Marsha, 1–2. *see also* Williams, Marsha Posner
Pride events, 16, 18, 25, 28, 56, 81n, 98, 160, 201
Procter & Gamble, 116–117

Q
queer people. *see* LGBTQ+ people
"Que Sera, Sera," 82
Quinn, Colin, 182–183

R

radio networks, 247–248
rainbow flag, 46
Randall, Tony, 139
Ratzenberger, John, 120
Reagan, Ronald, 116, 209, 249
Reality Bites, 132
Red Scare, 169
Richards, Renée, 100
Richman, Jeffrey, 240–242
The Ritz, 49, 120
Roberts, Doris, 136–137
Roc, 6, 240
The Rocky Horror Picture Show, 49, 59
Rodwell, Craig, 18
Roker, Al, 221–222
Romer v. Evans, 184, 195
Roseanne, 5, 183, 198, 240
Roundtree, Richard, 6
Rove, Karl, 232
Rubenstein, William, 174
Russo, Vito, 250–251

S

Saks, Matthew, 162
same-sex couples
    commitment ceremonies for, 186, 196–197, 240–241
    legal rights/protections for, 174–175
    marriage by (*see* marriage equality)
    as parents, 89, 111–113, 230, 233
Sandrich, Jay, 140, 210
Sargent, Dick, 21–22, 24–25
Sarria, José, 15–16
Saturday Night at the Baths (film), 59
Saturday Night Live, 119, 182–183
Sawyer, Diane, 203
Scher, Steven, 155
Schiappa, Edward, 226–227
Schiller, Bob, 52
Schitt's Creek, 249

Schneider, Alfred, 58, 75–79
Schuster, Sandy, 114
Schwarzenegger, Arnold, 239
Schwimmer, David, 180
Scorsese, Martin, 52
Screen Gems, 68
secrecy
    about sexuality, 5, 24, 40, 88, 107, 127–128, 192–193
    on *Bewitched*, 10
    in *The Golden Girls* episode, 146–147
    in 1960s, 11
Segal, Mark, 31
Seinfeld, 125, 133, 144, 184–185, 189, 222
Seinfeld, Jerry, 4, 184–185
Seomin, Scott, 216
sexual orientation
    civil rights protections covering, 195
    gender vs., 108
    secrecy about, 5, 24, 40, 88, 107, 127–128, 192–193
"Sexual Psychopath Law," 169–170
Shannon, Lori, 34, 47
Sheen, Martin, 75
Shepard, Matthew, 215
Sibbett, Jane, 128*n*, 186
Silverman, Fred, 100, 119–120
The Simpsons, 166
sitcoms, 4–6. *see also individual shows*
    homosexuality broached in, 51–52, 133
    LGBTQ+ characters on, 125–126, 183, 224
    as metaphor for social change, 11–12
    portrayal of families in, 10–11, 142
    at turn of millennium, 229
Smakov, Gennady, 87–88
Smith, Bob, 187
Snip, 50, 61
Snow, Kevin, 201

Soap, 1–2, 5–7, 9, 93–118, 120–125, 151
soap operas, 96
Some Like It Hot, 34
Some of My Best Friends Are . . ., 123, 139, 224
Sonny Comedy Revue, 76–77
Soo, Jack, 68
Southern Baptist Convention, 190
Spelling, Aaron, 50
Spin City, 192
Standards & Practices (S&P) departments, 74–76
Stark, Jonathan, 204
Starsky & Hutch, 35
Stonestreet, Eric, 234
Stonewall Inn uprising, 2, 31, 32, 67, 69–70
Struthers, Sally, 167
Supertrain, 119

T

Tales of the City, 64, 249
Tannenbaum, Eric, 229
Tarses, Jamie, 197
Tartikoff, Brandon, 137, 138
Taxi, 111, 120, 210
Taylor, Meshach, 141*n*
That Certain Summer, 24, 75–76
Then Came Bronson, 94
Thomas, Tony, 94–96, 100, 117–118, 147
Thompson, Karen, 171–175
Thompson, Scott, 187
Three's Company, 35, 126
Tie the Knot, 239
Today Show, 221–222
Torch Song Trilogy, 129–130, 138, 154–155
transgender people, 107–109, 186–187. *see also* LGBTQ+ people
True Blood, 225
Turner, Kathleen, 186–187

U

The Ugliest Girl in Town, 35
Ugly Betty, 225

V

values conflicts, 175–177
Vergara, Sofia, 234
Vida, Ginny, 99, 101
Vigoda, Abe, 68
violence against LGBTQ+
    people, 13, 42–43, 69–70,
    216
von Hoffman, Nicholas, 49, 64

W

The Wackiest Ship in the Army,
    68
Walker, Nancy, 50

Walter, Jessica, 167
Walters, Barbara, 130, 131
Waters, Harry, 96
Wayans, Marlon, 166
Wendt, George, 120, 131n
White, Betty, 139–140, 143, 148,
    149, 160–161
White, Dan, 43
White Night riots, 44
Wicker, Randy, 17
Wildmon, Donald, 3, 4, 97, 100,
    116, 118n, 191
Will & Grace, 132, 207–227
Williams, Marsha Posner, 6–7,
    96, 100, 102, 116
Wilson, Flip, 35
Wilson, M. Sue, 173–174
Winchell, Barry, 215
Winfrey, Oprah, 199

Winters, Jonathan, 35
Witt, Paul, 94–96, 100, 117–118
WKRP in Cincinnati, 126
WLBT, 57
Wolf, Dick, 198
Wolfson, Evan, 153
Wooten, Jamie, 160
World Championship
    Wrestling, 216

Y

York, Dick, 21
Young, Alan, 46

Z

zaps, 31–32, 46
Zimmerman, Stan, 143–144,
    146, 155